Civil rights activist, a vocal opponent of the Vietnam War, champion of gay rights, and author of over 30 books—including his spiritual classic *Are You Running with Me, Jesus?*—Malcolm Boyd gained prominence during the 1960s as the "Espresso Priest" for his readings in coffeehouses and his activism outside the confines of the institutional Church.

Based on actual spiritual direction sessions plus a series of e-mail exchanges between Boyd and the author, readers are permitted to eavesdrop as Boyd recounts narratives of his life as a celebrity priest, his battles against racism and homophobia, and the people and events that shaped his life, including his association with celebrities such as Mary Pickford and Hugh Hefner, plus his long-term partner Mark Thompson.

An unconventional biography of an unconventional life, **Black Battle, White Knight** also reflects the lively exchanges between Boyd and the book's African-American, heterosexual author as Battle seeks guidance for his own religious career and inspiration from one of the elders of the Church. In addition to reproducing many of the e-mails and transcripts of the oral exchanges, the book is enhanced by the inclusion of numerous rare photographs from Boyd's personal archives—many unpublished until now.

In the foreword, Archbishop Desmond Tutu notes that we read biographies to make sense of ourselves through others. Accordingly, **Black Battle, White Knight** is both an intimate portrait of an extraordinary life and a mirror in which to see our own reflection and life more clearly.

MICHAEL BATTLE is Canon Theologian in the Episcopal Diocese of Los Angeles and rector of The Church of Our Savior in San Gabriel, CA. He has served the church in many capacities, as priest, seminary dean and professor, writer, speaker, and retreat leader. His ministry covers the globe and focuses on Christian non-violence, human spirituality, and Black studies. He was ordained by Archbishop Desmond Tutu, earned his PhD from Duke University, and is the author of eight other books, including *Ubuntu: I in You and You and Me*, also from Seabury Books.

Black Battle, White Knight

Black Battle, White Knight

The Authorized
Biography of
Malcolm Boyd

MICHAEL BATTLE

Foreword by Desmond Tutu

Seabury Books
NEW YORK

Copyright © 2011 by Michael Battle

All rights reserved. No part of this book may be reproduced, stored in a retrieval system, or transmitted in any form or by any means, electronic or mechanical, including photocopying, recording, or otherwise, without the written permission of the publisher.

Unless otherwise noted, the Scripture quotations contained herein are from the New Revised Standard Version Bible, copyright © 1989 by the Division of Christian Education of the National Council of Churches of Christ in the U.S.A. Used by permission. All rights reserved.

Scripture quotations marked KJV are from the King James Version of the Bible.

Every effort has been made to trace the copyright owners of material included in this book. The author and publishers would be grateful if any omissions or inaccuracies could be brought to their attention for correction in any future edition. They are grateful to the Malcolm Boyd Archives placed at Boston University for permission to use excerpts from Boyd's works, and the archive at the Episcopal Diocese of Los Angeles for the photographs.

Many of the unattributed quotations in this book are conversations or e-mails between the author and Malcolm Boyd, collected during the period of 2009 to 2011.

Image on page 239 courtesy of Janet Kawamoto. Used by permission.

Illustrations on pages 9, 12, 27, 31, 119, 127, 131, 136, 141, 173, 195, and 199 by Paul Conrad. Used by permission.

Cover image courtesy of Mark Thompson, photographer/author/editor. Used by permission.
Cover design by Laurie Klein Westhafer.
Typeset by Beth Oberholtzer.

Library of Congress Cataloging-in-Publication Data
Battle, Michael, 1963–
    Black Battle, White Knight : the authorized biography of Malcolm Boyd / by Michael Battle.
        p.   cm.
    Includes bibliographical references (p.).
    ISBN 978-1-59627-226-2 (pbk.) — ISBN 978-1-59627-227-9 (e-book) 1. Boyd, Malcolm, 1923– 2. Race relations—Religious aspects—Episcopal Church. 3. Battle, Michael, 1963– I. Title.
BX5995.B66B38   2011
283.092–dc22
[B]
2010053252Seabury Books
445 Fifth Avenue
New York, New York 10016
www.churchpublishing.org
An imprint of Church Publishing Incorporated

Contents

Acknowledgments		ix
Foreword by Desmond Tutu		xiii
INTRODUCTION:	Horse with No Name	1
CHAPTER ONE:	Running with the Horses	35
CHAPTER TWO:	The White Horse of Pestilence	57
CHAPTER THREE:	The Red Horse of War	117
CHAPTER FOUR:	The Black Horse of Famine	153
CHAPTER FIVE:	The Pale Green Horse of Death	189

*Looking at your own life is something
most of us cannot really do.*
–MALCOLM BOYD

Acknowledgments

I would like to thank Church Publishing for accepting this book and then turning around and holding it high for many to see. In particular I am in debt to the publisher, Davis Perkins, for being with Malcolm and me every step of the way through finalizing this book. In addition I am in deep appreciation for the fine editorial work of Dennis Ford and the astute production assistance of Ryan Masteller. They've worked very hard on the book—and to good advantage for all concerned.

Malcolm and I wanted to find the right publisher so that the vital themes and lessons of Malcolm's life would not be lost or gradually fade away. We also wanted to find a publisher willing to risk the fusion of genres, biography/autobiography—especially since much of this work comes out of Malcolm and Michael's spiritual direction sessions. Like Malcolm's own writings, my intent in this biography is to honor how he broke new ground. This biography attempts to break new ground in how a biography is depicted in conversation between the writer and the principle life being depicted. In this regard, I am especially grateful for Malcolm's acquiescence to my "postmodern" use of direct e-mails between Malcolm and me and the concurrent use of digital images and text. I applaud Church Publishing for publishing this unique book that breaks new ground in its depth of honesty and inclusiveness. Before we decided on a publisher (and before we approached Davis), Malcolm sent me the following message:

> Dear Michael: Sitting here waiting for word of the book. Not easy! Our fate seems to be in the hands of complete strangers who, frankly, may not give an honest damn about us. Yet one must persevere.

Our immediate goal, I believe, is to have the book published. Hopefully by someone who at least likes it, hopefully loves it. The book is an original, i.e., there is nothing remotely like it in the book market. It ploughs new ground. It opens up doors and windows. It also concerns major historic and contemporary issues. If there are a few structural problems, surely they can be addressed successfully in an editing process.

It isn't a time for us to refuse to be flexible. The goal is publication and quite soon. An editor who cares (and hopefully loves) seems to be a requirement. By its very nature, the book is a literal statement about openness and inclusion and relevance and honesty. We need a decision so that we can shift gears, engage in final editing, place all our resources in the debut of the book, and be moving forward. It will be deleterious and spiritually damaging to us not to do this. We need to weigh our actual options and, frankly, make a decision. To clear the air. To be creative again instead of stuck. As a matter of fact, what could be helpful right now would be placing the mss. in some semblance of final form (which doesn't mean not continuing to edit it), and sending it to a select group of persons who are qualified, asking them for input, reaction, suggestion, perhaps sharing vision. This could enable the book to be as absolutely and nearly fine as possible. I like "community." I like the idea of a small number of persons who honestly care about the book's issues actively contributing, in a real sense, to its taking a public bow.

As I write this I don't know if you are on Mars or Saturn or even Venus. I am here in the City of the Angels. Just finished reading one of the best novels in years, *The Invisible Bridge* by Julie Orringer. It appears that the Sausalito Film Festival will be inviting me in August to read from my work (as I did in Anaheim at the Jazz Kitchen) and to be accompanied again by the same jazz group. Isn't that exciting? It is also the fiftieth anniversary of the Freedom Rides and my presence there will symbolically include all the other Freedom Riders too. So new life beckons! Time Marches On! All best—Malcolm.[1]

In closing I am in debt to everyone who granted me interviews. I am grateful to Mark Thompson for his ability to assist my writing process and his grace in handling profound subject matter. I also want to acknowledge

---

1. Malcolm Boyd, "Message from the Edge of the World," e-mail message to author, July 19, 2010.

three particular books by Malcolm that contributed to this work in a meaningful way: *As I Live and Breathe: Stages of an Autobiography*, *Take Off the Masks*, and *A Prophet in His Own Land: A Malcolm Boyd Reader*.[2]

The Episcopal Diocese of Los Angeles and Bishop Jon Bruno were invaluable for providing infrastructural help. Especially, I want to acknowledge the help of Janet Kawamoto and Bob Williams. Thanks to Kay Conrad for permission to include a number of editorial cartoons originally published in 1973 in the book *When in the Course of Human Events*. It was co-authored by Malcolm and Pulitzer Prize–winning journalist, Paul Conrad. The Howard Gotlieb Archival Research Center at Boston University was also invaluable in providing detail and nuance to this work on Malcolm. And I am grateful to my wife, Raquel, who supported me in this work to hold up Malcolm's life as a shining light for as many as possible to see and in so doing, be transformed.

---

2. New York: Random House, 1969—Malcolm feels this is one of his best books; Brooklyn, NY: White Crane Books, 2007; Brooklyn, NY: White Crane Books, 2008.

Foreword
Archbishop Desmond Tutu

One of the most difficult tasks is to know yourself. This biography beauti-fully provides such an examination. Michael Battle invites you into a journey not only of seeing the extraordinary life of Malcolm Boyd, but consequently seeing yourself. After all, isn't this why we read biographies—to make sense of ourselves through others? In South Africa we call this sensibility *Ubuntu*. We say this because a person is a person through persons. We need each other to be human . . . to be a child of God.

Michael will describe later in this book about his first encounter with Malcolm. I was indirectly involved. For about two years (1993 and 1994), Michael lived in residence with me near the end of my time as Archbishop of Cape Town and before my chairmanship of the Truth and Reconciliation Commission. I have since learned from Michael that these were formative years in his own life in the discovery of spiritual direction. I think what Michael means is that he saw how I regularly engaged my own spiritual director and learned to apply such direction to the difficult journey of knowing myself in the world.

I pray that Malcolm proves to be as powerful to Michael as my own spiritual directors proved powerful in my life. One in particular was the Rev. Francis Cull. Francis was like a character out of a Tolkien novel—short, stocky, and with a white beard. Francis's words were measured as he would tell me the work of the spiritual life was not so much to find something as to be someone in God.

I learned early in my vocation the difficult task of looking at self through the eyes of others—the greatest other being God. Without such engagement (often times confrontation), I would not have had the longevity and quality of life entrusted to me.

Although many may see me as a political agent against apartheid, I learned to see my agency more as a spiritual battle, hence my vocation occurred through habits of deep spirituality. This reminds me of a story given to me about desert spirituality.

One day two desert mystics were walking beside the sea. The younger mystic was thirsty and said to the older one, "Father, I am very thirsty." The older one said a prayer and then said to the younger, "Drink some of the sea water." The water proved sweet when the younger mystic drank some. He even poured some into a leather bottle for fear of being thirsty later on. Seeing this, the old man asked the younger one why he was taking some. The younger mystic said to him, "Forgive me, it is for fear of being thirsty later on." Then the old man said, "God is here, God is everywhere. You do not need to be afraid."

This biography (and in some ways autobiography) is more like these two mystics searching for water and God. Michael is the younger one and Malcolm the older. Malcolm's genius has been to show the world that God is everywhere, even for those who say they do not believe in God. The prayers in Malcolm's spiritual classic *Are You Running with Me, Jesus?* have deeply affected human lives throughout the world. He writes poignantly and powerfully about the human condition of becoming a slave of self, with one's soul parched, dreams crumbled, and energy stifled. Yet at the same moment one can pray (Malcolm tells us) "for a voice to cut through heavy silence, hear laughter, see a burst of light, and start to care again."

On the surface, Malcolm and Michael seem to be an odd couple. One is an octogenarian, and the other a late baby boomer. One is gay in a long-term partnership and the other is heterosexual, married with three children. One is white and the other is black. But the similarities far outweigh the differences, the chief similarity being their mutual search for God here and everywhere.

Because I have been with Michael through many of his own rites of passage—ordaining him an Anglican/Episcopal priest, officiating his wedding to Raquel, baptizing their three children, Sage, Bliss, and Zion—I am deeply invested in the outcome of Michael's life. Therefore, I am happy that Michael has found himself a spiritual director in Malcolm. Incidentally, Malcolm is celebrating the twenty-seventh anniversary of his partnership-relationship with noted gay journalist-editor Mark Thompson.

As I have learned more about Malcolm's life, I understand now how he in fact knows where the water is . . . where God is. Malcolm searched wide and far, often in dangerous places. He was ahead of his time, being a white civil rights prophet on behalf of people of color (Malcolm was a Freedom Rider for African-American justice in the U.S. in 1961), protesting against tyranny and war (he was arrested in the Pentagon during a Peace Mass to protest the Vietnam War), asserting God's inclusivity for all people including gays, and offering prayer in actions as well as words.

Lastly, Malcolm is a fellow elder; this is important. We have responsibilities to the younger generations much like a North Star responsibly guides us beyond treacherous waters. May you follow Malcolm in this book and in so doing discover yourself in a much deeper way. But be warned. This will be a difficult and demanding journey, requiring spiritual direction. If you're not willing to look at your own life, this will be a challenging book to read, hence its title *Black Battle, White Knight.*

INTRODUCTION

Horse with No Name

Growing up, one of my favorite songs was "A Horse with No Name," written by the rock group in the seventies known as America. It's curious that a forty-seven-year-old African American like myself would like such a song. After all, the stereotype is for me to love Luther Vandross, Whitney Houston, and Barry White. Defying the stereotypes, I found "A Horse with No Name" to be a brilliant, hypnotic song. The chorus in particular invites you into the subject matter of this book—the boundary-breaking life of Malcolm Boyd. The hypnotic chorus of the song recalls imagery of a desert and a horse with no name. The rider feels good to be in the desert where you can remember your name (out of the rain) where no one can give you no pain. Perhaps this imagery was recalled in some drug-induced state of a typical rock group, or maybe it was gained through the insight that all of us need guidance out of a wilderness that often becomes known as ordinary life. Strangely enough, I found myself in such a wilderness listening to a voice crying in the desert.

Like many folk musicians and famous musicians, Malcolm's voice was boosted in strange places. One such place was called the "hungry i." The hungry i was a nightclub in San Francisco, owned by Enrico Banducci. The mysterious name "hungry i," with the lower-case "i," is said to represent "intellectual." On other accounts, Banducci came up with a Freudian meaning implying "the hungry id." In a more humorous account, the sign "the hungry i" simply was not finished in time for the club's opening, and next-day reviews in the San Francisco papers cemented the name for all time.

The club was located at 546 Broadway Street, and was instrumental in the careers not only of Malcolm but for the actor/comedian Bill Cosby; the Kingston Trio, who recorded two famous albums there, including the first live performance of their version of "The Lion Sleeps Tonight"; and jazz legend Vince Guaraldi. They were all given career boosts from their appearances at the hungry i.

When the comedy and folk music scene declined in the mid-1960s with the rise of hard rock and Vietnam War protests, Banducci closed the club and sold its name to a topless club at another location nearby. Banducci and many of the club's performers reunited in 1981 for a memorable one-night performance, captured in the nationally televised documentary *hungry i Reunion*, produced and directed by Thomas A. Cohen and featuring separate reminiscences by Maya Angelou and Bill Cosby.

Malcolm's voice crying from the wilderness started in strange places like the hungry i. But what was he saying at the time?

Malcolm Boyd, author and Episcopal priest, is a social critic whose work has appeared frequently in the pages of the *New York Times,* the *Washington Post,* theological journals and mass-circulation magazines. As an Associate Fellow in residence at Yale, he wrote a weekly column for the *Yale Daily News*. Nationally recognized as a social activist, he is also a playwright, film critic and well-known television personality.

He is author of furteen books, including *Are You Running With Me, Jesus?*, which has been hailed as a modern religious classic.

Paul Conrad, 49-year-old editorial cartoonist, was born in Cedar Rapids, Iowa. He served with the Army Corps of Engineers during World War II and was graduated from the University of Iowa in 1950.

Upon graduation he moved directly to the *Denver Post*. In February of 1964 Mr. Conrad joined the staff of the *Los Angeles Times* and is now syndicated five days a week.

Previous honors bestowed to Mr. Conrad are the 1964 and 1971 Pulitzer Prizes for editorial cartooning, and the 1963, 1968 and 1970 national awards from the Sigma Delta Chi, national professional journalism society.

On a chalkboard in Malcolm's office is this printed notice: "Who Said?" There's a statement that could have come from one of three persons: "It is better to know some of the questions than all of the answers." The three persons listed who might have made the statement are Malcolm Boyd, Gottfried Leibnix, and James Thurber. Maybe all three came up with the words. I don't know. Whoever said the words, they accurately convey Malcolm's voice.

Openness to change seems essential for Malcolm. Change is the answer for bureaucracy without focus, irrelevant answers to nonquestions, continuing to do things "as they have always been done," a jaded attitude, and a numbing loss of spiritual energy. A classic Japanese film, Akira Kurosawa's *Rashomon,* portrays the human dilemma of trying to arrive at "the truth." The film depicts the rape of a woman and the murder of her Samurai husband through the widely differing accounts of four witnesses. The stories are mutually contradictory. These four perspectives are also instructive of the four horsemen who frame the texture of Malcolm's life. Seeing life from different perspectives often causes panic in the seeker for one kind of truth. This brings up the classic question posed by Pontius Pilate in his confrontation with Jesus: "What is truth?"

Malcolm writes me:

> Fundamentalism comes up with "one" irrevocable answer. There is a singular interpretation. Yet in multilayered and highly complex life, I choose to remain open to various interpretations rooted in complex and dismayingly different views and experiences. This can extend to looking at a singular person or event as "good" or "evil," "promising" or "hopeless," "creative" or "destructive," a "positive" sign or a "negative" one. I never like "either/or." I prefer "both/and." Is the above clear? Do we need another sentence or thought? If so, maybe you can come up with it. I just find life itself so amazingly "open" instead of sealed shut and "closed." Usually it includes possibilities. Anyhow, I thought we should get *Rashomon* in here.[3]

Indeed, Malcolm sought the truth—come what may. His voice in doing so was often heard as caustic and jarring. "I'm white," Malcolm said. "Did I murder six million Jews in Nazi Germany? Did I lynch, castrate, starve, burn, knife, hang, disembowel, rape, and murder thousands and thousands of black people in America? Do I stand today in the way of black progress, social equality, and liberation in the U.S.?"[4]

---

3. Malcolm Boyd, "New," e-mail message to author, October 25, 2010,
4. Malcolm Boyd, "Funky," *Yale Daily News*, February 19, 1969.

This voice attracted me to the desert. It was an apocalyptic voice, irritatingly honest, calling for conscious attention to the ills of the world. It was the voice of an apocalyptic horseman galloping in the desert. Malcolm's was a voice demanding that he better study (and learn) White history because his identity was shattered when he confronted the invisible among us—those lesser identities that Ralph Ellison referred to in the *Invisible Man*—such as undocumented workers and the downtrodden. Malcolm attracted me to the thought that the White Experience has been built on labyrinthine myths that now drive him to his fellow compatriots like white psychotherapists who corroborate such myths in the White Experience. Malcolm put it this way, "I try to look deeply into the White Experience but am unnerved by what I see. I had been told it was all apple pie, prayers, cleanliness, decency, morality, righteousness, goodness, a just but not overly loving god (you know, a father image), law, order, converting the natives, and it wasn't. Am I therefore a masochist instead of the righteous ruler? What is to be 'my role'?"[5]

These were my same questions, but unlike Malcolm, an eighty-eight-year-old, white, gay, celebrity priest, I was a black, forty-six-year-old, married heterosexual wannabe celebrity priest. I am an African-American Episcopal priest. For many of you, this is a strange identity, especially given the context that I should not be who I really am writing this book. Wouldn't the reader think that a white, gay liberal is most qualified to tell Malcolm's story? I don't think so. Because of who Malcolm is (not either/or but *Rashomon* from all angles), it fits that I write this book—even if one of the crucial aspects of Malcolm's life was his coming out as gay during a violent and turbulent period in human history. Malcolm provides me the following account that makes his life all the more vivid and real. It is contained in a letter Malcolm writes to a friend:

> Dear Chris: It occurs to me that, as gays with tragic histories and innumerable problems linked to the past, we are a bit like Zionists confronting—again and again—the Holocaust. Is it forever the Rock of Gibraltar, the Tsunami that strikes without warning and casts a giant shadow, indeed, one's very history imbedded within oneself. This is far more than a question of a "happy ending." This is essential being. But the question remains: can we move forward, seek and perceive a new direction, achieve and maintain some solid and meaningful balance in one's life?

---

5. Conversation I had with Malcolm during spiritual direction, January 6, 2011.

A night that I visited Cheyenne, Wyoming, in 1959 remains locked in my memory. Of course, I was in Brokeback Mountain territory. And Matthew Shepard territory. I drove up to Cheyenne from Fort Collins, Colorado, with a male friend. I didn't know him well, assumed he was not gay. We were not on a gay seek. I felt vulnerable because, in a sense, I was always on a gay seek (even if I buried that deep in my consciousness). We drank a lot; I think it was beer. I'm sure our visit had no common purpose. (Why were we making this visit to Cheyenne?) Clearly, I was extraordinarily vulnerable. I felt I couldn't let my guard down. The guy was a part of a social structure in which I moved as a chaplain at Colorado State University.

At that time I felt sure I would never be able to come out. It simply wasn't a remote possibility. I was imprisoned. Yet here I was drinking a lot with this guy and aware that, as a closeted gay man, I was in deep enemy territory. I really had to watch my P's and Q's. Not let my guard down. Not react to anything. And then the sense of actual danger grew in me. This was truly "enemy territory." We didn't stay the night but drove back rather late. I have some vague memory of his making a possible sort of pass (in the context of a lot of alcohol) that I knew I had to ignore. He was a colleague at work in the university system. He was political. My best defense was to be free from gossip and innuendo in "the man's world" in which I found myself. So that night in Cheyenne was hellish because it inadvertently brought up so many issues, made me confront my reality once again (hell, why go through that shit again?), rendered me helpless, and all this was taking place in the deep, deep shadow of—yes—Brokeback Mountain territory. . . . So this is another slice of gay history, gay experience. But even in an ambience of male bonding-cum-alcohol, it was necessary to keep the lid on.

I wonder what a few of those guys who later killed Matthew Shepard thought of us, two men together visiting their bar, strangers from the nearby university, good-looking men without women. Why were they here? What were they looking for? They were strangers. Do we want strangers like that to come into our turf? Indeed, this is a part of gay history. Can we lift the shadow a bit? Instill good memories into bad? Become a bit more trusting, a bit more positive? In fact—whether it's a holocaust or a Brokeback Mountain—dare/can we surrender a chunk of our vulnerability?[6]

---

6. Malcolm Boyd, "A Bit More on Brokeback," e-mail message to author, May 7, 2010.

Constantly in writing this biography, Malcolm pushed me toward vulnerability, which in turn created a common ground for seemingly disparate persons like Malcolm and me. Our common ground was more than being priests. Even if you are not religious, what I am about to say is fascinating because it points to how boundaries around human identity have changed. What I mean is: the Episcopal Church has historically meant a white European church in which my kinds of identity (for example, Negro, colored, black, African American) were not anticipated as becoming vibrant members. Surely, the original founders of the colonizing Church of England did not foresee my ancestors, African slaves, as the average Anglican. And yet, today, the mean average of an Anglican around the world is a thirty-six-year-old Nigerian woman. An African who is an Anglican is a crazy juxtaposition. An African Anglican is really an oxymoron since for much of human history, these two identities could never be mutual.

Malcolm's genius is in how his vision of the world and God's creation was such that there could be room at the table for all people. I remember an example of this when I was having dinner with fellow Anglicans at a church conference. To a table full of strangers, I mentioned that I was doing this biography on Malcolm. Even though I shouldn't have been, I was surprised that the majority of the table knew about Malcolm and even more that a couple at the table told me that they wouldn't have gotten ordained in the Anglican Church if it had not been for Malcolm. One of the persons who made this confession sent me information from an honors thesis she was writing. The thesis was about a Hawaii-born man named Masao Fujita, of Japanese ancestry, who entered the process to become an Anglican priest in 1950. After interrupting his seminary training to serve in the military in 1954–55, he was ordained in 1957. In isolated, rural areas Fujita served Grace Church, Molokai, and the Kohala Mission on the north side of the Island of Hawaii.

It was on the mainland in 1963 while doing postgraduate study that he visited Malcolm, with whom he had become friends while in seminary. During his visit Masao related to Malcolm that it was impossible for an American of Japanese ancestry to get a good church position in Hawaii, because all the good spots went to Caucasians. Shortly thereafter an article appeared in the *Los Angeles Times* accusing the Episcopal Church in Hawaii of racism. Malcolm wrote the article. Though the story never got major play in Hawaii, the Bishop of Los Angeles sent Bishop Kennedy a copy of the article. Reacting with horror at this accusation, Bishop Kennedy called the other clergy of Japanese ancestry into a private meeting at a clergy conference. Without showing them the article, he asked, "This isn't true, is it?" Another priest, Norio Sasaki, relates that, "We were all scared to disagree with the Bishop. I know that I was just out of seminary. Now I think that maybe I didn't support Masao enough."[7] In retrospect today, Masao's concerns were difficult to hear by those in power. To criticize a Bishop in the *Los Angeles Times* caused much tension, especially among those who valued good public appearance as essential. Yet, there is another aspect to be considered. Masao and Bishop Kennedy, coming from different worldviews, did not have the same perceptions of vocation. Similar to Malcolm's insights about *Rashomon,* one of the chief tasks in life is to understand each other coming from different world views. Bishop Kennedy had valued his days in small, rural missions as some of the happiest days of his life. Masao wanted an up-and-coming city church as much as any other priest in Hawaii in those days. Also, it was not custom for people from a Japanese culture to confront their superiors directly with a complaint or criticism. Probably if Malcolm Boyd had not written the article, Masao Fujita would never have complained to the Bishop—and improvements in his vocation may not have manifested.[8]

Doing my research on the life of Malcolm Boyd led me continuously to such strange occurrences of meeting many people whose lives were deeply influenced by Malcolm's voice crying out in the wilderness. I found myself in this new strange territory singing that rock group's reframe, "I've been through the desert on a horse with no name." Of course my context was different. The black experience was hard to name in a church with a predominantly white British identity. The difficulty of having no name in this world was compounded by the fact that I didn't want to blame white people. After all, everyone is trying to survive in the desert. Who needs another voice of blame when you're simply trying to drive your kids to school, survive an economic meltdown, and keep your cholesterol under control? Nevertheless, I felt like I was playing a role. I was the expert on black experience. I was the token voice for the appendages of history in which the colonized represented reconciliation with the true church (of European descent). This was the sarcastic spirit clanging in my soul.

Malcolm became my spiritual director. "I learned from black liberation," Malcolm told me, "that I do not have to play a 'role.' It is not only

---

7. Carol M. Arney's Interview with the Rev. Norio Sasaki, March 2, 1995.

8. Carol M. Arney, *The Episcopate of the Rt. Rev. Harry S. Kennedy, Bishop of the Missionary District of Honolulu, 1944 to 1969* (Honors Paper, The School of Theology, University of the South, 1995), 45–46.

my black brother who can be free. I, too, can taste the freedom, liberation, release, and meaning that transform my existence into a life." In our regular sessions of spiritual direction, Malcolm taught me that God gave me freedom to be human, hence my new name, human being. In my freedom as a human being, I can transcend roles that would imprison me—if I have enough courage to cut myself free from ties in the mind, the body, the personality, and the society.

> Malcolm prays, "Whoever receives one such child in my name receives me." Jesus, help us to receive you.[9]

Although I grew up in North Carolina when segregation was a fresh memory, Malcolm taught me that I have the power to turn away from a white god who resides in temples of whiteness, white purity, white truth, and white holiness without having to feel guilty for hurting white people's feelings. After all, Malcolm is white—and his feelings weren't hurt. But the key to Malcolm's spiritual direction was that in my new freedom, I shouldn't go to the opposite extreme in my freedom and turn to a black god who resides in temples of blackness, black purity, black truth, black holiness. Nor, really, do I need a green god, a red god, a yellow god, or a blue god.

Also, I do not need a white ghetto, a black ghetto, a green ghetto, a red ghetto, a yellow ghetto, or a blue ghetto. Malcolm states strongly, "I will fight all these lousy damned ghettos. Because I know that I cannot speak of freedom as an individual if I cannot live in a free society."

"But Malcolm, why should I be black in a white church, a white universe? Shouldn't I fight against this idolatrous worldview?"

"No. I do not have to fight anybody. Anger is almost as much a landmine as self-righteousness. Battles concern me only within the context of war. I must convey my humanness to others, not my 'Christianity.' I must convey my humanness to others, not my 'Americanism.'"

"How can I do this if I am not human—if I have no name in some human systems?"

Malcolm answers by describing his own experience. "To be human, I must understand that my whiteness is secondary, along with my 'Christianity' and 'Americanism.' As a human, I have human contacts with other people. I have as many close black friends as white ones; our

---

9. Malcolm Boyd and Paul Conrad, *When in the Course of Human Events* (New York: Sheed and Ward, 1973), 22–23.

Nothing unusual happened on the way to school again today . . .

blackness and our whiteness are vitally important in defining our individual humanness and our social relationship, but the blackness and whiteness finally do not separate us but instead become the factor of binding our painful humanity together. I cannot truly enter the human experience if I do not comprehend (and partially live in) the Black Experience as well as the White Experience. The human experience is, in its fulfillment, a unity."

Eldridge Cleaver, a famous black power activist, speaks of a world that has become virtually a neighborhood. Martin Luther King Jr. calls it a World House. Both Cleaver and King conclude that if this planet is to survive, the concept of humanity segregating is really something that can't continue indefinitely. "Injustice anywhere is a threat to justice everywhere," preaches King. Archbishop Desmond Tutu puts it this way, "Humanity is inextricably linked together. A person is a person through other persons." I think this is why one of Tutu's best friends is the Dalai

Lama of Tibet. Strange relationships develop when the worldview is cooperation rather than competition.

Malcolm concludes, "I do not wish to be naïve about my humanness or my whiteness (indeed, my 'Christianity' or 'Americanism'). . . . I do not speak of utopias, I am not even explicitly idealistic. Survival is hard pragmatism. Freedom and liberation are hard as nails, not airy generalities. If a black person abrasively rejects me—on the basis of my whiteness, not on the basis of knowing Malcolm as a person—it is inhuman and dehumanizing of me to react in outrage, protest, cries of self-pity and deprecation, and unholy preachment. We can, the two of us, maintain our humanness in the creative tension of separation. Isolated we will not be, for our mutual consciousness of one another is a burning thing. And, if we seek a mutual goal, we can remain human within tactical separation."

Malcolm refused to be separated from all black people at the height of the Civil Rights Movement. With those black folk open to friendship with Malcolm, he joined the struggle, the Civil Rights Movement to join Black Experience with White Experience (even a Martian would have to be treated well!). "After all," Malcolm says, "it is the funky human experience that defines, kills, and resurrects us."

I think it is in this realization that I cannot be human alone that I approached Malcolm Boyd to be my spiritual director. I knew I needed someone, himself complex enough, to help me navigate turbulent waters of identity. I needed someone with a strong name, a strong identity, who could help me know my own. I feel as though I am a member of a church like America's song "A Horse with No Name"—a church whose name has changed or perhaps, no longer has a name. This journey is key to this book.

Malcolm writes me:

> Dear Michael: I don't know how you're literally planning the book. It seems to me you need a short, succinct introduction to follow the foreword—and precede chapter 1—in which you introduce yourself, explain "who" you are and "why" you're writing this book. The entire book hinges on this.
>
> You need to move deep, deep, deep into yourself. Tell us your story/stories. Total authenticity here. The reader must "know" you. Otherwise you are just another abstract "thing" such as an "Episcopal priest" or "a scholar." Actually, why did you become both? What else did you become? What does race—and faith—have to do with it? What is our relationship (yours and mine) and what is something strange and esoteric called "spiritual direction"?

This involves the relationship with me, too. Where/when did you first hear of me? What have been your feelings or impressions? I remember when we met and when you asked me to be your spiritual director. When did you think of writing the biography? Why?

This leads to some self-examination in terms of your own life. (A writer must be open and vulnerable.) Where are you heading in your own life? (What do you want? What do you feel God wants from you?) "How" do our lives intersect? (Do they intersect in the book?)

Once this kind of thing is firmly established in the reader's mind, you can refer back to it again and again as you progress through the entire book. Finally, what are you progressing toward as you complete the book? Will there be any "answers"? What will be the big questions?

It boils down to that classic line in the classic film *Alfie*: "What's it all about, Alfie?" The book is a terrain. You are moving (across) it as a kind of pilgrim or wanderer. What in your past has motivated you to do this? What skills or insights do you possess? Have you a sense of a destination? (What form might it take?) I'm really talking about your whole life—the wholeness (holiness?)—of your entire life experience.

I'll look forward to what you will be sending me in the coming days. All best. . . .[10]

Whenever I do speaking engagements, usually on the themes of reconciliation and human spirituality, I like to tell my audiences that the reason I am an Episcopalian is because I grew up in the black church denomination National Baptist, and attended the University of Notre Dame my freshman year—being Baptist at a 99.8 percent Roman Catholic University cooked me into an Episcopalian. The confluence of Baptist congregationalism and Catholic ubiquity set me on a course for an Anglican middle way.

As a result of my own anomalous life, this biography was born in spiritual direction, looking for God in the desert. As a spiritual director myself, I realize the demand of the naming process—of learning your real name. After all, there are so many stereotypes given to me as my names. In many ways it's easy for me to just accept them and move on. It's hard to find those individuals who refuse the false names, the masks we hide behind. I needed such an exemplar to know my own unusual name.

Similar to the beauty of the rite of passage of a Native American vision quest, I set out on a journey in search of a sage who could guide me.

---

10. Malcolm Boyd, "Maybe most important . . . you," e-mail message to author, December 21, 2009.

Being an unusual person myself, I required an unusual spiritual director. I was picky. So, when I needed to find God, I approached Malcolm Boyd.

For you this may seem a strange occurrence for all kinds of reasons—chief of which could be: who is Malcolm Boyd anyway? Or you may say my voice is not all that unusual; after all, many African Americans do not fit the stereotypes.

> Malcolm prays, "Enable us to see complex people instead of simple images, Christ. Enable us to be complex people instead of simple images, Christ."[11]

Look at the popular black singer Tina Turner, for example; she's a Buddhist! Even if you do know Malcolm Boyd and recognize no irony in my voice as his biographer, the burden is no lighter in trying to con-

You know nothing about Watergate, which group would you most likely suspect of burglary, theft, breaking and entering, wiretapping, election law violations and conspiracy?

---

11. Boyd and Conrad, *When in the Course of Human Events*, 34–35.

vince you to read a biography in which you may feel uncomfortable because, for many, finding God in Malcolm is blasphemy. How could anyone find God in a gay, political, rebellious, celebrity priest? I say to all of you who approach this biography from a myriad of perspectives, come into a desert with a horse with no name and I think you will be surprised by the new identity you discover in yourself and in Malcolm Boyd. The irony, of course, is that Malcolm has a world renowned name. Malcolm bashfully writes me:

> Apropos of nothing, I've listed a few major and fascinating personalities with whom I've (to say the least) "interacted" on one occasion or another. In other words, there are "good stories" here. *The Washington Post*'s Katharine Graham ("America is not an imperial power," she thundered at me as she bolted from the TV studio in Chicago). Rosemary Radford Reuther, the Catholic theologian (and great person) who, in a meeting in East Harlem, announced: "The problem with Malcolm is he wants to be loved." Well, yes, damn it—as a faggot and queer and leper, YES, I DID want to be loved!!! Hugh D. Auchincloss, Jackie Kennedy Onassis's step-father, muttered to me in Newport Beach: "Why don't you write some prayers for stockbrokers?" You already have in the manuscript the classic scene in Hollywood where I come too close to opening a window and shouting at Howard Hughes and Samuel Goldwyn to "SHUT UP!" And there's an utter classic scene with sainted Mary Daly that is almost too awful to recount. . . . Where would a paragraph of these fit in the manuscript? Oh yes, and the time when I introduced Bishop Donegan of New York to the vodka martini??? (Which he then drank every evening for the rest of his life). I've marked the entire chapter in each instance of doing editing. So I'm ready for our meeting Friday 15 at 1. All best . . . M.[12]

What's fascinating about Malcolm is that although his name is great, it can evoke pain.

Malcolm once told me about a particular portrait of him painted by world-renowned artist Don Bachardy. Malcolm wondered what the artist would see when he examined him closely, paintbrush in hand? Malcolm drove to the artist's home feeling like the proverbial Cowardly Lion. Sitting in a chair facing the artist, with a view of the ocean over Malcolm's

---

12. Malcolm Boyd, "Have finished chapter," e-mail message to author, January 13, 2010.

Malcolm Portrait 1 by Don Bachardy.

shoulder, Malcolm sat for his first portrait. For the second, Malcolm sat on a couch and propped himself against pillows. For the third he lay down on a couch with his head resting on a pillow. Later, when Malcolm saw the portraits, he liked the first and third. But he had an immediate negative reaction to the second. Malcolm explains, "I didn't like the 'me' it reflects." That is to say, it didn't resemble Malcolm's own idea of what he looked like—or wanted to look like. Malcolm concludes, "Yet I had to face the fact that perhaps this picture showed a part of me I chose to reject. Maybe I didn't want to deal with this person (a part of myself) at all. As a further complication, was it possible I hadn't a clue how this person could be an integral part of 'me'? Who am I? This remains a central question in all our lives." When asked specifically if Malcolm could identify what "part" of him he found in the portrait that he didn't like, he responded, "No. Only the awareness or an opening up to a different reality of self that you didn't see before often scares you."

Malcolm was born in New York City in 1923 as the child of a prosperous investment banker. His parents divorced by the time of the Depression and he went with his mother to Denver, where he graduated from high school in 1940. Bronchial trouble kept him out of military service during World War II and led him to the University of Arizona. An indifferent student, he graduated in 1944 with a major in English and a minor in economics.

From Arizona he went to Hollywood and a $50-a-week job with the Footer Cone and Belding advertising agency. After directing a homemakers' hour on radio, he moved to Republic Pictures, where he became a publicist, an excellent entry position in the film industry. Republic Pictures was (and still is, in-name-only) an independent film production-distribution corporation with studio facilities, operating from 1934 through 1959 and best known for its specialization in westerns, movie serials, and B-films emphasizing mystery and action. They were also responsible for financing one Shakespeare film, Orson Welles's *Macbeth* (1948), several films directed by John Ford during the 1940s and early 1950s, and for developing the careers and star-status of John Wayne, Gene Autry, and Roy Rogers.

By 1949 Malcolm was in New York and associated with Mary Pickford and Buddy Rogers in a venture organized to package television programs. Two years later, in 1951, he was in a hotel room in Tucson, Arizona, spending a weekend with the Bible. Shocking his friends and amazing Hollywood—he had seemed to be only starting a promising career—he decided to enter the Church Divinity School of the Pacific in Berkeley, California.

Three years as a seminarian were followed by a year at Oxford University. In England he discovered an Episcopal mission ministering to the needs of workers in Sheffield. From England he went to an ecumenical institute in Geneva and on to Union Theological Seminary in New York, "where every question was asked." Then he was back in Europe at the Taizé community in France, learning firsthand about spirituality and worker-priests.

Malcolm's first church was in Indianapolis. There in 1957 he took charge of a 150-member, all-white parish in a neighborhood that had become largely black, and there he became aware of the depths of the race problem when he traded altars one Sunday with a black priest and "the biggest question in his parish was whether they would receive the chalice from a nigger's hand."

In 1959 he became a chaplain at Colorado State University and received nationwide attention as well as his first ecclesiastical rebuke when he moved his ministry off-campus into the Golden Grape Coffee House and a student beer joint. Bishop Joseph Minnis decried "priests going into taverns and drinking and counting it as ministry."

Malcolm got the message that his kind of ministry was perceived as at best unorthodox and at worst blasphemy. Malcolm felt like he was expected to conform, to be quiet, and not to question or criticize anyone over him. In particular Malcolm vied with the power of Bishop Minnis. No longer did Malcolm feel welcome in the church by Bishop Minnis. Concurrently, Malcolm got the divine message about racism and the need for faith and religion to hit the streets. In 1961 Malcolm went on a Freedom Ride with twenty-six white and black priests who traveled from New Orleans to Detroit, where they attended an Episcopal General Convention.

From 1961 to 1963 he served as a chaplain on the Wayne State University campus in Detroit. While there he wrote five plays about racism (one performed on television). At one point, Malcolm took up modern dance when an essay of his on Christianity was being choreographed. But his writing got him into trouble, too, and Michigan Bishop Richard Emrich criticized Malcolm for using the words "damn" and "nigger" in his plays.

Early in 1964 Malcolm found friendly shelter when then Suffragan Bishop Paul Moore Jr., of Washington, D.C., took him under his wing and made him assistant priest of the historically African-American Church of the Atonement. From that base, Malcolm traveled to as many as 125 campuses in a year and became an unofficial chaplain-at-large to college students.

This initial portion of Malcolm's biography is an attempt to really see Malcolm, and in turn see ourselves. In the African sense, I want to know his real name—his real identity. That's the beauty of biography; the journey of a life always invites the discovery of self-identity for the reader as well. Much of this journey is about the reconciliation of disparate identities articulated so well by Malcolm: the "me" I want and the "me" I try to avoid. Where Malcolm helps all of us is in his tenacity not to rest until there is a synthesis. Although he calls himself the Cowardly Lion, Malcolm is a cauldron of courage. As you will learn, Malcolm's tenacity requires sustained courage and grit. To illustrate this, one of the best descriptions of Malcolm comes from his friend Paul Monette, who won the National Book Award in 1992 and died too young at age forty-nine. In Monette's book *Last Watch of the Night*, he describes Malcolm in these words: "He wrestles God as Jacob wrestled the angel, till the breaking of the day."

In this biography, I seek to reconcile the God so easily encountered in Malcolm with the angst in Malcolm's unique life due to his encounter with racism and xenophobia, especially toward gays. Malcolm's life is the image of God in that there are so many different perceptions of him and yet there exists one large geographic identity. To see such identity requires a quiet place, like a desert. Malcolm tells the story of sitting under a 400-year-old tree and learning to not use words. The tree didn't move, but Malcolm crossed his legs. The tree simply remained there with him. In so being, Malcolm came to realize that, like him, the tree's identity isn't simple at all but is immensely complex. Malcolm and the tree share this complexity in common. However, by its very existence, the tree makes the strongest possible statement. It is anchored here and now. Malcolm states, "I ask the same for myself."

Before we begin the biography in earnest, more context is still in order. I first heard about Malcolm when I lived with Desmond Tutu in Cape Town, South Africa. Tutu modeled for me the health that derives from staying in spiritual direction. Tutu's tremendous impact against apartheid would not have occurred apart from his own deep spirituality. With the backdrop of Table Mountain outside, I sat in Tutu's office looking through his writings and constant requests for book endorsements. On one particular day, I ran across a book sitting on Tutu's desk entitled *Gay Priest: An Inner Journey*, written by Malcolm Boyd. Even in 1993, I found this a provocative title. Neither Tutu nor I are gay, but as I explored why this book was in Tutu's office, I discovered that Malcolm had blessed both me, an African-American heterosexual, and Tutu, a world-renowned African saint. We were deeply impressed by the Holy Spirit in Malcolm's life. As I look back to 1993, this is where the seed for this book was planted. Malcolm recognizes this seed as well.

> Dear Michael: Since the book is about US (the two of us, our spiritual direction work, our mutuality, our connectedness), it seems essential that you include Tutu in the celebrity chapter.
>
> He is a great figure in your life—and also in the world. Such links need to be made. Actually including him should make your work easier because obviously you have material about Tutu on hand that you

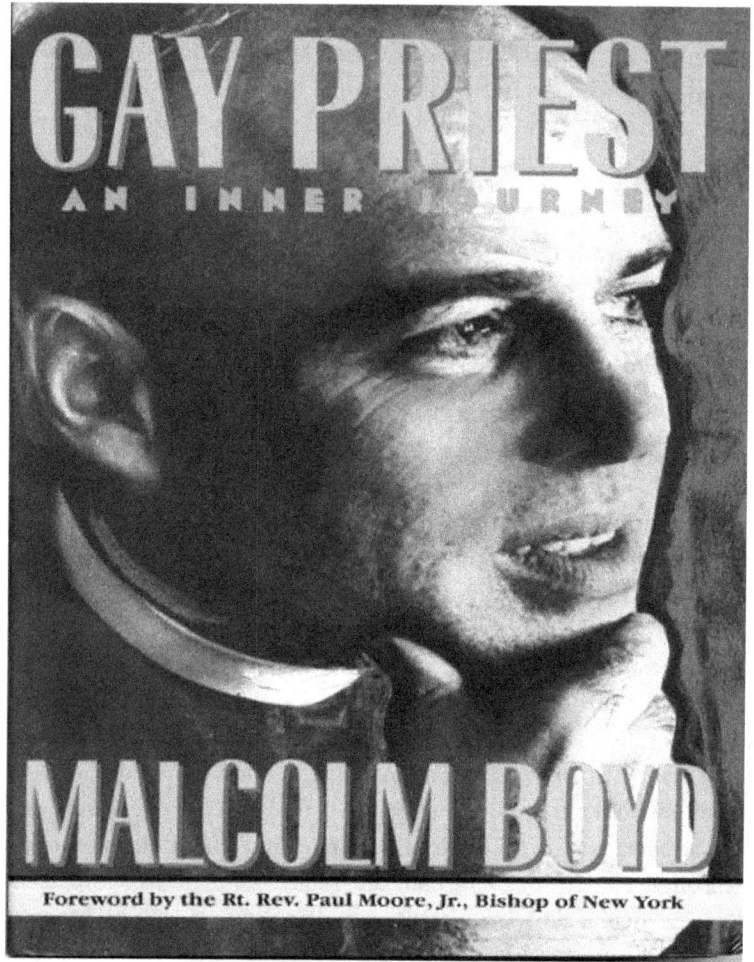

can incorporate here. This heightens interest and excitement, assists the task of communication, and draws you closer into your necessary orbit. The book becomes ever and ever more fascinating. It's far more than "a biography."

All this is becoming infinitely more fascinating than either of us initially had in mind. A truly original, creative work.[13]

Fortunately, I didn't need a spiritual director for my two years in South Africa because I used Tutu's own spiritual director, the Rev. Francis Cull. It was fascinating working with Cull, who resembled a character from

---

13. Malcolm Boyd, "Big News," e-mail message to author, August 17, 2009.

Tolkien or C. S. Lewis stories. His very presence stimulated a sense of unusual reality which helped in spiritual direction. It was easier to talk about God and unusual things with Francis.

When I returned to the United States in 1995, I no longer had a spiritual director. And sadly, my Nome-like spiritual director had passed away. As my public ministry developed as a professor of spirituality, retreat leader, theologian, and Episcopal priest, I was living in the hypocrisy of giving spiritual direction without being in it myself. These years accumulated because I was too picky and could not settle upon an ordinary spiritual director. One day, in August 2007, as I was walking through the Cathedral Center in the Episcopal Diocese of Los Angeles, I overheard someone say that Malcolm Boyd gave spiritual direction. Malcolm became my spiritual director.

How Malcolm discovered his gifts as a spiritual director was interesting and surreptitious. It wasn't as if he signed up for a course in spiritual direction or climbed a Tibetan mountain to attain a particular acumen to do it. In the 1980s Malcolm served as an associate priest at the parish of St. Augustine by-the-Sea in Santa Monica, California. The Rev. Fred Fenton, rector of the parish, invited Malcolm to "come out" as a gay priest in his first sermon there. Some people walked out and some pledges were cancelled, but Malcolm remained there for nearly fifteen years. In past years Malcolm had counseled dozens, if not hundreds, of men and women in Indianapolis and Colorado and as a college chaplain. Yet he had never thought of this work as "spiritual direction." In other words, he had not engaged a group of individuals in spiritual work over a sustained and lengthy period of time as a regular, ongoing enterprise.

At St. Augustine, he was sought by an Episcopal priest who had long been a member of an Anglican religious order. He asked: could Malcolm become his spiritual director? Although he felt untrained and perhaps inadequate, Malcolm said yes. He would give it a try. He and the priest/monk entered into what became a fifteen-year spiritual relationship. Malcolm says: "I had the finest on-the-job training in the world." Soon several other men and women requested that Malcolm enter into a dialogical pattern of spiritual direction with them. Malcolm says his approach has always been improvisational rather than tightly scripted or adhering to a rigid mode. In a seemingly idle conversation, suddenly a nerve is struck; maybe a childhood experience comes to the fore in a startlingly relevant way; an "elephant in the room" stirs and is identified.

Now Malcolm acts as spiritual director for a dozen men and women. His range has included bishops, both younger and older persons, a

Lutheran pastor, a Methodist pastor, gays and straights, mostly Episcopal clergy but also deeply committed lay people. Individual sessions can run to three hours. Malcolm's approach is to be as open to his directees as they are to him. So the sessions are intimate rather than distanced, impersonal, or bureaucratic. Spiritual direction, as Malcolm practices it, is less a process of crisis management than it is a long, ongoing, patient process of discovery and self-discovery. It is marked by both simplicity and humor. Faith is not perceived as a museum piece but as a living and present force.

In a letter to someone seeking spiritual direction, Malcolm describes his own unusual style of doing spiritual direction. Malcolm writes one of his directees:

> I honestly don't know who would be a good spiritual director for you! My own approach is so out of the ordinary, not formal, built on relationship and dialogue. I've simply related to a number of individuals who asked me to "be" that role in their lives. However, I'm not a "member" of a "group of spiritual directors." God knows who could "be" this for you. (God undoubtedly does, yet that doesn't help us very much right now.) Take a deep breath, look around (and closely, and pray).
>
> Someone is writing my biography! This is a strange, altogether new experience for me. Requires much emotional and mental digging into my past.
>
> Mark is fine (and, of course, has a new book just out). Diocese of LA is chugging along well. The two new suffragan bishops are splendid. All blessings, Malcolm.[14]

Malcolm's style of spiritual direction was indeed that of being—being present to the seeker of God. There was no pretense of technique or getting the words exactly right. As I asked my own narcissistic questions about prayer, God, justice, bad religion, and much more in front of Malcolm, narratives and wisdom flowed from Malcolm's life experience. It was impossible to be self-absorbed while hearing Malcolm's staccato laugh or to despair while listening to him read one of his provocative poems. After a year of being in spiritual direction had almost passed, I experienced an epiphany. "Malcolm, you need a biography," I said. We both pondered the thought. A few days later Malcolm writes the following letter:

> Dear Michael: Pursuant to our conversation re: a book you might write, I have some thoughts. I don't "want" or "need" a biography,

---

14. Malcolm's handwritten letter to "Rob," October 20, 2010.

which seems pretentious and premature. Nobody (including myself) cares about all the intricate details of my life!

What has my life represented? Its "Rosebud"—its deepest significance—seems found in my somewhat unexplainable passion for justice which found basic expression in my participation in what we call civil rights. I'm also thinking along similar lines as a possible focus of your work and in line with both your skill and your image.

I'm thinking of a book title: "Black Struggle, White Knight." Obviously this is a suggestion. My point is: I was not "unique" in this. There were many "white knights," volunteer men and women who sacrificed in different ways to enable a movement. I am not an "exemplar" or "role model." I was (and am) one of many. All of us, in our small and varied ways, paved the way for the phenomenon of Obama.

I remember often being told by blacks in the movement "Your job is with whites, not blacks." I disagree because I see this as not being "either/or." I have always seen it as "both/and." I believe it is time for a prominent/skilled black figure to write about deep white involvement in the historic and ongoing movement. In beneficial ways this could open up a more meaningful racial dialogue.[15]

Biography cum Autobiography

In postmodern literature, we have learned that the genre of memoir or testimony is the best vehicle of truth telling because it provides the context of a particular perspective coinciding with multiple interpretations. Such a genre written in the first person creates art out of concrete experience. Malcolm's art is in his articulation of the beauty of this strange brooding world that we live in. Like Malcolm's own writing, this biography is an attempt to break new ground in how one learns about a significant life. I do not attempt to tell a chronological story. Nor do I want you as the reader to think that I am an innocent narrator. In some ways this is both autobiography and biography at the same time. Malcolm writes me a letter and puts it this way:

> Dear Michael: After our highly beneficial meeting yesterday, a few thoughts.
>
> I think what sets this book apart is that it's NOT a biography per se, it's a dialogue, and it stems from spiritual direction. It's two people engaged in both life and discussion. Yesterday you seemed to feel chapter 1 might be on race, chapter 2 on gay. BUT I think chapter 1 MUST

---

15. Malcolm Boyd, "Rosebud," e-mail to author, February 17, 2009.

be on celebrity. It's the driving force in a global dance with celebrity in the media age. Also we have my utterly unique engagement with celebrity: first with Mary Pickford, second with a best-selling book and resulting celebrity. This is NEW for a spiritual or religious kind of book. Race is no longer new, nor is gay. They are of central importance but, for an opening chapter, I think celebrity cries out to be the theme. (Can you manage this in terms of your plan for the book as a whole?)

If we set up celebrity at the outset, and pursue it, you have—and hold—wide reader interest. Celebrity is an enigma. It can be considered a curse, it can be considered a blessing. Certainly, it's unfair! If you make chapter 1 on celebrity, then making chapter 2 race and chapter 3 gay follows logically. (Both are areas in which I have encountered, and worked with celebrity.) My life with celebrity has overlapped my life with both race and gay (and, indeed, contributed to it).

In this sequence, does "the anemic church with its institutional structures and lacking religion" follow logically? (Does it follow for you?) I want to avoid the pitfall of our ending up with "an Emerging Church experience" which I feel is a decoy or simply misleading. Do you remember a book called *A Generation of Vipers*? It was big when I was a kid. I remember it very well. It cut through all the bullshit. It just said, correctly, that we ARE "a generation of vipers." It didn't come up with a Disney ending. I feel this book can be honest with itself and end with the right questions instead of the wrong answers. In fact, "it is better to know some of the questions than all of the answers."

Anyhow. Chapter 1 can be celebrity, 2 can be race, 3 can be gay, and 4 can be the well-meaning but out-of-touch institutional religion that is failing to connect with people caught in the crisis of living. Glory be, have we avoided a Polyanna ending offering palliatives? Frankly, I have no answers. I have questions. You don't have answers either. You have questions.

Bishop John Robinson's *Honest to God* touched many lives. So did my groundbreaking book of prayers *Are You Running with Me, Jesus?* There aren't many books in this category. Let's stay in this category. BUT this means ASKING THE QUESTIONS everybody has but no one is being listened to. This means opening up all the closet doors. This means dealing with reality. (And there is no more persistent reality in the world today than the reality of celebrity, warts and all.)

Does this give you your 4 chapters? Can you wrap yourself around these 4 related themes? Finally, when the smoke clears, there can be a short-but-smashing post piece (just possibly written by someone else if we feel the Spirit so moves).

Above are thoughts for the day. For chapter 1, I'd tear into celebrity—its rawness, its tears and laughter, its relentless presence. This should give you the gift of your readers' rapt attention. When you've looked at the photos, please just give me a reaction as to their usefulness. Ditto when you've broken into the box of memories. . . .[16]

This is not a static biography in which the biographer is objectively removed from his subject matter. On the contrary, this is written in my experience of looking for God and finding Malcolm. Although the sequence of dialogue and chapter flow is written primarily to reflect my encounter with Malcolm's voice, it should be noted that my voice as the biographer has not been co-opted by my subject matter. In other words, I do not present to you a flowery work that only sings Malcolm's praises. Malcolm's own nature and particular voice would not allow such a biography anyway.

I am a Christian, and I care deeply about this identity. But I am also aware of how such identity has colonized and subjected others to horror and bloodshed. Likewise, I am an African American, and I care deeply about this identity. But it is an amphibious identity that I actually discovered when I went to Africa and discovered that I was an American; and yet, being in the United States made me feel more like an African. In order to understand my own development, these two identities have to be interrelated.

Most of my life has been spent in the discovery of how African-American identity and Christianity help us better see practices of peacemaking and reconciliation. I started this discovery with Desmond Tutu, an exemplar of someone who lives African and Christian identity together. In white society, Tutu profoundly negotiated how Christianity helps us better see practices of peacemaking and reconciliation. Such an exemplar has led me to think that one of the unnerving issues of contemporary theology is how scholastic and separated from the actual lives of people theology has become. This leads me to the organizing theme of my spiritual development: the formation of self through communal prayer. This is where Malcolm enters the picture. I needed a spiritual director. So, I have taken to heart the advice of the true sages of our day to make my own spiritual journey. I needed a spiritual director who could resist the pathologies of religion and help me not repeat the same old mistakes of religious oppression.

---

16. Malcolm Boyd, "Post-Thursday thoughts," e-mail message to author, August 14, 2009.

One of my chief concerns is: what is my particular vocation? What this question implies for me is the difficult matter of measuring what it is that I do when I lead in a religious world. Am I a dispenser of information? Do I disciple others into a communal theology? Am I a coach, coaxing the less enlightened into maturity? Or am I, simply, a mentor? Parker Palmer's insight into these matters is helpful.

> Then I ask the question that opens to the deeper purpose of this exercise: not "What made your mentor great?" but "What was it about you that allowed great mentoring to happen?" Mentoring is a mutuality that requires more than meeting the right teacher: the teacher must meet the right student. In this encounter, not only are the qualities of the mentor revealed, but the qualities of the student are drawn out in a way that is equally revealing.[17]

My answer to my opening questions about identity is to begin with my understanding of being a black Christian. It is this **being** that is crucial because it is a "being" in community. In sum, Malcolm helped me make sense of my amphibious-self through how I have been formed **to be** an African-American scholar, a priest, a professor, and a spiritual guide. The following is a statement of such development.

A Complex Self

To understand how my character corresponds with Malcolm's, one must understand two particular identities: African and Anglican. In my African-American identity, I challenge some of the divisions that characterize theological and religious discourse today. One may see this challenge in my books on Archbishop Desmond Tutu.[18] Tutu's thought is grounded by religious experience in which God creates what is good by creating what is different. Consequently, there is no legitimacy in an apartheid narrative (itself a homogeneous theology) which forms people into believing that otherness—for example, racial difference—is the foundation by which one race may dominate another. Relating my African identity to my Anglican identity proves to be another challenge. Having lived for two years in residence with Archbishop Tutu in Cape Town (1993–1994), I, as an African American, experienced Tutu's mode of the-

---

17. Parker Palmer, *The Courage to Teach: Exploring the Inner Landscape of a Teacher's Life* (San Francisco: Jossey-Bass, 1998), 21.

18. Michael Battle, *Reconciliation: The Ubuntu Theology of Desmond Tutu* (Cleveland: Pilgrim Press, 1997); *The Wisdom of Desmond Tutu* (Louisville, KY: Westminster John Knox Press, 2000); and *Ubuntu: I in You and You in Me* (New York: Seabury Press 2009).

ology firsthand. I was given the unique research experience of having complete access to Tutu's personal writing archives. Having such access and living in an African community afforded me the opportunity to present African Christian thought and practice from original data. This was one of my formative experiences as a scholar to understand myself as an authority in African Christian spirituality. This profound experience, however, provides its share of curse in the midst of blessing.

The curse entails two aspects. The first is the difficult process of synthesizing African and Anglican identities in light of colonialism. This is an acute concern since I was ordained a priest in a colonial church, the Anglican Church, by Archbishop Tutu in Cape Town at St. George's Cathedral on my birthday, December 12, 1993.

In light of the above, perhaps, one may begin to see the context of my development. Who I have come to be as a person cannot be divorced from my African and ordained Anglican identity. African identity is particularly charged from the outset as to whether negative, imposed identities—especially identities caught in the ambiguity of legitimate or illegitimate humanity—are to be accepted. To work against this ambiguity, there can be no concept of African and Anglican identities without full disclosure of their contingent, politically oppressed histories. In other words, to understand myself, I will also need to understand how one resists seeing me. Tutu helps me see this when he states, "Who you

Archbishop Tutu and Michael, Cape Town, 1993.

are affects and determines to a very large extent what you see and how you see it."[19] What I intend in my biography of Malcolm is to deepen my thought about the complexities of being human, especially in the midst of a hostile environment shaped by bad religion and colonialism.

The second aspect of the curse is in the toil of successfully presenting a spirituality from an oppressed people. The guiding idea behind my view of Malcolm is that he too toiled to present a spirituality of an oppressed people. For Malcolm, an extraordinary thing happened in that he both embodied an oppressed spirituality being gay and he chose an oppressed spirituality by identifying so profoundly with black people during the Civil Rights Movement. I am like Malcolm in such an embodiment and choice, but for me, my embodiment was being black and my choice was to be Anglican. Spirituality is needed to make both the embodied identity and the chosen identity toil synchronically toward the desired effect of reconciliation and transformation. Herein lies the salient task of my work on Malcolm, to expose to the world a profound life capable of synthesizing disparate identities.

Why Apocalyptic Four Horsemen?

As this book was being finalized, my editor wrote me that my apocalyptic theme kept him up at night. The haunting question was: why did I decide to use the images of the four horsemen (White Knight, Red Knight, Black Knight, and Green Knight) as an organizing principle rather than writing a more conventional, chronological bibliography? I shared this question with Malcolm, who wrote, "Regarding the four horsemen. They made me want to do the book with you! A conventional biography about me would almost be 'missing the point.' I am not conventional. Nothing about me is actually conventional. I am not a conventional priest or a conventional writer or a conventional gay person or a conventional civil rights worker! I am different, unique, I suppose one could say 'queer.' I believe the horsemen 'form of organization' does provide more insight into my life than a 'mere conventional biography.'"[20]

A life capable of synthesis of disparate identities like the four horsemen is crucial for our world today, a synthesis that no longer measures a

---

19. Tutu's undated handwritten speeches, "Perspectives in Black and White." Tutu illustrates further with this story: "A little boy excitedly pointed to a flight of geese and shouted, 'Mummy, Mummy, look at all those *goose*.' 'My darling,' Mummy replied, 'we don't call them *gooses*. They are geese.' Then the little darling, nothing daunted, retorted, 'Well they still look like *goose* to me.'"

20. Malcolm Boyd, "In Response to Dennis Ford," e-mail message, February 3, 2011.

life through the typical dualisms (for example, black vs. white, male vs. female, rich vs. poor, Asian vs. globalism) that lead to competition and war. It is interesting how Malcolm's life represented a struggle against such dualisms. Similar to Martin Luther King Jr., when one pursues civil rights for black people you can't avoid how such work dovetails on issues like victims of the Vietnam War and other injustices. Many of Malcolm's speaking engagements on college campuses focused upon helping young people make such connections—that injustice anywhere is a threat to justice everywhere.

Malcolm prays, "You lost in Vietnam, didn't you, Christ? Why do we say that we won?"[21]

Instead of a worldview of dualisms, Malcolm invites synthesis. As we measure Malcolm's profound synthesis, we encounter the angst of having

---

21. Boyd and Conrad, *When in the Course of Human Events*, 26–27.

to go beyond stereotype and routine. Mathematical teachers may assess the progress of their students by observing how well they reason-out a particular formula. In biology, a professor will see the results of a student's lab. In spiritual disciplines, however, what results could ever satisfy the quest to know mutuality with the greatest of disparate identities, the creature and the Creator?

What do I mean by mutuality? Frederick Buechner helps me explain my meaning of mutuality through his definition of vocation as "the place where your deep gladness and the world's deep hunger meet."[22] The concept of vocation proposes a kind of mutuality in which teacher and student behaviors are congruent not only with words and ideas but also with commitments and practices. A spiritual teacher like Malcolm is one who readily admits the incongruence of words and ideas as a virtue and a form of deeper knowledge. In other words, the spiritual teacher sees the world differently by learning to see "what is not there." By learning to see "what is not there," we learn to see "what should be there." For example, marginalized and minority identities have often not been there or, if they are, they are invisible.

As an African-American Christian theologian, I argue that how I continue to see "what is not there" is informed by my commitment to God's communal image. From the perspective of God's mutuality, I practice "what is not there" in many difficult places (for example, being the only black person in my school and church)—namely, my vocation of being African American and Christian. This leads me back to Buechner's definition of vocation. Those who teach in a spiritual way have an opportunity to develop the world into "the place where your deep gladness feeds deep hunger." By being mutual with Malcolm, I also facilitate the revelation of Buechner's concept of vocation in my own complex persona. This revelation of vocation honors many others in their own complex journeys in which they innately know that mutuality can only be known through vulnerability. We cannot know mutuality through conflict and disorientation. We know mutuality by first knowing what it is not. Therefore, to teach the spiritual life well requires the ability to create mutuality in such a way that both teacher and student acknowledge the impossible task of knowing God outside of the miracle of mutuality.

How then do I understand myself as a spiritual teacher? One can synthesize an answer only through the mutual search for communal ways of

---

22. Frederick Buechner, *Wishful Thinking: A Seeker's ABC* (San Francisco: HarperSanFrancisco, 1993), 119.

knowing. In other words, my quest for the Spirit always leads me to diverse communities. Unfortunately, the normative course is intended for autonomous learning among individuals only or siloed communities (for example, white, black, gay, straight, poor, or middle-upper class). For example, many persons are often irritated with the question: how are we to design spiritual experiences inclusive of diverse communities?[23] To answer this question demands a response to the assumption above in which Eurocentric educational design privileges the individual or competitive communities. Patricia Cranton illustrates this assumption:

> I recently discussed the idea of being an authentic teacher with a seasoned science education professor—a man who was looking forward to retirement within the next year after thirty years of teaching practice. He was almost appalled at the notion of being oneself with students. "I don't think I could go for that," he said, startled by what he saw as my naiveté. "Who I am in the classroom and who I am outside of the classroom are two different people. Students don't need to know me, they need to know how to teach science." Perhaps my raising the topic provoked images of personal self-disclosure or an emotional sharing of feelings with students, things that had no place in his mind in science teaching, but more likely, he simply saw teaching as something he does rather than who he is.[24]

Malcolm invites us to embrace the cultivation of learning in community that does not delete difference. This is his profound contribution as a spiritual teacher. There is an emerging consensus that the repertoires of teaching strategies most effective and responsive in socially and culturally diverse settings can be the very same strategies that are identified as characteristic of teaching excellence for traditional students. For example, the creation of space conducive for learning remains an important strategy for multicultural courses. Jack Mezirow states, "The more reflective and open we are to the perspectives of others, the richer our imagination of alternative contexts for understanding will be."[25] Malcolm teaches me that I should be just as concerned about relational interaction

---

23. When I attended a conference in 2002, Apiwa Mucherera, assistant professor at Asbury Theological Seminary, phrased this as a "Here we go again" mentality in which one may dismiss the other before she even speaks.

24. Patricia Cranton, *Becoming an Authentic Teacher in Higher Education* (Malabar, FL: Krieger Publishing Company, 2001), 43.

25. Jack Mezirow and Associates, *Learning as Transformation: Critical Perspectives on a Theory in Progress* (San Francisco: Jossey-Bass, 2000), 20.

and communication style as I am about the content. In fact, I do not see the two as separate. Students expect the instructor to identify with them as students and as individuals in a holistic way. I have become Malcolm's student. The crucial question Malcolm helps me answer is: how can I participate in serving the world without making matters worse in the world, especially by patronizing those I encounter? When thinking about how better to serve, one should distinguish between charity work and community service. Charity work implies "detached beneficence"; whereas community service "conjures up images of doing good deeds in impoverished, disadvantaged (primarily Black and Brown) communities by those (mostly White students) who are wealthier and more privileged." My role as spiritual leader, taught by Malcolm, is to challenge the perceptions of both community service and charity, replacing them with spiritual and human responsibility in a pluralistic but unequal society. By doing so, community service shifts from an individualistic experience into a social responsibility.

Malcolm prays, "Help me not to be dead while I am still alive, Lord."[26]

In terms of further defining community service, one may go back to 1969 to the Southern Regional Education Board in Oak Ridge, Tennessee, who defined it as "the accomplishment of tasks that meet genuine human needs in combination with conscious educational growth." Current theorists on service learning still seem to agree with this definition, although a problem remains.[27] There have been many ways to describe community service. Although descriptions of service learning appear to be politically neutral, of course service learning, as multicultural education also demonstrates, is deeply political. All of this points toward ideological considerations behind any notion of service. What moves such programs beyond "charity" work is the intentional and critical focus of spiritual work.

This biography breaks new ground in walking out on the ledge of biography cum autobiography. It offers you a perspective on a significant life both through Malcolm's own perspective and mine. Even more, Malcolm gives us his unadulterated voice in a way that is unavailable

---

26. Boyd and Conrad, *When in the Course of Human Events*, 14–15.

27. The following educational theorists contributed deeply to the integration of service learning into the academy: John Dewey, Jean Piaget, David Kolb, and Paulo Freire. See C. W. Kinsley and K. McPherson, eds., *Enriching the Curriculum through Service Learning* (Alexandria, VA: Association for Supervision and Curriculum Development, 1995).

"What did you do to stop the war, daddy?"

outside this biography. At some points, however, you may not like his voice. Similar to a voice crying in the wilderness, the secret-bearer disturbs us. As we will soon learn about Malcolm's life, some will find his spiritual direction either blasphemous or divine. I pray this book will shed more light on the divine life of Malcolm Boyd—a life that should have much more public acclaim.

> Dear Michael: I like your progress. The way you are so much a part of this. In a sense, then, our dialogue, our common/shared experience. Maybe the best way in the moment is for you to start each of the different chapters and see how they lead you. And, how each encompasses you as well as me.
>
> Clearly, you need to flesh this stuff out (for example, see the trove I gave you of old papers, etc.) What may help most of all is the way EACH CHAPTER seems to grow and develop in its own way.
>
> Most interesting, I think, will be the chapter on Celebrity. It is the cornerstone. Celebrity has changed the world. (Is it a virus?) You have

the opportunity to explore the "Hollywood" side of this in my material, and how it deeply affected my life. Then, utterly ironically, how I "happened" to write a book that became not only a best-seller but a celebrity itself. Then, link this with you and Tutu (irony upon irony, if you will). So we're in the midst of this. Where does it lead? What can we do about it? Can we make it work for "good" instead of our being simply slaves or victims of it? I think you need to shut out the world briefly, concentrate, focus, and do a damn fine first draft of the Celebrity chapter—which should, in reality, lead off the book itself. It gives the book its glamour, its immediacy, its hard challenge, its utter relevance. It simply combines sacred and secular by DOING it instead of merely "talking about" it. . . .

You need to be unafraid to bring yourself into the center of things. Including your fears, inadequacies, confusions, awakenings. In a sense the book is a thrilling trajectory of spiritual direction as well as a biography. You're looking into your own life as well as into mine. So what does "success" mean? What can/does one do with "fame"? Include Tutu. "What's it all about, Alfie?" But why are "success" and "fame" so often suicidal and self-destructive? (Why do they often seem to bring out the worst in people?) Indeed, why are they seen as selfish? How is this related to Jesus—and, especially, to the cross?

There is so much involved here! Isn't it fascinating????[28]

So, here, in this book, is my response to Malcolm. This is not just another black book or gay book. This book is born on the miracle of the election of Barack Obama, which no doubt makes both Malcolm and me reflect more deeply about the repercussions of the Civil Rights Movement. For example, is it over? Also, this book emerges in the threshold of the debate for full inclusion of gay and lesbian persons. Can they marry? Is marriage a good idea? And could a gay or lesbian person be a head of a church? The answers that a reader discovers in the life of Malcolm Boyd are deeply contemporary (he is way ahead of his time)—and more importantly deeply divine.

Beyond getting to know Malcolm as a modern-day prophet, I have now enjoyed the privilege of receiving spiritual direction from Malcolm. Because of the life of God that I have learned from Malcolm, I think it is appropriate that I give some of this spiritual direction to the reader as well. I, therefore, write this book as it is intended to be read—with new

---

28. Malcolm Boyd, "Black Horse of Famine," e-mail message to author, September 4, 2009.

perspective while at the same time testing current and past realities. So, read this biography as a focused reflection upon a person conscious of unnecessary hierarchies and false gods. By doing so, the genius that you will discover is that none of us are called to worship false gods.

> Dear Michael: I realize for the first time what an extraordinary book you have here. It is a part of (has grown out of) spiritual direction. Quite aside from the book itself, this is simply extraordinary.
>
> The book is not only my biography. It is also your autobiography in numerous ways. You must place yourself (as well as myself) in these pages. I believe you already are doing this. So it can be informal in places, intimate, unpretentious, natural, even conversational. This is the progression of your own spiritual development growing out of our conversations and our looking together at similar issues and themes. Here, the very title of the book comes alive. I'm wondering if perhaps the subtitle should be changed from "A Biography of Malcolm Boyd" to "Biography-cum-Autobiography."
>
> This can make the book itself a matter (and example) of global and international interest. This can be of intense interest. What is going on here? Something altogether fascinating, unique—that teaches virtually everyone new directions, insights, questions, approaches. It also opens up countless "old" questions and dilemmas, illustrating how to approach them in altogether fresh ways, with new attitudes and insights.
>
> SO you place yourself in the book from the outset. (I think you're doing this.) There's dialogue (with me) instead of monologue. As we trace our public course, I've also offered you—step by step, detail by detail—spiritual direction. I love the scope and naturalness and depth of this. Actually, all sorts of people in all sorts of places may want to read and share this book.
>
> Your chapters are your own genius. Pursue them. (Talk about gravitas.) Next week I'll have an opportunity to delve into chapter one and respond specifically to you in detail.[29]

---

29. Malcolm Boyd, "The Book," e-mail message to author, July 22, 2009.

CHAPTER ONE

Running with the Horses

*If you have raced with foot-runners
and they have wearied you,
how will you compete with horses?*
(Jeremiah 12:5)

In light of the title of this book, Malcolm's life reimagines the four horsemen of the Apocalypse described in the Bible. In the book of Revelation, chapter 6, ride the four horsemen of Pestilence, War, Famine, and Death. The image of the four horsemen gives shape to the chapters of this biography. After the glowing accolades of Malcolm already mentioned in the foreword and introduction, why this dark tone and chapter structure to describe Malcolm's life? Simply put, the four riders of the Apocalypse help me to connect the dots of Malcolm's deeply textured and nuanced life. Malcolm's life seems symmetrically organized around the continuing apocalyptic threats that still wreak havoc on planet earth. Before we look at the four horsemen and how they correspond to Malcolm's life, a short story is in order. The primary imagery and metaphor of the four horsemen invites the reader into the apocalyptic presence that Malcolm often brought to his audience.

The questioner was a girl, about twenty, with somber brown hair, big droopy eyes, and a thin-line quivering mouth. She was sitting, straight-backed and intent, in the Dwight Hall Common Room at Yale University beneath the tapestries and heavy architecture which make the room seem smaller than it is.

She was pleading with Malcolm, who was sipping coffee as the week's guest sermonizer must at the coffee hour. What she wanted, and what everyone wants out of Malcolm, was an answer—something solid, a

Nightclub Priest Bids Church 'Get Down to Earth'
By GEORGE DUGAN
New York Times (1857-Current file); Sep 17, 1966; ProQuest Historical Newspapers The New York Times (1851 - 2005) pg. 32

Nightclub Priest Bids Church 'Get Down to Earth'

Boyd Warns Christianity May 'Die' in 2 Generations

He Calls for Urban Centers and Modern Discussion

By GEORGE DUGAN

The Episcopal priest who opened a month-long stand this week as a paid performer at the hungry i, a sophisticated nightclub in San Francisco, is convinced that the Christian church will be dead in two generations unless it "comes down to earth."

The 43-year-old priest, the Rev. Malcolm Boyd, gave up a career in television and radio 11 years ago to enter the ministry.

An intense, nervous man who seems never to be quite sure that he is doing the right thing, despite his strong convictions, he has frequently been in hot water with some of his colleagues.

Unpopular With Superiors

He ruffled his superiors five years ago when he heard confessions in a bar, organized a series of "espresso nights" in a converted garage and publicly charged Christianity with "smugness" and "snobbishness." As a result, he was asked to resign as chaplain for Episcopal students at Colorado State University.

Moving to Detroit, Father Boyd got into trouble with his superiors there for writing and appearing in plays that used "vulgarity and profanity." He was politely asked to take his evangelism elsewhere.

His headquarters are now in Washington, where he holds the title of Episcopal chaplain-at-large to college campuses.

At the hungry i, the controversial priest is making his first appearance as a paid performer. His $1,000-a-week salary will be turned over to agencies concerned with the civil rights movement.

The Rev. Malcolm Boyd

coffee and old-fashioned "bull sessions" on love and sex. He favored what he described as "bar evangelism," wherein a roving minister might supplant the bartender as a psychological counselor.

According to Father Boyd, seminaries are at least 50 years behind the times. He said that students for the ministry now come out of "isolation" without the slightest idea of how to relate themselves to the world into which they are suddenly thrust.

His latest book, "Are You Running With Me, Jesus?" published by Holt, Rinehart & Winston, drew critical applause.

A collection of private prayers, completely informal and ranging from civil rights to unwanted pregnancy, the volume was described by a New York Times reviewer as, "to my considerable surprise, a very moving book."

Father Boyd's plays are directed mostly against racial discrimination and "institutionalized" church life. He holds that the media of the theater and motion pictures have far more impact than pulpit sermons.

The Episcopal priest, short and a bit on the stocky side, with receding gray hair, was born in Buffalo.

He was graduated from the University of Arizona in 1944, and went to Hollywood, where he embarked on a public relations career with Mary Pickford and Buddy Rogers. Radio and television writing followed.

In the early 1950's he began studying for the priesthood at Union Theological Seminary here and at Oxford University in England.

New York Times *article where Malcolm predicts the death of Christianity.*

bedrock to refer to when everything else is crumbling. She wanted a bright light, a quick conversion, a truth.

She was looking earnestly to Malcolm probably because she had read his "prayer book"—*Are You Running with Me, Jesus?*—and knew his struggle was hers. She asked the short, almost bullet-shaped priest what were his "absolutes."

Malcolm's answer was simple and misleading. "God, I guess, and community, and probably Jesus." One might think he meant heavenly father, sacred church, and holy son, if one didn't hear what followed.

"But I can't believe love and justice are absolutes, although I once did. This morning I read about Orangeburg, South Carolina. The Orangeburg massacre occurred on February 8, 1968, when nine South Carolina Highway Patrol officers fired into a crowd protesting local segregation. Three men were killed and twenty-eight more were injured (mostly shots in their backs). After the massacre, two others were injured by police. And a pregnant woman later had a miscarriage due to being beaten. The Orangeburg massacre predates other major civil rights revolts such as the Kent State shootings and the Jackson State deaths."

Because of these violent contexts, Malcolm's jolting candor bars him from handing out easy answers to the hung-up. He can't talk about heavenly father or sacred church because he doesn't understand them in terms of "crisis" or "napalm." He didn't even want to climb the Battell pulpit in Yale's chapel earlier that morning, because he couldn't see the reason why he should be up there. He's too impatient to cope with boring liturgy, unheard music, and velvet-laden gowns.

Two weeks earlier in New York, *Readers' Digest*, of all groups, sponsored a discussion of "religion in a world of change," whatever that means, and Malcolm was one of the panelists.

The questioner this time was a Kent-smoker, fiftyish, with no lemon juice in his yellowy-white hair. Frankly troubled, like any normal vestryman, his normally sedate nervous system was jumpy and he could sit no longer. A kindly woman had asked Yale chaplain William Sloan Coffin, another panelist, what he would tell a young man who wanted to become a minister. Coffin answered by saying he could not tell anyone what to do, he could only ask questions the young man might not have already answered. The Kent-smoker's normally pink face was reddening. He had to interrupt.

"If you church leaders don't attempt to lead, then who . . . ?" This was Malcolm's cue.

"We're not leaders, man. How could we be? *Readers' Digest* just got us together to talk some things over."

Malcolm is irony. He is a "leader" of the "alienated," but he refuses the onus of leadership. He is a priest, but he hasn't the concrete faith of a Coffin. He is the only campus lecturer who is likely to say "I don't know" a half-dozen times every night.

"Boyd's a sensationalist," says one Yale student. Another adds, "Boyd's an ass. I just can't handle an Episcopalian minister who says 'bitch.'"

Malcolm is masterful in front of an audience, born and trained. When he was concluding his talk in Battell, he had even the easy doubters and cool sophisticates moving to his beat. He uses the shock effect because it keeps the audience with him and because that is often the only way to communicate. He is seldom at one campus for more than two days and never at one university more than twice a year. He must be bluntly honest, because there is no time to cajole and persuade.[1] Because of how Malcolm affects his audiences, I perceive Malcolm's life in the framework of the "Four Horsemen of the Apocalypse."

The beginning of the book of Revelation tells of a scroll in God's right hand that is sealed with seven seals. Jesus opens the first four of the seven seals, which summons forth the four beasts that ride on white, red, black, and pale-green horses symbolizing conquest, war, famine, and death, respectively. For some, the interpretation of the Christian apocalyptic vision is for the four horsemen to wreak havoc upon the world as harbingers of the end of the world. Such interpretations are dangerous among those who may not fully understand the complexity of power revealed in this surreal book of Revelation. For example, the influence of this Armageddon theology is reflected in a Federal Bureau of Investigation report that certain individuals have acquired weapons, stored food and clothing, raised funds, procured safe houses, prepared compounds, and recruited converts to their cause, all in preparation for foreign attacks. Many believe in the militia movement in the United States that the Antichrist will attempt to take over the world in the near future. There were over 100 extremist militias that the Southern Poverty Law Center has identified as active in the United States in 2009. In March 2010, one of these militia units, called the Hutaree, had several members arrested for planning an attack on the police.[2]

So, interpretation of the book of Revelation must be entered into carefully. Each of the four riders is summoned onto human history by one of

---

1. Malcolm Boyd, "991/2 Irony and Mr. Boyd," *Yale Daily News*, February 14, 1968.
2. "Hutaree Militia Members Arrested in Plot to Murder Police," *The Southern Poverty Law Center, Intelligence Report*, Summer 2010.

the heavenly living creatures. The opening of the first four seals reveal the four horsemen of the Apocalypse. Each one of the four living creatures reveals a horseman, the first three horsemen are summed up by the fourth horsemen, "They were given power over a fourth of the earth to kill by sword, famine and plague, and by the wild beasts of the earth." But remember, power in heaven is strange, if not seemingly unstable.

Although the four horsemen of the Apocalypse are described in just eight verses of the book of Revelation (chapter 6:1–8), which is the last book in the Bible, they are also eerily foretold in the same chapter and verses of the Hebrew Bible, from Zechariah (6:1–8) in which there are four chariots pulled by variously colored horses, conveying the four spirits of heaven proceeding from God to the world. The four horses also travel in four directions, that is, they affect the whole earth. For Zechariah, the horses appear in the following order, red, black, white, and finally the pale horse. Zechariah's horses differ from Revelation's not only in their order but also they do not indicate anything about their characters since they are more like sentries than like agents of destruction or judgment.

In Revelation, the four horsemen appear when the Lamb (Jesus) opens the first four seals of a scroll. A seal was a security measure used when a letter was dispatched from a royal office. Often this seal was made using a signet ring, hence the word signature. Such imagery is fitting for the Revelation of John since the biblical message was often conveyed through epistles or letters. In the strange vision of Revelation, the seals were not just security measures. Such seals meant something much more. John's Revelation contained all together the following seven seals:[3]

1. The white horse
2. The red horse
3. The black horse
4. The pale horse
5. The martyrs
6. Anarchy
7. The fanfare of trumpets

---

3. The first four seals pertain to the four horsemen. The fifth seal reveals those who had been slain because of the word of God and their testimony, which is the persecuted church. The sixth seal reveals the day of the Lord, which brings the Lamb's wrath to those on the earth. The opening of the seventh seal reveals silence. The seven seals sum up human history from the viewpoint of heaven and the church. There is war, famine, and pestilence in general and on the church in particular, there is persecution, and when the end comes, it will bring terror to the world; this probably accounts for the silence of the seventh seal.

As each of the first four seals are opened, a different colored horse and its rider is revealed. And yet, earlier in John's Revelation (chapter 4) we see God seated on the throne in heaven, but also sovereign over earthly events. A paradox of power occurs as the Lamb (Jesus) appears in chapter 6 and takes the scroll from God. This is a paradox because how can a lamb be powerful? And yet the Lamb not only snatches the scroll, he also breaks the seals, a privilege only for Kings. To further the paradox, especially as practiced by the less divine, the first horse and rider, white in color, is interpreted as good, representing either Jesus or the church going out, in victory, sharing the gospel. The time, however, eventually came when the church became a persecuting power, mutating to a second rider on a red horse with a sword in his hand. The paradox here is in how the first horse and rider is juxtaposed to the second, who represents a history in which the church turned on its own members. The crime of many who were killed was the "crime" of reading the Bible. For example, in the year 1215 Pope Innocent III issued a law commanding "that they shall be seized for trial and penalties, who engage in the translation of the sacred volumes, or who hold secret conventicles, or who assume the office of preaching without the authority of their superiors; against whom process shall be commenced, without any permission of appeal."[4] Innocent "declared that as by the old law, the beast touching the holy mount was to be stoned to death, so simple and uneducated men were not to touch the Bible or venture to preach its doctrines."[5]

Rather than promoting erroneous interpretations of this important book of the Bible, the key to interpreting Revelation is Jesus. This is Malcolm's key interpretation as well. Similar to the way the first century had a difficult time interpreting the Messiah as someone meek and mild like Jesus, so do we have complexity in interpreting Revelation, the second coming of Jesus. What is described by the seals is similar to the signs of the end of the age as described by Jesus in Matthew 24. There will be wars, famines, and earthquakes (Matt 24:6–8); persecution (24:9–14); and the heavenly bodies will be shaken (Matt 24:29): "Then the sign of the Son of Man will appear in heaven, and then all the tribes of the earth will mourn" (Matt 24:30). After the opening of the seven seals, the scroll can be read and we will find more detail, but this starts in chapter 8. The seven seals describe tribulation that is largely the result of human foibles

---

4. J. P. Callender, *Illustrations of Popery* (New York: Francis F. Ripley, 1838), 387.

5. Philip Schaff, *History of the Christian Church VI* (New York: Charles Scribner's Sons, 1910), 723.

(wars, famine, and persecution) but under the control of God. The fact that the seven seals are opened by Christ indicates his sovereignty over the future. Jesus is the Alpha and the Omega, the First and the Last, the Beginning and the End (Rev 22:13); he is sovereign from the beginning to the end of history, and everything in between.

Focus on Jesus in the book of Revelation should prevent militia and extremist groups because John's vision indicates that these strange occurrences all occurred under the sovereignty of God. I think this is strange; after all, the Lamb is the most powerful one. Even if we do not understand the message of Revelation, the reader is obligated to give assent to God whose strange sovereignty lasts from the start to the finish. The Lamb's enemies end up defeated and punished while the saints are vindicated and rewarded. The revelation ends with a new heaven and a new earth where there will be no more death, crying, or pain. The vision all along was for a different use of power in which a Lamb sits on the throne of heaven. God's plan for the future of the world, especially as the apocalyptic vision is progressively revealed, is not to destroy, but to create. This revelation comes with the instructions to record the prophesy so that it can be used to encourage a struggling first-century church. In many ways, Malcolm fits this progressive apocalyptic vision—especially as Malcolm seeks to create rather than destroy.

This detailed review and interpretation of the seven seals is necessary for understanding Malcolm because so much of Malcolm's public impact was either interpreted as creative or destructive. The verdict seemed to be in the eye of the beholder. Similar to the early church's apocalyptic literature, how one interprets the end times of an empire often depended upon having power or not. On one hand, if you were invested in the power structures of the empire, of course apocalyptic realities were seen more as a horror movie. On the other hand, if you were marginalized or oppressed (like the early church), apocalyptic realities meant something else entirely. The oppressed longed for the toppling of the empire. For the marginalized and oppressed, the Apocalypse is actually a creative act.

Today, especially in our Western culture, it is difficult to be encouraged by apocalyptic worldviews. Malcolm's genius in many ways represents the divide between how apocalyptic worldviews seek to encourage societies out of ruts and how modern-day society has a difficult time receiving such worldviews as constructive and creative. Of course, any society struggles with its own end; after all, who can really handle "extra-reality" judging our current reality? Our particular struggle in the Western world comes because we expect an empirical revelation full of complete and technical accuracy. We were the masters of such revelation, but now we are beginning to see Chinese and Indian children out achieving our own. Instead of being insecure, Malcolm is helpful to the Western worldview. Malcolm's apocalyptic worldview entails judging the world according to extra-wordly or transcendent standards. In other words, instead of seeing others as a threat to our existence, why not simply understand that the world never stays the same?

Malcolm's mission was in fact one of encouraging the church, but not in ways that she often wanted. Malcolm's word of God revealed God as one who could transcend all of us and yet sit in a coffee shop and a bar, a God who could love us equally in Sunday morning worship and Friday night laughter. Consequently, Malcolm approaches God's revelation without too much anxiety about whether he has gotten such revelation precisely correct. His mission is simply to make known that there is indeed a revelation from God.

This revelation often comes across as apocalyptic to those who cannot accept truth and reality as coming beyond self (and even Western culture). Malcolm's vision is akin to the writer of Revelation who envisions four horsemen galloping through the desert on a horse with no name. But Malcolm accepts the judgments that are coming and tries his best to help us do so as well as he gleans what has been given to him in the poetic imagery of God who transcends us and yet drinks coffee with us.

Though the faith-minded might find comfort in my interpretation of Malcolm's impact, there is also a challenge to us as well—namely, the imminent side of God (the One who drinks coffee with sinners) is not all there is to God. God is also transcendent. So, although the faith-minded may look for the seven signs of the Apocalypse as taking place in the order in which they appear in Revelation, there is little need to actually follow this order. To understand that God transcends us should actually take the pressure off. Belief in God alerts us to the fact that our interpretations of reality usually carry with them self-fulfilling prophecies that often end us in ditches rather than flourishing places. In other words, God keeps us honest between hope and despair. Malcolm irritates the faith-minded just as he does the empirically-minded in that no one can be self-sufficient, really. In addition, for many faith-minded, Malcolm could never be their brother due to their never being able to accept his identity as a white, gay Episcopal priest. Keep in mind that Malcolm's impact comes through his poetic, apocalyptic literary style that paints a picture of how God's kingdom accepts a person wherever they are.

When Malcolm prays, "Are you running with me?" he prays to a Jesus who came to fulfill the promise that God made to Abraham that his descendents will be impossible to count. In fact, Malcolm's message does not bring us a new revelation, but rather places in writing the same message that Jesus brought us, but does so in a wonderful and colorful literary style.

White Horse

In my first chapter I look at the first horseman of pestilence who rides the white horse. The writer of Revelation describes it this way, "When the Lamb had opened the first of the seven seals, I heard the first of the four beasts say with a thundering voice, 'Come and see.' And I beheld, and lo a white horse; and he that sat on him had a bow: and there was given unto him a crown, and he departed as conqueror and to conquest" (Rev 6:1–2). **Malcolm is this White Knight representing pestilence because of his "queer" identity, his celebrity, and his shocking words.**

The white horse and its rider are ambiguous images that create polarities between good and evil, depending on one's interpretation. For many biblical scholars, they see the White Knight as civil war and internal strife. Some go so far as to say the rider of the white horse is the Antichrist, or a representation of false prophets. Pestilence follows wherever this White Knight appears. Malcolm's appearance certainly caused strife as he came out in public as a gay priest. Of course, I cannot write this biography without exploring Malcolm's gay identity. Such identity becomes complex in light of his secular witness as a civil rights leader and his religious identity as an Episcopal priest. Malcolm writes, "My presence as a gay man and elder should be thought through in light of someone like Bayard Rustin, who organized the March on Washington, but whose role was never really acknowledged." And so, this biography seeks to acknowledge Malcolm's role in the Civil Rights Movement—and even more, to shed some light on Malcolm's groundbreaking wisdom in understanding the relation of civil rights to gay rights.[6]

As already mentioned, another aspect of Malcolm's pestilence is in his celebrity status. Malcolm offers groundbreaking wisdom due to his ability

---

6. See especially Malcolm's book *Gay Priest: An Inner Journey* (New York: St. Martin's Press, 1986). The Right Reverend V. Gene Robinson, Bishop of New Hampshire, wrote the foreword of *A Prophet in His Own Land: A Malcolm Boyd Reader* (Brooklyn, NY: White Crane Books, 2008).

to reach large publics without watering down his authenticity. This ability invites us to reflect upon Malcolm's life as a celebrity figure. For example, a reporter shoved a microphone in Malcolm's face and asked, "They just announced that God is dead. Do you have a comment?" This dynamic of celebrity is true, especially, following the publication in 1965 of the spiritual classic and international best-seller *Are You Running with Me, Jesus?*[7] For many, the combination of being both gay and a celebrity priest is an abomination or is just plain sick. The rider of the white horse (or the White Knight) fits Malcolm because there are concurrent meanings: white for goodness, but a pestilence because his words frequently shocked and offended. The White Knight causes polarities between good and evil, destruction and creation. Among the civil wars concerning full inclusion of gay identity, interpretations swung between extremes as to whether gay people could be fully human, married, serve in the military, and even be Christian. Malcolm's life demonstrated such pendulum swings. In terms of the pendulum swinging toward goodness, according to Revelation 19, the rider on the white horse is depicted as the Word of God. In the end, however, the White Knight not only represents Malcolm's queer identity and celebrity status, it also represents the pestilence of the white horse because of his shocking words. Much of Malcolm's work was deemed controversial and apocalyptic because Malcolm's word of God shocks—words like, "Jesus had a penis."[8] "Malcolm proclaims that we minister to Jesus—the Jesus who comes in Matthew in the guise of the needy, the thirsty, and the naked—when we minister to a "nigger," a "kike," a "dago," a "queer," a "dyke," or a "faggot."[9] Such a word from the Lord made people **sick** of Malcolm. The pestilence of Malcolm's words drove many to extremes. So, not only was Malcolm a White Knight bringing pestilence, he was doing this through the controversy of his poetry, theology, and prophecy. The White Knight proclaimed that the end of the world and judgment day would occur if people did not repent for racism, a continuation of hunger, torture for masses of people, environmental collapse, and the division of people into warring tribes.

Thus the rider of the White Horse seems to appropriately represent Malcolm in at least three aspects: his gay identity, celebrity, and shocking language. The symbol of the White Knight is crucial to begin reflection on Malcolm's life.

---

7. 40th Anniversary ed. (Cambridge, MA: Cowley Publications, 2006).
8. Malcolm Boyd, *Take Off the Masks* (San Francisco: HarperSanFrancisco, 1993), 163.
9. Boyd, *Take Off the Masks*, 202.

Red Horse

In my third chapter, Malcolm is also the apocalyptic rider of war. The red color of his horse represents blood spilled on the battlefield. He carries a powerful sword that represents battle. **Malcolm is also this red rider of war because of his courage to fight against racism and war, conformity and indifference, the misuse of religion, and a flagrant worship of false gods.**

I am happy that Malcolm approved the first part of the title of this book, "Black Battle." In so doing, he has allowed this creative biography in which my name is also a part of the book. Malcolm's keen mind was always aware of the pun of my name as he writes:

> Dear Michael: I'm at the Cathedral Center and the coming storm is ominous, hovering around stone towers, threatening all peace and security. Armageddon. The Final Battle (oops! Don't take that personally) looms. Where shall I hide? Actually I won't, I think I'll just go home and wait out the whole bloody thing. I can already hear the Final Rain start beating on the roof.
>
> Well, however, we have a meeting tomorrow. (The Final Battle will have to wait, won't it?) Apparently I will await you at home around 1 PM. This is an important one in our mutual progress. Don't forget to park on Tracy where there are no meters. All best—Malcolm[10]

The genre of this biography is unusual because of my spiritual direction with Malcolm. More importantly, my voice is here. This proves to be unusual but helpful. This is unusual because I am a younger, black, heterosexual writer describing the converse of myself. And this is helpful because Malcolm's life witness can be made more available to those populations more like my own who have not been privy to Malcolm's genius and divine words. But Malcolm's battle is more than engagement with me. Like theologian William Stringfellow, Malcolm went to war against the powers and principalities. "And there went out another horse that was red: and power was given to him that sat thereon to take peace from the earth, and that they should kill one another: and there was given unto him a great sword" (Rev 6:4, KJV).

As I have researched Malcolm's life, many see him as civil war incarnate and internal strife—even the Antichrist. A letter to Malcolm read, "You should *never* use the word gay with the same breath with the Lord.

---

10. Malcolm Boyd, "The Final Battle," e-mail message to author, January 20, 2010.

He *hates* gay." And another: "The Jesus in me loves you. But as I watched you on the TV set, I wept openly that the sweet and tender Jesus that I love so much would be distorted and misrepresented."[11] All of this is complicated by Malcolm's own inner strife. For many years, Malcolm saw himself this way. "I repressed my own feelings for a long, long time, thinking God viewed homosexuality as ugly, demonic, and sinful. Now I know it's beautiful and God loves it."[12]

In this biography, one of the identities of Malcolm as the purveyor of war comes from his days as a civil rights activist. Malcolm asked me to recognize—and pinpoint—the role of the white volunteers and followers in the Civil Rights Movement. In Malcolm's case, a key highlight came in 1961 when he was a Freedom Rider.[13] Malcolm narrates how he and several others moved from the Freedom Ride itself to a subsequent visit to the University of the South (Sewanee).

> The staunchly traditional undergraduate student body remained all white. Encouraged by the interracialism of the nearby Highlander Folk School, local seminarians had been pressing for a full desegregation of the campus for several years, but university and church officials had refused to confront the issue, including a strict color bar at a popular on-campus restaurant leased to a local segregationist. As soon as Boyd and the other pilgrims arrived on campus and discovered that the restaurant remained segregated, he announced plans for a sit-in and a hunger strike. By Friday morning, however, Boyd had received assurances from church and campus officials that all of the university's facilities would be desegregated in the near future. After the Presiding Episcopal Bishop of the United States, the Right Reverend Arthur C. Lichtenberger, issued a strong public statement endorsing the prayer pilgrimage and condemning racial discrimination, Boyd and his colleagues canceled the planned protests and departed for the (General) Convention in Detroit.[14]

Malcolm writes me and comments on this historical account during the civil rights period. He laments that very little apology has taken place in institutional structures regarding racism. Malcolm writes me:

---

11. Boyd, *Take Off the Masks*, 161–62.
12. Ibid., 142.
13. His role is documented in Raymond Arsenault, *Freedom Riders: 1961 and the Struggle for Racial Justice* (New York: Oxford University Press, 2006).
14. Ibid., 433.

It does seem to me that Sewanee has decided and tried to "bury" this and not include it in its public "history." Remember the woman from Sewanee attending a conference in LA, and with whom I lunched one day, who had "never heard of" any of this? You'd think that I might have been invited at some time since 1961 to "visit" Sewanee as an "honored guest" to participate in a discussion of racial issues and seek together to find new ways of "coming together and healing." I feel as if the entire Sewanee incident had never happened or taken place![15]

However, this biography does not so much seek to provide a detailed description of such events as to display an authentic white, gay, and Christian identity known as Malcolm Boyd that emerged over many years. I am especially grateful to Malcolm for offering the reader the archives of history that document a deeper vision of his life, especially the early events in his life that set the trajectory for his courageous witness against American injustices. What we discover here is encouraging to many of us who discover that Malcolm is extraordinary in his ordinariness.

Black Horse

In my fourth chapter, Malcolm rides the third horse, the black horse called Famine. The black color of the third horse represents the grim circumstances of malnutrition. "And when he had opened the third seal, I heard the third beast say, 'Come and see.' And I beheld, and lo a black horse; and he that sat on him had a pair of balances in his hand. And I heard a voice in the midst of the four beasts say, a measure of wheat for a penny, and three measures of barley for a penny; and see thou hurt not the oil and the wine" (Rev 6:5–6, KJV). **Malcolm is the black rider of famine because of his constant theme that the institutional church could no longer feed people.**

An example of such a famished church was in how the institutional church lacked sufficient sustenance to remain intact over issues like slavery. Many Christian denominations resulted because of the split over slavery (e.g., Presbyterians of America, Presbyterians USA, Southern Baptists, National Baptists, the African American Episcopal Church, the Episcopal Church [ECUSA] etc). A church with a strong body would not easily split over whether or not a black person should be a slave or free. A strong, well fed church would not split during the Civil Rights Move-

---

15. Malcolm Boyd, "Material on 1961 Freedom Ride," e-mail message to author, December 28, 2009.

ment. Such splits would not occur if the church body were secure in its primary identity revealed in Jesus. When baptized in Jesus, primary identity is revealed as the corporate identity of Jesus who organizes all of our other particular identities (e.g., male, female, black, white, slave, free, etc.). The problem, however, is that the church often fails to demonstrate primary Christian identity—instead revealing a weak and divided body of people in conflict.

This famine aspect of Malcolm can be seen in Malcolm's role as an Episcopal priest. Malcolm wrote me, "I was on the Freedom Ride as a priest (it was called a 'Prayer Pilgrimage'). Through the 1960s I was as deeply involved in civil rights as any human being could be."[16] As we met weekly, I explored Malcolm's times and places as a priest, especially in the unusual circumstances of Malcolm serving with Martin Luther King Jr. Then, continuing to follow MLK, Malcolm's involvement against the Vietnam War, including an arrest inside the Pentagon while engaged in a Peace Mass in a corridor. What was unusual was how such events occurred through Malcolm's identity as an Episcopal priest.

Since much of Malcolm's life has been devoted to the civil rights of African Americans, I think it appropriate that this biographer is an African American who is different from Malcolm in age, race, and sexual orientation and yet resembles Malcolm's identity as a writer, anti-war activist, theologian, civil rights advocate, and Episcopal priest in the institutional church.

Being gay in the institutional church made Malcolm "black." Malcolm's identity as a gay white man remains a stumbling block for many, especially those in institutional religion and more communal societies that socialize their members to see gay identity as an aberration. Such communities are often patterned around ethnicity and socioeconomic status. I also think it profound for me as a black heterosexual male to reflect upon Malcolm's life in that much of the current tensions in religion are between more ethnic-minded identities—such as black and brown people—and white, liberally minded people who tend more to accept gay and lesbian people.

Malcolm taught me that all institutions are about self-preservation and perhaps this why he has been such an apocalyptic figure in relationship to

---

16. This is documented in two books: Michael B. Friedland, *Lift Up Your Voice Like a Trumpet* (Chapel Hill: University of North Carolina Press, 1998), and Gardiner H. Shattuck Jr., *Episcopalians and Race: Civil War to Civil Rights* (Lexington: University Press of Kentucky, 2000). Much more research could be done in Malcolm Boyd Archive at Boston University.

what counts for religion today. "I don't know why I am that way," Malcolm told me (April 9, 2009). Being an institutional person myself (and in need of the epiphanies that Malcolm offers), I should not offer literary analysis or ruin your own epiphanies with my own; however, I have learned from Malcolm not to conclude from the demise of institutional religion that life is bleak and deterministic. Appropriate to Malcolm's own character, there is an inherent optimism or hope in these pages. Like rigorous archeological digging, we may need to unlearn a lot of our own caricatures and stereotypes in order to see the hope in this book, but it is here. We need only to let God be God in order to escape the famine of institutional religion.

Pale Green Horse

In my fifth chapter, I describe the last horseman that Malcolm resembles, the fourth horseman who rides on a pale horse explicitly named Death. However, the Greek word translated in this context as "pale" is elsewhere in the New Testament translated as "green," leading to some confusion. Such confusion fits Malcolm nicely. As one columnist wrote, "Malcolm is fast. Very fast. For 10 years he spins and fakes and breaks into the open field, fist clenched and the muse throbbing in his heart. The crowd cheers wildly as he sprints toward the goal, but just as he is about to cross the line, it evaporates." Another columnist describes Malcolm's ambiguity this way, that his "manner suggests the turbulent waves of the storm breaking over man, church and the American life."[17]

Such confusion is normal, however, when you deal with Malcolm. When death occurs, you inevitably bear the brunt of chaos. The writer of Revelation explains, "And when he had opened the fourth seal, I heard the fourth beast say, 'Come and see.' And I beheld, and lo a pale green horse; and he that sat on him was called Death, and Hades followed with him. And power was given to them over a fourth of the earth, and that they (the four horsemen) should kill with sword, and with hunger, and with death, and with the beasts of the earth" (6:7–8).

In his Pulitzer Prize–winning book *The Hours*, Michael Cunningham writes, "There is something worse than death, with its promise of release and slumber." After reading the book and this particular quote, Malcolm writes me, "Incredibly painful and revealing work! I find this *significant* but I *disagree* with Cunningham's conclusion. Is this relevant to this book?" I think this indeed is relevant. First, Cunningham provides the most remarkable performance piece about growing up white and gay in

---

17. Boyd, *Take Off the Masks*, 118.

South Africa. Such crosscurrents of being gay in apartheid South Africa was indeed relevant to Malcolm's own life.

Second, the quote from Cunningham initiated one of Malcolm's deepest insights that runs through this book, that there is something worse than death. In death as in Malcolm's life, he believes there is a peace that contains a deep restlessness. In other words, the goal of life is not a death in which people find static peace. In Malcolm's Christian worldview, the goal is not for such peace. He likes to recall theologian Karl Barth's words that there is sinking and suffering, and being lost and rent asunder, in the peace of God. He writes about this in "To a Prophet Dying Young."

> It wasn't easy knowing you, or even hearing you. I felt, in fact, that you were often strong-willed, uncharitable, and impolite.
>
> I saw you pouring out your life. I resented that, too, as I safely clutched my own. But I *did* see you, though I sometimes didn't want you to know it.
>
> Yes, I heard the criticism—and joined in. At times I thought I hated you, because what you said and did cut so painfully against my mask, my security, my being.
>
> I miss you very much. Thank you—for who you were and whose you were. You wouldn't want me to wish you "peace," and I could never think of you in any misalliance with a false truce or easy compromise.
>
> But I do, with all my heart, wish you peace with deep restlessness, a cock crowing at dawn to announce battle, and love to heal the necessary wounds.[18]

Malcolm rides this Green Horse of Death because of his deep spirituality in which at some point in his life he was no longer afraid of death. Being eighty-six years old, Malcolm has cheated death and offers the reader the wisdom to do the same. Malcolm's wisdom concerns the paradoxes that we all must face of gaining our life by losing it; and losing our life to find it. Having cheated death, Malcolm offers twenty-first-century people deep wisdom. To begin with, nothing can be resolved regarding racial, religious, and sexual identity until we can all confess the absurd. How does one confess the absurd?

When I was a student at Princeton Theological Seminary, I heard a fellow seminarian preach in a maximum-security prison unit in Trenton,

---

18. Malcolm Boyd, "To a Prophet Dying Young," in *Free to Live, Free to Die* (New York: Signet Publishers, 1970), 87.

New Jersey, when an inmate interrupted the sermon to rebuke the inconsiderate inmates talking in the corner. "Shut up!" he growled, while staring at them with wild eyes. The others laughed while he gritted his teeth. This was the same inmate I saw earlier beating the top of his head with both hands to the beat of *Blessed Assurance.* A black man, ill-clad, wearing white and faded blue jeans, he lived in a different world than the rest of us and he wanted to get on with "church." But his interruption did not seem to stop the others from talking.

With peculiar gyrations he continued his command to "shut up," his arms flinging like a symphony conductor. This black conductor looked at the other black men, a majority of whom continued to talk, and screamed at them in the middle of my friend's sermon, "Are you in church or where you at?" A peculiar question I thought. How could he really expect others to believe this was a real church service in the middle of a maximum-security prison unit? Sure, they had sung hymns, there were ministers in the room, there was a lectern posing as a pulpit, there were musical instruments for praising God, the chairs were lined up in the room for an assembly of people, and they even prayed to God as if God were truly there. But how could he really expect to be "at" church when an armed guard stood by the door? The rational explanation is that he does not fit in the normal world. The prisoner's world is intentionally meant not to be a free person's world; however, I soon discovered that the world within that prison that can make room for a "church service" can often do it better and more meaningfully than the world outside the prison walls.

Malcolm's life facilitated my reflection on my own normality of trying to fit my vocation with my identity. I seek to do that by making peace and revealing truth and reconciliation, which for many is absurd. In a world full of elite survival and business skills, my vocation of making peace and revealing reconciliation is as unlikely to succeed as the prisoner's church is to fit into a maximum security unit. Malcolm's life helped me to see how the prisoner's command to "shut up" and his question, "Are you in church or where you at?" is a challenge to analyze the nature of what absurd and bold things we are all called to be and do. Malcolm's life also invites the reader to reflect on how one may seem to be living the contradiction between vocation and a stifling job in the "normal" world. When listening to Malcolm's wisdom, perhaps we will only be perceived as a deranged prisoner in pursuing the living God, but that is a chance we should be willing to take.

Malcolm's stroke of genius, akin to other exemplars like Desmond Tutu and the Dalai Lama, is to disarm our false selves and make us pay attention to the often painful reality of authenticity. He does this through deep humor, profound social awareness, and responsible social activism.

An example of Malcolm's sense of humor and social awareness occurred back in his twenties when he worked in Hollywood for a major advertising agency and would eat lunch at a well-known restaurant where the biggest names in the movie industry gathered. One was Ronald Reagan's older brother, Neil, who was an ad agency executive.

Neil was gracious and helpful to Malcolm, a young guy starting out, and always greeted Malcolm publicly in a friendly way. One noon Malcolm had lunch with a man who asked him to introduce him to Neil. Malcolm said OK but cautioned that Neil did not like to be identified as Ronald's brother. He was very fond of Ronald but wanted to stand on his own two feet and not cash in on his brother's celebrity. Malcolm suggested that Ronald Reagan's name not be mentioned.

Later, they stopped at Neil's table. Malcolm smiled at Neil, then at Malcolm's friend and said, "I'd like you to meet Ronald Reagan." It took Malcolm a while to understand the laughter and then join in.

Malcolm's life is appropriate for the United States as it awakes to its first black president, a reality very few saw coming—even black elders of America. There were very few clues for these elders to think that America was ready for a black president. The host of the public radio show "Wait, Wait Don't Tell Me" even remarked that it was like a *Star Wars* episode when he awoke on November 5, 2008, to the news that Barack Obama had been elected president. The host said it was like hearing the news that President Obi-Wan Kenobi was now leading the Galactic Empire. He joked that that it was just as unexpected to hear Obama's name as the president of the United States as it would be to hear that Jabba the Hutt in *Star Wars* could be a king.

Indeed, the courage of America to elect a black man as president remains fragile. That fragility is illustrated by the story of Malcolm coming across a copy of *Vogue* magazine with a photograph of Michele Obama on the front cover. He doesn't normally buy these magazines, but he did buy this one.

As he meditated on the cover, the epiphany came to him that this woman would normally represent the archetype of a house servant or maid rather than the First Lady of the White House. This book points to how exemplars like Malcolm helped a country find the courage to discover a new identity in an Obama age.

This book describes a life that has longed for and worked toward the realization of the previously unimaginable. Through the example of Mal-

Study in color (Malcolm is the white man in the middle).

colm's life we discover how current political tensions remain archaic, if not medieval. He teaches us that if we are not spiritually vigilant, at the drop of a hat we, too, will burn people at the stake.

> What went through the minds of mothers, what happened to the lives of children, what stabbed at the hearts of men when they were caught up in a sea of flame?
>
> What was Auschwitz like, Jesus, when the crematoriums belched the stinking smoke from the burned bodies of people? When families were separated, the weak perished, the strong faced inhuman tortures of the spirit and the body. What was the concentration camp like, Jesus?
>
> Tell us, Christ, that we, the living, are capable of the same cruelty, the same horror, if we turn our back on you, our brother, and our other sisters and brothers. Save us from ourselves; spare us the evil of our hearts' good intentions, unbridled and mad. Turn us from our perversions of love, especially when these are perpetuated in your name.

Study in color 2 (Malcolm in black mask with Woodie King Jr. in white mask).

Speak to us about war, and about peace, and about the possibilities for both in our very human hearts.[19]

In our twenty-first-century setting of the Western world, Malcolm makes me reimagine these four horsemen and their apocalyptic deliveries. These are our four horsemen of the Apocalypse screaming for us to conform. Malcolm's life is such that he has constantly taken on these four horsemen in battle, hence the title of this book. He is the White Knight in a Black Battle. As I mentioned earlier, there is a pun in the title of this book—namely, I am a black person named Battle. There is also irony in the question: is Malcolm black? Although Malcolm is a white man, this is not a trivial question. As one reads the Episcopal Church's archives, one is led to assume that Malcolm is African American because of his intense leadership during the civil rights era. Among black patristic figures like Richard Allen and Absalom Jones is poised the picture and profile for

---

19. Malcolm Boyd, "What Was Hiroshima Like, Jesus, When the Bomb Fell?" in *Are You Running with Me, Jesus?* (Cambridge, MA: Cowley, 2006).

none other than Malcolm Boyd.[20] When one goes to the website of these archives to peruse the pantheon of black leadership in the Episcopal Church for the past 200 years, one quickly understands that my question about Malcolm's racial identity is indeed complex. Malcolm remembers one occasion when, because of Malcolm's deep association with the fight for civil rights, a black protestor told him, "You'll have to live as a nigger like we do." Malcolm recounted this story with a chuckle and then concluded, "We couldn't find a church that wanted us that day because our group contained both black and white people; so we found moldy bread and warm beer to use for our Sunday communion in a poor shack out in the country."

For this authorized biography, Malcolm provided me unlimited access to his writings, resources, and current thinking on a variety of subjects. For example, he provided several oral histories of his life and I was given permission to record oral interviews with Malcolm and others. I also had access to all of his writings. Early in my research, Malcolm especially recommended that I read his autobiography, which I would also recommend to the reader.[21] Because of his generosity in providing me with full access, Malcolm has enabled me, as a writer, to create a historic, original, and significant biography. I simply don't know of another book like it. You don't need to visit Malcolm's archive at Boston University or his website or dig into all of Malcolm's books to learn about the passion of his life. Hopefully, this biography indicates the events in Malcolm's life that are relevant to how we as global citizens also need to see our own

---

20. The Archives of the Episcopal Church, The Church Awakens: African-Americans and the Struggle for Justice, accessed December 16, 2010, http://www.episcopalarchives.org/Afro-Anglican_history/exhibit/leadership/boyd.php.

21. Malcolm Boyd, *As I Live and Breathe: Stages of an Autobiography* (New York: Random House, 1969). Also, journalist William Jacobs and Malcolm were co-winners of a Catholic Press Association award for a series of articles in the Roman Catholic magazine *Ave Maria*. (These are held in the archives of Boston University.) Malcolm wrote "Maintaining Humanness in the Freedom Movement" in a book *Witness to a Generation—Significant Writings from Christianity and Crisis (1941–1966)* edited by Wayne H. Cowan (Indianapolis, IN: Bobbs-Merrill, 1966). The chapter "The Black and White Blues" in Malcolm's book *The Hunger, The Thirst* (New York: Morehouse-Barlow, 1964) can prove useful to readers trying to explore Malcolm further. It contains information on the 1961 Freedom Ride. "The Battle of McComb," in *The Christian Century* (Nov. 11, 1964) is a major civil rights piece. A series of columns Malcolm wrote in the 1960s for the *Pittsburgh Courier*, the national African-American newspaper, are especially vital. The title of Malcolm's column was "Blind No More." Malcolm describes his coming out as a gay man in *Take Off the Masks*.

complex identities—and actually celebrate them. Malcolm's wisdom needed to be mined for treasure and I am grateful to God to be charged with such a task. As I began working on this book, Malcolm was eighty-five years old. At the time of submitting this book for publication, he was eighty-seven years old (and will be eighty-eight on June 8). He told me to hurry up and get going because "the tape is rolling—I request making this a priority!" Indeed, completing this book became a profound priority in my life and I hope reading the finished work will become a priority for you as well.

CHAPTER TWO

The White Horse of Pestilence

And I beheld, and lo a white horse;
and he that sat on him had a bow:
and there was given unto him a crown.
(Revelation 6:2)

Although crowned, this White Knight brings pestilence. Normally, someone honored doesn't do this—bring deadly disease. The White Knight is the first of the apocalyptic riders to wreck havoc upon earth, causing all life to tremble with fear. This white figure is enigmatic because in many cultures to be "white" is to be good, and yet this White Knight man brings sickness. Due to the enigma of the White Knight, more time is spent on this first horseman than the others in an attempt to situate Malcolm's life and the conflicting interpretations that result from such a life. The problem is deepened further in my comparison of the White Knight to Malcolm, who brings his own pestilence of gay identity to many. For those on the receiving end of Malcolm's provocative life, many refuse to see any benign identity at all in Malcolm, only the abhorrent, sick, sexual behavior called homosexuality.

Another kind of pestilence that Malcolm cast upon the earth was celebrity. The irony of Malcolm's celebrity is juxtaposed to his struggle to become public with his gay identity. In this bipolar world of celebrity and the closet, Malcolm discovered his own pestilence working in not letting the pendulum swinging between the closet and celebrity destroy him. In fact, Malcolm learned to use the tension between celebrity and the closet to make the world free of other oppressions, such as the segregation of black people. In Malcolm's early days of celebrity, many grew agitated by his civil rights work championing the goodness in black people. In respect to both Malcolm's gay identity and civil rights role, those who experienced Malcolm encountered the Apocalypse.

In 1963, long before Marlon Brando became the pivotal antagonist in the blockbuster film *Apocalypse Now*, he marched for civil rights in the company of Malcolm. On one particular occasion, for two and a half hours, Malcolm and Brando protested against segregation in an all-white residential area and were arrested with picketers from the Congress of Racial Equality. Instead of using their celebrity to gain more fortune and fame, Malcolm and Brando made the camera point to the pestilence of their day—legal racism. On that day in 1963, Malcolm and Brando attempted a sit-in in driveways of this segregated area. The owner of one residential property had both Brando and Malcolm arrested, along with forty-five others, on a trespassing complaint. The *Los Angeles Times* reported, "The singing Negro and white sit-ins adopted passive resistance techniques, making their bodies limp and forcing a squad of 10 police officers to lift them bodily into a paddy wagon." As they were carried away, they were followed by three boys in white robes and three American Nazis carrying their own picket signs which read: "Brando is a stooge for Communist race mixture."[1]

During one of Malcolm's earlier marches, he provided the following meditation:

> There was almost a definite rhythm to our marching, Jesus. About twenty of us had been marching in a snowstorm, in a constant circular movement in front of the apartment house, for nearly three hours, on an afternoon in 1962.
>
> We were African Americans and whites, men and women, students, professors, clergy, and schoolteachers. We carried signs reading "Negroes Can't Live Here," "We Oppose Discrimination," "End Segregated Housing," and "Freedom."
>
> The reason we were marching was that a young black woman, the daughter of a faculty member at the large urban university located one block away from the site of our demonstration, had been denied housing in the apartment building which we were now picketing.
>
> The demonstration was similar to other picketing in which I had participated. Some passersby were friendly and smiled, others coldly

---

[1]. "Brando Joins Rights March; 47 Arrested," Paul Weeks, *Los Angeles Times*, July 28, 1963; *Los Angeles Times*, E1.

Malcolm (holding sign) at the Episcopal Society for Cultural and Racial Unity (ESCRU) demonstration in Chicago, 1965.

refused to accept handbills we were handing out, a few stopped to ask questions, and at least one man started shouting.

A TV cameraman stepped out of a car parked nearby and started shooting some clips for the eleven o'clock news that night. A reporter arrived, talked with several of us, and jotted down notes on pieces of paper.

It got colder. The snow was falling quickly now, blanketing the sidewalk, and the wind blew it into our eyes. I had to take off my gloves and dig my bare hands deep into my overcoat pockets, briskly flexing them to restore circulation. My feet were cold and my breath became a small cloud of vapor in front of my face.

We prayed for you to give us courage, Jesus. We felt our prayer was answered when the young black woman was invited to move into the apartment building a few weeks later. Thank you, Jesus.[2]

---

2. Malcolm Boyd and Chester Talton, eds., *Race and Prayer: Collected Voices, Many Dreams* (Harrisburg, PA: Morehouse Publishing, 2003), 108.

Despite the pestilence of bodies going limp and black people being segregated, scripture is correct that the white rider was nevertheless crowned, and I think in Malcolm's case, with celebrity. I learned that in the early seventies and late sixties Malcolm was one of the most popular and famous clergypersons in the United States, speaking to thousands at a time. He had achieved the odd combination of being a priest and a celebrity. During my conversations with Malcolm, I learned that such a combination of celebrity and spiritual vocation leaves one exhausted, both physically and emotionally. The peak of Malcolm's celebrity lasted three or four years and carried with it physical and emotional exhaustion. For example, when Malcolm was on the college lecture circuit, he was constantly approached for interviews. During this peak period of his fame, he conducted around 3,000 interviews for print and other media. He said, "At dawn I'm on the local today show, then a printed interview happens shortly thereafter. I'm then scheduled for a lunch interview for the featured radio broadcast. Then a TV station films me in the afternoon to air at night on CBS. I could be doing nine interviews in a day—that was crazy," he laughs.

Was there anything healthy about being famous? Malcolm answered that having access to the media, he could offer a different point of view that cut against the grain. In other words, he could say something that needed to be said that very few either could not say or were not willing to say. Malcolm is quick to note, however, that there are not many positive aspects to having celebrity. But isn't celebrity given, I asked? Don't we attribute celebrity to others? My questions to Malcolm were my insights that without such celebrity, God would've had even a more difficult time imparting the epiphany of Malcolm's genius of imagination and social awareness. There is reluctance on Malcolm's part to receive my compliments and my meta-narrative of his impact upon worlds.

Malcolm responds that celebrity doesn't mean power. He proceeds to rattle off examples. For example, a bishop in an institutional church may be powerful but not have celebrity. How many know the name of the Episcopal Bishop of New York? Ironically, a figure such as Bishop Paul Moore may not be a celebrity but can nevertheless be a powerful person. Moore served Malcolm extremely well. One of Moore's gifts was authenticity. He simply refused to take himself too seriously. When Malcolm was named honorary canon by Bishop J. Jon Bruno, Paul sent Malcolm a note: "Boom! Boom! Congratulations."

Malcolm recalls that Moore filled the role of older brother in his life. He guided Malcolm, protected him, and was always there for Malcolm. "If it weren't for Paul," Malcolm said, "I wouldn't be an Episcopal priest, engaged in my work of spiritual direction, even writing books and columns."[3] Especially as an older brother, Moore would write Malcolm when he was invited to be writer-in-residence at the Cathedral Center of St. Paul in Los Angeles: "My you ARE dignified and venerable and holy etc. etc. etc. Glad you like your new nest." This note exemplified an absence of pretension in his manner and style. On September 29, 2000, Paul sent yet another of his classic notes: "For the only Malcolm, Dear Friend, Brave Colleague, Troublemaker . . . with gratitude for a wonderful friendship of 45 years . . . Blessings."

Malcolm told me that during some of the hardest points in his life, Moore was a living power that rescued him. Malcolm's apocalyptic impact of gay identity and civil rights work aroused sharp, sometimes angry, opposition and criticism. At certain low moments in Malcolm's life, he found himself unemployed and at the bottom of his self-esteem. Moore had the living power to change those circumstances. I stopped Malcolm there, and asked, "But can't a person be dead and still powerful?" Yes, Martin Luther King Jr. and Albert Einstein illustrate such a phenomenon.

I asked Malcolm what he was up against in the apocalyptic times of the civil rights era—especially at a time when to be gay carried no translation that civil rights also applied to sexual orientation. When I pushed Malcolm on this, we inevitably meandered our way back to the provincial worldview of the institutional church. Malcolm's experience as a celebrity was helpful in discussing my service on an Episcopal Church committee, especially in trying to figure out the proper processes of discernment for someone to become a bishop.

"Should someone desire to become a bishop?" I asked Malcolm. After all, it seems opportunistic to make such a wish known in public. And yet, there are biblical references in which St. Paul describes in 1

---

3. Malcolm Boyd, "Everyday Saints: Paul Moore," Episcopal News Online, Diocese of Los Angeles, e-Newsletter, June 2008.

Timothy that it is a good thing to aspire to be a bishop. But Malcolm said in the early church that what was meant by bishop was different than being a celebrity. "The whole bishop scene is sick as hell," Malcolm said. This is important because if so-called spiritual leaders can't handle celebrity who can?

Malcolm cuts to the chase when he asks, "Isn't it monarchial when we talk about clergy?" The separation of the clergy and laity offends Malcolm. There are some clergy who act monarchical when in a clergy setting—it sort of brings out the diva role. The epiphany that Malcolm gave me and his world was the obvious answer to the question: can a spiritual leader act like a monarch anymore in Western culture and get away with it? The obvious answer is no; and yet Malcolm clarifies that the pestilence in postmodern religion is the extent to which individuals pretending to be religious can still get away with such despotic behavior.

Part of what Malcolm finds objectionable is the pretence that leads to the acting out of false piety—for example, clergy dressed up in gowns, fake voices delivering sermons, people still pretending a building is a church rather than the people of God. But things are changing, Malcolm and I agreed. I had recently attended a clergy gathering and found it interesting that a third of the clergy had no gowns. Voices were not fake when they delivered sermons. And sacred space was more at the beck and call of the people instead of the other way around. Malcolm's Apocalypse is such that he has little patience for the hypocrisy of religion. In fact, Malcolm says that he personally doesn't own any clergy attire in which he can dress up and look good. He has no cassock, no alb, although he does have two stoles that were given to him. Malcolm writes me about a dream he had:

> I am a young man about to go somewhere—take a voyage, a momentous trip that will change my life. As I race on foot to the railroad station, I realize I've left my briefcase upstairs in the house where I stayed. In it are the essential documents of my life—papers, address book, identifications, indispensable things.
>
> Yet I realize that I can get along without them. I've also left behind my suitcase and clothes, so possess nothing as I rush to the station. But I feel peaceful in this realization: I've got myself, and I'm going to get on the train. I will make the trip. I want to get there, wherever it is. The new place is good, exciting, inviting. My life is changing. I'm going.
>
> I am glad to be leaving the accumulated luggage of my life. I have been carrying it on my shoulders for so long. I am ready to start my

journey, to begin a new life. (Note: I did this when I came out as a gay man and moved into the unknown.)[4]

Malcolm is the apocalyptic rider on a white horse because he constantly shocked people's stayed identities. He even shocked his own gay community as he challenged them to move beyond their own stereotypes and civil wars. Surely, the reader has already seen how it is difficult to caricature Malcolm as a gay man—especially one who doesn't like to dress up! It is because of Malcolm's ability to live in many worlds and cultures that we can learn how Malcolm created a frame of reference out of a people's prior naiveté. But he couldn't have done this, ironically, apart from his own celebrity. After all, who would've listened to Malcolm's provocative words had he not been famous? Without celebrity, wouldn't he have been seen as a blithering idiot or an irrelevant prophet?

Malcolm told me that the problem with celebrity is that "you are a tape doing the essentially the same thing every night." As I learned more details about the unusual person of Malcolm, I naturally could see his dilemma. Malcolm is pure creativity, and such a nature cannot be tamed by the socialization of celebrity or for that matter, as we will learn, the institutional church. Malcolm refused the things necessary to maintain celebrity. He told me that this refusal goes back to the decision that Malcolm made in a hotel where he came to terms with the trajectory of his life. In that hotel room he realized that celebrity was absurd, unsatisfying, and pointless.

The Pestilence of *Playboy*

When I first approached the subject of Malcolm's relationship with Hugh Hefner, he was reluctant. Malcolm wrote me:

> Suggest you read the Hefner chapter in the book you borrowed and figure out exactly what you "want" in the book regarding him. You might ask me two or three questions about Hef and my relationship to him; this could provide what you wish to use in the book. I don't find him particularly relevant in my life, yet I realize what intrigues you is the fact he is in my life at all! In other words, he is a clear example of my "outreach" to all kinds and varieties of people. . . .
>
> Just wrote a piece on "Death" that I will share with you.[5]

---

4. Malcolm Boyd , "New," e-mail message to author, November 23, 2009.
5. Malcolm Boyd, "Hefner Etc.," e-mail message to author, November 10, 2009.

Naturally, Malcolm would be reluctant to tread into these controversial waters due the easy misunderstandings that a general audience would have. After all, Malcolm is a Christian priest. "What's he doing being with a sinner?" I decided to pursue this enigma of Malcolm and Hefner anyway.

It was a dark and stormy day in New Haven when Malcolm made his decision. It would be controversial for sure. He was anxious to get started on a new project outside of the ivy walls of Calhoun College at Yale University, where he had been in residence as a guest fellow. On this rainy day, Malcolm was eating lunch with a Yale senior, a young woman who was curious about Malcolm's next book. "I will soon go out to Chicago to work on it, and to interview Hugh Hefner."

"God, I detest him," the young woman said.

Another male Yale student said, "I don't see how you can spend any time with him or let him have any space in your book."

The young woman broke back into the discussion, "*Playboy*'s whole attitude toward women is disgusting. Hefner must be against women. I loathe him."

The Yale male student said, "Jesus, he's so materialistic. *Playboy* glorifies everything that's lousiest about America. Those hairless, frozen blondes—made up to look like the girl next door, and photographed in a phony, out-of-focus way. And those goddamn conformist ads. Everybody is sort of supernigger, with his unbelievable chick, his goddamn expensive car, his shitty correct suit and shaving lotion and pad. Christ. You shouldn't do it."[6]

Malcolm did "do it." He interviewed Hefner, Hefner's mother, old friends, and *Playboy* staff members. He sought to know genuine human beings, and in particular to know the enigma of Hugh Hefner, a man who is both a mirror image and a challenge to an earlier myth of American innocence. Here is an example of Malcolm's dilemma of being a priest and a celebrity. Malcolm always traveled coach, not first class. He said he would have been embarrassed to be in first class. Hugh Hefner's chauffeur, a genial Irishman, came to pick him up at the airport, taking Malcolm's bag to load into a sleek black limousine. Malcolm settled back for the drive, happy to see the *Wall Street Journal*, the *Tribune*, and the *Sun-Times* stacked neatly at his feet. The chauffeur asked Malcolm if he wanted a Pepsi-Cola. Malcolm said he would. The chauffer proceeded to

---

6. Malcolm Boyd, *My Fellow Americans* (New York: Holt, Rinehart and Winston, 1970), 16.

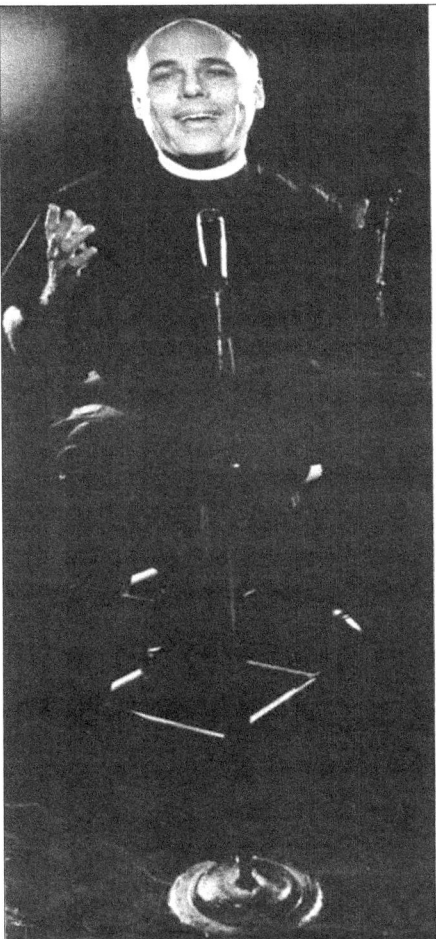

Playboy *issue Fall 1966 A.*

open an iced bottle and pour it into a large paper cup and said, "Is there anything else?"

"No," Malcolm responded as he navigated the controls on the back seat for the air conditioner and the psychedelic screen next to the radio.

Malcolm thought about how ludicrous this all was—traveling in economy class and then having a chauffeur treat him like Donald Trump. This sensitivity to the poor is morally mature of Malcolm, but what about the implication of being associated with Hugh Hefner, I asked?

The first time Malcolm met Hugh Hefner was when he was in Hefner's Chicago home—the Mansion. Hefner had expressed an interest in meeting Malcolm, and Malcolm accepted the invitation.

The mystique of *Playboy* was burdensome to say the least. Controversy surrounded Hefner, his sexual magazine, his mansion, his philosophy, and the company he kept. Especially for Malcolm as a Christian priest, *Playboy* presented many landmines of troubles. Malcolm states, "I did not feel free, as I set out for our meeting; I was overwhelmed in advance by fragments of his fame which lunged out of my recollection." What I admire about Malcolm pursuing Hefner is in how virtually no other major Christian figure sought to simply listen to Hefner and understand how and why he became so powerful. Malcolm did say that Hefner, the man, cut against clichés concerning Hefner's image as a Howard Hughes type of recluse because he had other Christian figures visit the Mansion. Harvey Cox, a well-known theologian, came by one night and stayed until 3 AM. On another occasion, Bishop John Robinson from England and author of *Honest to God* stayed up talking half the night. The Rev. Jesse Jackson dropped by on another occasion with animated discussion following well into the night. Malcolm said it was Hugh Hefner as a human being rather than a collection of images whom he was writing about for his book. Malcolm was brave enough to go on record with his observations. Malcolm gives a powerful quote to this effect. "I think that the Playboy Mansion in Chicago serves a marvelous purpose," A. C. Spectorsky, associate publisher and editorial director of *Playboy* magazine, told me, "It's like a blank screen onto which our critics project their fantasies of what they would do if they had the money and freedom."[7]

Malcolm spent nearly three weeks living inside the Playboy Mansion, where he conducted in-depth interviews with Hefner for Malcolm's book entitled *My Fellow Americans*. The various subjects of the book represented vastly different fields, yet Malcolm selected all of them on the basis of having made seminal contributions to contemporary American culture.

When he first arrived at the Mansion, Malcolm was taken on a tour by an editor of the magazine. Malcolm saw the giant living room where, on Sunday afternoons, Hefner showed his friends the latest Hollywood movies which were made available to him. Then he toured the exotic pool, the oriental bar off the pool area, the billiard room, the master bedroom with its circular bed, and the TV room where video programs were monitored and taped for later viewing.

Malcolm and the editor had lunch. A menu was placed before Malcolm. Malcolm was asked to order, but there were dozens of items to choose from. Malcolm was told the steak sandwich was good.

---

7. Malcolm Boyd, "Three Weeks in the Playboy Mansion," *Yale Daily News*, June 1, 1969.

Malcolm describes what proceeded this way: "Hef and I, when we met, talked for hours. I can't remember exactly how many. I think it must have been four or five hours. It was one hell of a good conversation. I drank scotch, he drank Pepsi."[8] Finally it was late, but they hadn't finished their conversation. Malcolm states, "We hadn't, damn it, even begun!" It was decided that Malcolm should return the next night. Malcolm did, and they talked again. About what? Everything: religion and the Church, politics, sex, ethics, blacks, war, publishing—you name it.

"I am a night person," Hefner told Malcolm while chatting in the penthouse apartment atop the Playboy Club on the Sunset Strip.

Malcolm said, "As my 4 PM appointment was his first of the day, he was dressed in pajamas and a bathrobe."

"On a typical day," he continued, "I get up at 3 PM and go to bed at 7 or 8 AM They say some people are physically night people. Night to me is the more romantic and interesting time. It's when things are happening that excite me and turn me on. It's easier to be awake and operating when other people are sleeping."

Hefner told Malcolm: "The rhythm of the Mansion is the rhythm of the people living inside it, not of the sun and moon and the world outside. It's a world unto itself and within itself. Man is the only creature who can control his environment. I control the clock with a 24-hour staff. Audio-visual equipment collects data for me to see later. Nothing says the day has to have twelve or sixteen hours, or begin at 7 AM, 3 PM, or midnight. The house can function as an extension of the man instead of committing him to do certain things at certain times."[9]

While Hefner talked, he drank bourbon with Pepsi-Cola, Malcolm had scotch and soda, and, when their hour-and-a-half conversation was winding up, they moved into the bathroom where Hefner shaved.

Malcolm wondered whether Hefner had become radicalized by a highly publicized incident on a Chicago street during the Democratic National Convention when he was attacked by a policeman. "The radicalism was already there," Hefner responded. "But because of my reputation as a cloistered guy in a mansion, the idea of my taking a walk at night and running into trouble was not without irony." The whole incident occurred in the following manner. Max Lerner and Jules Feiffer were houseguests of Hefner. The two of them, Hefner, a secretary, and an executive on the magazine decided to take a walk. They walked down to Lincoln Park and over to the old town area. They saw a few police

---

8. Malcolm Boyd, "Hefner of *Playboy*—Part 1," *Yale Daily News,* January 28, 1969.
9. Boyd, *My Fellow Americans,* 18

around. Things seemed quiet. Then they saw a crowd of people ahead of them being chased by the police. It was obvious the police were very uptight. Hefner describes the scene:

> The cops were calling people names. Helmeted police started going over a guy. There were, you know, some 200 working members of the press out that night. Sixty of them were attacked. I saw it firsthand and I know, as the commission report indicated, the police were out of control. They were acting as individual hoodlums. We got out of there. But a squad car came down the street. Cops leaped out of the car with shotguns aimed at us. "Get on your knees," a cop said to me. "That's what I'm trying to do," I replied. He hit me on the backside with his billy. Feiffer and Lerner ran off in other directions.
>
> The police car was bristling, packed with cops. They were out for blood for fun. They were venting their frustrations about Vietnam, race, and bad press. They didn't know me. I wasn't being singled out. What happened in Chicago could obviously have happened elsewhere. To anybody. My reaction was one of shock. Incredulity. It happened so quickly that there wasn't a chance for real fear.
>
> I was left with a feeling of great sadness. This was a sign of the extent to which our society has become polarized. We don't have a leader of the stature of John Kennedy. But we've got to find ways to communicate again.[10]

As Malcolm and Hefner became acquainted, Hefner in Technicolor vanished from Malcolm's imagination. Beneath the legend was very much a human being. They became friends. Malcolm and Hefner remained friends, with Hefner even inviting Malcolm to appear on the TV series *Playboy After Dark*. Malcolm told me, "I had earlier joined Bill Cosby, in fact, as a guest on the program."

Surely for many readers, they share the sentiment of that Yale student toward Malcolm—why in the hell be in the presence of Hugh Hefner and the exploitation of *Playboy*? Malcolm answers with provocative conversation and interviews with Hefner. For example, many would have never guessed that Hefner had certain views. "Kids are the only hope for the future. Thank goodness there are so many of them," Hefner said. In this particular conversation, Malcolm and Hefner were seated in the penthouse apartment atop the Playboy Club catching up on current affairs. Malcolm felt that Hefner had changed over time. Hefner describes it this way:

---

10. Boyd, "Hefner of *Playboy*—Part 1."

"I moved into my 40s and began taking stock of my life," Hefner said. "I had a wonderful success in the first 15 years of *Playboy,* but I was literally killing myself. I was down to 175 pounds and spent most of my time in the mansion. I took amphetamines. They allowed me to stay awake and made me hyper-conscious. It was wonderful to be able to sit at the typewriter for 24 hours. I used to go for 36 hours at a stretch. But I realized I was working too hard. I really consciously decided that so many things were happening, I wanted to be around to participate in them. I said to myself, you're at the midpoint of a lifetime that can be rich and fulfilling. So, I purchased the plane and started the television show in order to bring me out. I gained 40 pounds. I got exercise equipment. I haven't gone back in the same work pattern and don't know that I ever will. You can say that I suffer from good health.[11]

Hefner's insights were surprising as he continued to talk about the health of leadership. He said that we need sensitive leadership to take humanity out of the doldrums. "If there's repression in one area, it occurs in all other areas of living," Hefner said to Malcolm. This insight was surprising because many feel as though Hefner is simply hedonistic and self-absorbed.

Hefner applies his insights to politics. The people who voted for George Wallace are uptight about everything that makes people free and happy. According to Hefner, there's a very dirty business of fascism trying to take away the rights of other people and not let them enjoy the freedom of a democratic society.

Hefner reminisced about his college days at the University of Illinois. In those days of youth, Hefner landed a $45-a-week job with a carton company, interviewing other people for jobs. "But they didn't want to hire Jews or blacks or anybody with a long name," Hefner recalls. Returning to school, Hefner did graduate work at Northwestern and thought he might enter teaching. In a paper he did for a sociology course, Hefner compared Kinsey's findings with U.S. sex laws. His professor gave him an A for research, B-plus for his conclusions. A few years later, the American Law Institute issued findings similar to Hefner's.

As Hefner came into power with his Playboy Foundation, he launched an "activist arm" of his philosophy. Its intent was to change suppressive legislation as well as to fight and defend specific cases. "Sodomy laws are like drug laws," Hefner said. "Penalties are like 12, 14, and 20 years for

---

11. Malcolm Boyd, "Hefner—Part II," *Yale Daily News,* January 29, 1969.

oral and anal intercourse, homosexual or heterosexual, husband and wife. In one case, a guy had had anal intercourse with his wife. She had given her permission. But he was sentenced to something like 14 years in prison for it. We questioned the constitutionality of the matter and got the guy out on a technicality."

Malcolm not only brought out Hefner's views on sexuality, the Vietnam War came up as well. Concerning the Vietnam War, Malcolm learned from Hefner that America's basic flaw began after World War II in not being for democracy but against communism. In so doing, we developed habits of misinterpreting true democracy as we focused solely on the enemy. As a result, we ended up on the wrong side in the Vietnam War. Hefner told Malcolm, "It would be nice to see a little law and order internationally. We've got to see a way to establish a world government. We learned to destroy one another before we learned to live together. There is no solution in continuing to arm or disarmament. There has to be a working world government which has the safeguards and controls."

In several of our spiritual direction sessions, Malcolm struggled to make sense of these years of the late 1960s. Malcolm's creative spirit was seemingly fearless, taking on subject matter that was taboo to the world, much less the church. And yet, as we will see later, there were definite fears that Malcolm had to overcome. Despite these fears, Malcolm seemed fearless as he, as a clergyperson, embraced taboo subject matter like Hugh Hefner and *Playboy*. Malcolm writes me:

> Dear Michael: Yesterday, when I e-mailed you a few ideas—stressing the importance of my experience at Yale in 1968–69—I hadn't yet heard from Boston University about finding my *Yale Daily News* columns. Well, just after I e-mailed you, a large package arrived from Boston—containing a trove of those very columns. They stunned me. They reflect what I was thinking in 1968–69, and apparently I've lost track with the person I was then! In other words, reading the old columns abruptly updated me. I think you'll find them fascinating (a couple are even on Hefner). I won't be surprised if you get 3 to 5 pages of good material from this stuff. ANYHOW, I'll give them to you when we meet this Thursday at 1 PM. Best—M.[12]

Malcolm writes that in the weeks he stayed at the Mansion, there would be so many divergent opinions expressed about Hefner, but more

---

12. Malcolm Boyd, "New trove from Yale," e-mail message to author, December 15, 2009.

significant than any single view was the awareness that even many of those living or working at the Mansion found it hard to discern between Hefner the man and Hefner the celebrity. In particular, Malcolm writes, "Why did these men in Hefner's own organization speak so critically of him? Partly out of frustration, I thought. They worked for the magazine too, yet had not made millions of dollars or achieved world fame."[13]

In one of Malcolm's late night interviews with Hefner in the Mansion, Hefner cut to the chase, "In a very real way, the thing that sets *Playboy* apart is the idea that sexual emancipation and female emancipation go hand in hand. The old Judeo-Christian concept kept women in slavery; they were seen as nonhuman, chattel. A woman's virginity was prized because, if she wasn't a virgin, she was used property."[14] Hefner's basic philosophy is that American behavior is based upon Puritanism. Hefner is anti-Puritanism not just in relation to sex but the whole idea of play and pleasure, this extending to materialism. Puritanism outlawed the theatre, for example. It couldn't stand the idea that somewhere someone was having a good time. "We are opposed to a view that sex is either sacred or profane, and not a normal part of living," concludes Hefner.[15]

Hefner defends his enterprise on moral grounds. He was proud that his nightclubs were the most successful internationally. "But we've done a few other things, too; we started the black comics, for instance—Dick Gregory was the first Negro comic to be booked in a white circuit. And we have black bunnies in all the clubs, including those in the south. In New Orleans and Miami, we had to buy back the clubs from franchise owners because of racial discrimination."[16]

Not only did Hefner defend himself on moral grounds, he also articulated the demise of religion in light of democracy. He states:

> Religion is based upon faith; democracy is based upon reason. America's religious heritage stresses selflessness, subservience to a great Power and the paying of homage to Him in long-established, self-defined, well-organized ways; democracy teaches the importance of self, a belief in one's self and one's own abilities. Religion teaches that man should live for others; our democracy's free-enterprise system is based on the belief that the greatest good comes from men competing

---

13. Malcolm Boyd *My Fellow Americans* (New York: Holt, Rinehart and Winston, 1970), 21.
14. Boyd, *My Fellow Americans*, 35.
15. Boyd, "Three Weeks in the Playboy Mansion."
16. Boyd, *My Fellow Americans*, 60.

with one another. Religion offers a special blessing to the meek and the promise that they will inherit the earth; democracy requires that men speak out and be heard.

Most religion in America teaches that man is born with the stain of Original Sin upon him; a free democracy stands on the belief that man is born innocent and remains so until changed by society. Most organized religion in the U.S. is rooted in a tradition that links man's body with evil, physical pleasures with sin, and pits man's mind and soul against the devil of the flesh; the principles underlying our democracy recognize no such conflict of body, mind and soul. Religion tends to de-emphasize material things, discourage a concern over the acquisition of wealth, bless the poor and promise that they shall dwell with God in the Kingdom of Heaven; our free-enterprise system is founded on the ideal that striving to materially better oneself is worthwhile and benefits not only the individual, but the world around him. Most religions are based upon the importance of the next world; democracy is based upon the importance of this one.[17]

Malcolm asked Hefner why organized religion in the West had tended to be anti-sexual. Hefner responds, "Christianity took a nonhumanistic attitude from the dualism of St. Paul. Of course, you can work out some after-the-fact rationale for this. At the time families and nations were dependent on the number of offspring for strength in an agrarian society. Young men were needed to fight the wars. All this helped emphasize sex exclusively as procreation. They were afraid of enjoyment, maybe because Christianity started as a religion that suffered. And it came out of a Judaism that suffered. In the Middle Ages, of course, life was even lousier than before. And remember, in all of this the people were told over and over that they have been conceived in sin."[18]

Malcolm's relationship with Hefner and such a secular worldview attest to his ability to live in so many worlds and yet resist the extremes or pathologies found in them. I think this also was the genius of Jesus. It's very unlike Jesus to be pietistic and not associate with people most deem "evil and sinners."

While living in the Playboy Mansion, Malcolm also learned that Hefner's mother didn't like what her son was doing, but accepted her son nevertheless. The mother was Methodist. Malcolm got along very well with her. And Malcolm would interview many others in the mansion.

---

17. Boyd, *My Fellow Americans*, 56–57
18. Ibid., 57

Hefner wanted Malcolm to see different aspects of the *Playboy* philosophies. The Playboy Clubs had resorts; Malcolm flew to one of the resorts to get a sense of it. At the resort, he discovered that there was a "Bunny Mother" who took care of the girls, gave them Tylenols, and helped them sort through their emotional problems.

"This was a crazy world," I said to Malcolm. "How did you stay sane?" Malcolm joked, "Well, some would argue that I'm not sane." Malcolm doesn't claim to be a saint. He admits that he didn't think he'd been all that intelligent in how he lived his own life on some occasions, but it ended up well. "At least I've been honest," he said. "I've tried to be authentic. One of the benefits of Christianity is that it invites you to be authentic. Jesus got angry at a lack of authenticity."

In one of my spiritual direction sessions with Malcolm, I learned that a major documentary film on Hugh Hefner had been made. Malcolm was in it. Malcolm's major criticism of the film was that it went back to bunnies and clichés and could have aimed for more gravitas. In the documentary, Malcolm provides an insight: "Perhaps Hefner's Rosebud was love." Malcolm here alludes to the classic film *Citizen Kane*, which begins with a boy riding his favorite sled named Rosebud. From 1984 to 1986, I did my college work-study with Jane Gains, professor of literature and English at Duke University, where I was majoring in religious studies. Professor Gains taught many courses in film theory and history. I remember being her audio-visual work-study student, always beginning her semesters with *Citizen Kane*. She thought this film was the major catalyst for the whole Hollywood industry. The film proceeds to tell a story in which the boy is caught in a complicated web of relationships. The mother gives him over to handlers in order to relinquish her responsibilities as a parent. The spoiled, lonely, and tortured boy grows up the heir to millions of dollars. Needless to say, he acts out in dysfunctional ways, obviously seeking what was lost, which the audience could easily see was a lack of a foundation of kindness and love.

Malcolm teaches me that the reason *Citizen Kane* is a classic is that everyone has a Rosebud—that is, a deep desire from childhood. "Perhaps Hefner's Rosebud was love." Malcolm's own life is akin to *Citizen Kane* as he jokes, "I didn't have my own adolescence until I was fifty years old." As I will recount through Malcolm's relationship with his partner Mark Thompson, there is love; yet, Malcolm comes close to conveying a sense of melancholy in which to think about ultimate desire.

How Malcolm used his celebrity is a fascinating subject that warrants our attention to see how an unusual priest facilitated good in a society, although his actions were interpreted as pestilence. Malcolm's insight that Hefner's ultimate desire, though unfulfilled, is love leads us to an apocalyptic message. Before Malcolm delivers his message, it is important to say a word first about how complicated Malcolm's own identity was. Very few could receive anything good from such a complex identity. In other words, not only was Malcolm a priest, a civil rights activist, and an esteemed writer—he was also gay. This latter identity to this very day brings pestilence to many people's worldview. After all, in Malcolm's time, there was little if no reference point to understand the difference between sexual identity and sexual act. In the 1960s, even the American Medical Association still had homosexuality listed as a "mental disorder." So, a word here about how I think Malcolm was able to be heard despite the pestilence of his gay identity.

The Pestilence of Gay Identity

In 1999 Malcolm addressed the Episcopal House of Bishops in San Diego. He began with humor. He told about social arbiter Miss Manners who was asked: "If I am at a party and introduced to two homosexual persons who are in a longtime relationship—what should I say to them?"

"How do you do?" replied Miss Manners. "How do you do?"

Malcolm uses humor to detonate bombs, to make the conservative smile, even laugh concerning the contentious nature of the sexual orientation debate. Malcolm teaches them that gay people aren't new anymore, or even quietly locked up in closets. They're on primetime TV, the front page, in Doonesbury, the U.S. Senate, and even the House of Bishops. Malcolm states, "I remember when Billy Graham was asked some years ago, 'What do you think of a homosexual?' At the time he was quoted as saying, 'I don't know. I've never met one.' I felt I should telephone and say, 'Let's have lunch.'"[19]

Malcolm as a boy.

---

19. Malcolm Boyd, Address to the Episcopal House of Bishops, San Diego, California, September 20, 1999.

Malcolm receiving the Unitas Award at Union Theological Seminary in New York, October 6, 2005.

Malcolm is conscious that he has been gay all of his life. At the beginning it wasn't easy. There was no gay movement, no gay books or media, and role models were few and far between. All Malcolm knew was that he was different. As Malcolm grew older, he received negative images fairly constantly telling him he was a "bad" person who must disguise his real self in order to avoid being beaten up.

When Malcolm was a boy, he remembers one summer night leaving his house with his father to play ball with other boys and dads in a park nearby. But he could neither throw nor catch the ball. In fact, it was clear he didn't belong there. "The scalding truth was that any of the other boys was closer to being my father's son than I was. I walked home alone, leaving my father with the others." This existential knowledge of being alone at such an early age was devastating, particularly because there was no one with whom he could share his feelings. It would be years before Malcolm found out that countless other gay men had similar experiences with their fathers when they were boys.

Malcolm also recalls his relationship with his mother. Her greatest difficulty in Malcolm's coming out later was that she loved and was proud of her son, but how could she bear to have him appear publicly as a "faggot," a modern-day leper, someone who—according to Cardinal Ratzinger, who became Pope Benedict XIV—was "intrinsically evil"? Naturally, being described in such pejorative ways damages self-esteem, which can lead to a sense of utter worthlessness. Malcolm tells me, "One shifts uneasily between feeling merely unwanted in respectable society to knowing one is (in another's eyes) morally despised."

The pestilence of gay identity could be read in another's body language; a warm smile could change in an instant to a look of hatred, friendly eyes could quickly turn accusatory in the revelation of Malcolm's gay identity. Malcolm concludes, "I learned I could never really let down my guard or quit playing a hoped-for acceptable role in an effort to earn kindness or security." Of course, Malcolm understood that some Christians interpret scripture differently; and yet, Malcolm thought the spirit of the age was changing. The change was similar to the enlightenment around racial classification.

In 1900 the American Book and Bible Society published a work entitled *The Negro a Beast*, arguing from scripture that a black person was not a descendent of Adam and Eve but a beast without a soul.[20] Such an interpretation of scripture went hand in hand with the accepted spirit of the times. Similarly, we have witnessed the killing of Jews, the treatment and second-class citizenship ascribed to women, and the too often brutal and unloving treatment of gay people. Malcolm urged change in the spirit of the times through conforming to the will of God, which was not to hate but to love. We are currently in a spirit of the times in which there is a remainder of hatred toward particular groups, but we have the capacity to reshape such a spirit. How can we do this? Malcolm answers that we must turn away from stereotypes that dehumanize.

Gay people have been stereotyped as either sexual athletes, ready for the Rose Bowl, or else sexual monsters who are predators trying to destroy the world. One reason this stereotyping has occurred is because, among gays, a ghetto mentality developed as a defense against antici-

---

20. Charles Carroll, *The Negro a Beast* (St. Louis, MO: American Book and Bible House, 1900).

Malcolm and Mark's Blessing in Los Angeles Episcopal Cathedral Cente.r

pated attack, as did the in-your-face antics that became strategic to an eventual self-loathing.

Malcolm's twenty-seven year partnership with Mark Thompson is a balm in the midst of the socialization toward self-loathing. Mark, himself, has written several books on the subject, calling stereotyping an oppressive sickness that other minorities also have suffered from. Mark is a writer, an editor, a therapist, and a wonderful human being. Their relationship has been even more deeply affected by "in sickness, in health" because Mark is HIV-positive and has the AIDS virus and Malcolm is rapidly moving beyond being an octogenarian. Their relationship provides an experience of partnership and extended family in which unconditional love is discovered.

The question confronting the church is far more complex than trying to decide whether to bless gay relationships or whether a gay person can be an ordained bishop. Especially in academic discussions, these questions frequently revolve around concepts that understand the nature of gender to be dynamic, in which there is a continuum of identity. Such concepts have deep roots in many cultures, including, for example, the Native American concept of the *berdache* or "Two-Spirit People," as they were regarded. Recently, Malcolm believes that psychiatric help, probably more than the practice of religion, has helped many gay people acquire a mature wisdom and the skills needed for survival. Malcolm believes that some 80 percent of gay people are presently in committed relationships (or yearn for one); and they are responsible members of society, quietly honeycombed through most nooks and crannies of our common life. So, how can we reshape the spirit of the times: by resisting facile, inflammatory, and accusatory stereotypes through studying and learning more about gay people who are closer to most people than many who are not gay realize.

Malcolm feels that the ability to go beyond stereotypes will impact the future of spirituality and the church. "I remember a church in Michigan," Malcolm recalls "that had always been segregated. Not one African American was invited to enter, pray, or receive communion. Finally in the 1960s, the parish leadership decided the time had come when it had to open its doors simply to appear relevant. There were anxious vestry meetings, anger, tears, and prayers. The fatal Sunday arrived. African Americans were now welcome. The rector, vestry, and congregation braced themselves for a horde of newcomers to storm the doors. But no one came. Not one black apparently wished to be there. The question arose: 'Why should they? Did they feel that they were genuinely wanted?'"

Malcolm wants us to see the similarity between the black experience and the experience of gays. "The vast majority of those of us who are gay understand it as an essential part of our creation and being. We have survived long and virulent persecution. We are strong. We are proud of who we are in God's eyes and in the arms of Jesus and in the embrace of the Holy Spirit." Malcolm prays:

> Christ, as lesbians and gay men we stand inside your church and know a wholeness that can benefit it. We learned long ago that we must regard the lilies of the field, putting our trust in you.
>
> Pressured to hide our identities and gifts, we have served you with an unyielding, fierce, vulnerable love inside the same church that often condemned us.

Carefully taught that we must feel self-loathing, nevertheless we learned integrity and dignity and how to look into your face and laugh with grateful joy, Jesus.

Although we have suffered a long and continuing torture, we assert a stubborn, unshakeable faith in your holy justice.

Negativism was drummed into us as thoroughly as if we were sheet metal. We learned what it is to be misunderstood, perceived as alien, even sometimes hated. Yet, because of your grace and love, we witness to the fullness and beauty of all human creation, including ours, in your image.

We are alive and well and stand inside your church. Bless us, Christ, to your service.[21]

In Jesus' life, death, and resurrection, one finds the theology of inclusion and openness to social outcasts. Malcolm states, "I don't ask the church to become an advocate for a cause, but a witness to change. I believe at the millennium we are being issued a wake-up call from God." Questions about human sexuality inevitably enter into this. So, gay men and lesbians are inescapably bound up in this wake-up call from God. Malcolm feels that he has played a part in this all of his life. Baptism, confirmation, service as an acolyte, participating in the choir and as a young adult, becoming a seminarian, and the fifty-seventh anniversary of his ordination as a priest on December 21, 2010—Malcolm has witnessed throughout these years the creative presence of gay people permeating every aspect of the church's life. Malcolm believes, "For the vast majority of us, choice never existed as a factor. Nor do we follow what is euphemistically described as a lifestyle. The point is: our being gay has to do essentially with how we **know** ourselves in God's grace."

To some, Malcolm's life reflects being a saint. Others see him as controversial. Others see him as the spawn of the devil. So, if we aren't given the vision to see Malcolm for who he is, you may end up with no distinct clarity of his impact. In fact, you may easily become persuaded that the impact is indeed destruction. Strangely enough, Jesus helps us in this regard to understand Malcolm. Jesus, himself an enigmatic figure, was also described as holy, controversial, and demonic. He hung around "sinners" who quickly became his best friends. His words were poetic; and depending upon your perspective, his impact brought either liberation to the oppressed or anarchy to the powerful. In many respects, Malcolm imprinted on the Jesus who demonstrated how one could reside in multi-

---

21. Boyd, Address to the Episcopal House of Bishops.

ple worldviews. This is dismaying and difficult for many, however; it would be easier if Malcolm just followed a clear script of what makes a male hero. But he couldn't.

Malcolm couldn't follow the script because he wasn't at peace in Hollywood. I learned from Malcolm how Hollywood is a state of mind instead of a place. Hollywood was wide open in Malcolm's younger years, full of opportunities. Hollywood was creative, where Malcolm himself wrote scripts and had exciting jobs. He worked in a motion picture studio and major ad agency. Someone who wanted to be successful just had to work at it, especially given you had powerful relationships. Malcolm followed his Hollywood career and soon discovered that Mary Pickford, in a mysterious way, more or less adopted him. The irony, however, is that the more Malcolm worked at Hollywood, the more he realized he didn't want it and, according to his destiny, soon entered an Episcopal seminary. Few people can resist the lure of Hollywood, and yet Malcolm did. He even took on the moguls of his day, as when he publicly excoriated Cecil B. DeMille's film *The Ten Commandments.*

What made Malcolm give up on Hollywood? Malcolm's response opens your eyes to the trajectories in life we all encounter. "I didn't want to be like those people in five years," Malcolm told me. If Malcolm had stayed in Hollywood, he probably would have died early (like Michael Jackson) or become a reclusive on some Hollywood hill. Malcolm rejected Hollywood because he needed an element of service, meaning, and ultimately spiritual adventure.

Richard Bolles's *What Color Is Your Parachute?* became an influential book in Malcolm's life, especially in making sense of the elements needed to resist a negative life-trajectory. Bolles offered Malcolm a scholarship to a life and work planning conference. At this time, Malcolm was looking for something special to do with his life, especially since the church didn't seem to want Malcolm anymore. Ironically, what came out of this seeking period was the discovery that Malcolm's place was indeed in the church.

In the planning conference, Malcolm had to list the most important people in his life and in society. Malcolm worried over the first list he created of important people from the past, especially over whether to list Jesus because this could be seen as "corny and Disney." And then it occurred to Malcolm that he didn't really admire anyone else, so Jesus indeed got his name on Malcolm's historic list, along with Florence Nightingale. For contemporary people, Malcolm put down Eleanor Roosevelt. And then when it came time for Malcolm to think about his own

Malcolm and Cecil B. DeMille.

life influences, he said, "I sat there like a complete idiot crying because the few people I named touched my life so deeply." It was a simple exercise but enormously important for Malcolm. Also, part of the planning conference's vocational assignment was to name twelve cities you would like to live in. Naturally, Los Angeles was one of them.

If you think about Malcolm's formative years of growing up in the United States in the 1940s and '50s, he wasn't really naïve to list Los Angeles as a key city to live in. Despite the pathological nature of this city's celebrity, it helped Malcolm make his apocalyptic impact, especially on reimagining gay identity. One must remember the times in which Malcolm grew up and later affected so powerfully.

Malcolm's formative years set the apocalyptic stage on which he would offer his gifts to the world. Indeed, this would be a scary stage to be on, but thankfully, Malcolm discovered supportive people in his life.

The first gay person Malcolm knew was a "dyke," an unabashedly "out" lesbian. Malcolm recalls the scene, being so scared and alone, so unattractive in high school. All he had were books and the opera broadcasts Saturday mornings. Virginia was Malcolm's friend. She was sophisticated, beautiful, sure of herself. She had a theatrical cigarette-voice and was outrageous, going to bars and being quoted for her clever sayings. She loved Malcolm. She drove a red convertible and had black friends in 1938—way ahead of her times.

Virginia would pick up Malcolm and take him to the Pencol Drug Store in Denver where the beautiful people went for a coke. She wasn't afraid to be with Malcolm who was so insecure. Virginia (her nickname was Gin) took Malcolm into the public eye, loving him for who he was. She wasted time on Malcolm, which was one of the greatest signs of respect one could give. And Malcolm basked in the attention, playing over and over on the jukebox the song *The Man I Love*. He had no idea what significance this would later play in his life.

Gin was in med school. Sometimes he would visit her at home. She got married in a big wedding, but a scandal arose. Three weeks after the marriage, when her husband left her, Malcolm heard he was gay. She got kicked out of med school. They said she was a lesbian. Malcolm grew up, moved away, and came back to Denver only twice. Virginia was older, but still beautiful, and so sophisticated. She still loved Malcolm, who still felt alone and scared, but not so unattractive, having garnered the attention of millions of people. She took Malcolm's hand in hers, held it, and said his hand was lovely; indeed, even the loveliest hand. She told Malcolm she knew a man who would love to know him, love him. The three of them could go away together for a while, but Malcolm was scared and said no.

On his last visit to Gin, her old family home, that had once been aristocratic and in the best part of town, was now in a slum where it was dangerous to live. The paper left on the porch was stolen unless picked up quickly. On that porch, on Malcolm's last night there, Gin threw a party for him. She had an old card table with a fancy tablecloth. The good old silver was used. Malcolm describes the scene, "There was Virginia. Me. A dyke, a dyke army sergeant, an old lover of hers. We ate on the porch in the slum. Candlelight flooded the scene. Virginia had suffered a stroke, spoke with difficulty, used a cane. It was a glorious dinner. We laughed, cried. Tennessee Williams would have loved it. Geraldine Page could have played it."[22] The next morning Malcolm left. The next year Virginia died.

---

22. Malcolm Boyd, "Virginia, My Soul-Sister," *Christian Century*, Spring 2002, 17.

Malcolm had no other people like Gin in his life growing up and perhaps that's why he became a glutton for punishment as he joined the most macho fraternity in college.[23] Why? What was going through Malcolm's head to entice him to join such a fraternity in light of his own struggle with sexual orientation? Malcolm answers that as an outsider he felt that he had to fit in the most hostile of environments. Trying to belong and survive harsh conditions became his mission in life. Isn't this the ultimate way to survive for a gay person, to join the macho fraternity?

There was a young guy in another fraternity who was a friend to Malcolm. They had lunch together quite often and developed a platonic relationship. After graduation, Malcolm's friend went to war. During World War II, he was caught having sex with another male in the army. This was such a traumatic event for Malcolm's friend that he hanged himself in a jail cell. It would be difficult for Malcolm to know his own sexual identity apart from such tragic circumstances that seemed to inevitably arise.

After college Malcolm worked in Hollywood and then went to seminary at the Church Divinity School of the Pacific in Berkeley, California, where he graduated in 1954. Malcolm felt he had to unlearn lots of things, and yet still learn a great deal. A change of scene was clearly needed. "I was a 'seeker,'" Malcolm said. "It was arranged for me to be housed at Pusey House in Oxford, but I had no other direct plans—and certainly didn't want to be in 'a box' (academic or otherwise)." Malcolm describes himself at that time as a contemporary Marco Polo, who needed to find out "who in hell I really was." He made Oxford a base from which to explore.

Janet Lacey, a close friend in London, got Malcolm moving in all kinds of different directions on his journey. First, at Oxford itself, someone who influenced Malcolm greatly was Michael Foster at Christ Church. A sensitive philosopher who stuttered, Foster was infinitely gracious in tutoring Malcolm in life, theology, philosophy, and survival. Malcolm settled into a routine of reading and dialogue with several significant persons who were kind enough to take him under their wing and help him open up in life and vision.[24] This led Malcolm to discover the most

---

23. For explicit examples of Malcolm's behavior in his formative years, see *Take Off the Masks*.

24. One was an Anglican priest, Ernest Southcott, who developed the concept of the "House Church." Another was Bishop Ted Wickham, who pioneered the "Industrial Mission."

exciting theater in the world. "Later, I realized some of the best sermons I'd ever 'heard' were in the theater." At Oxford, Mrs. Graham Greene had Malcolm over for dinner—and showed him her tiny doll houses.

Malcolm took that winter to live and work at the Ecumenical Institute of the World Council of Churches at Bossey in Switzerland. This was a transforming experience in many ways. En route home to Oxford, Malcolm spent a month on Mount Athos—carrying only a knapsack—and staying as a guest in several of the ancient monasteries there and presenting to each a letter from His Holiness, Greek Orthodox Patriarch of Constantinople's Athenagoras, requesting that he be offered ecumenical hospitality. Then Malcolm went back to Oxford. So, Malcolm's year at Oxford changed his life and was an overwhelming experience, yet he was peripatetic, roamed quite freely, and didn't stay in place. Following all of this, Malcolm spent two more years at Union Theological Seminary in New York City, where Malcolm wrote his first two books.

In late summer 1957, Malcolm traveled from New York to Paris and then from there by train to a tiny farming village in rural France called Taizé. Taizé, however, is more than geography. It is a world-renowned spiritual community of contemporary monastic living. Malcolm could see a chateau, the center of the monk's life, at the top of a hill. Carrying his bag, Malcolm climbed the hill and rang a bell outside a wooden gate. He was greeted and taken to meet the prior, Brother Roger. "I didn't know exactly what I expected," thought Malcolm. This was uniquely a faith journey. Would Malcolm remain there and, as a young U.S. Episcopal priest, find a new spiritual home on foreign soil? Or would he return to his roots in North America? Malcolm lived with the novices, doing hard work in the fields during the morning hours, joined the Community for noon prayers, and served in the afternoons as a concierge (answering the bell when visitors rang), selling the community's art, modern pottery, and stained-glass windows.

The Taizé community believed that the presence of Christ is in each person; and such theology became the foundation for the community's Rule of Life. At Taizé, Malcolm discovered an altogether fresh sense of movement in Christian spirituality. The Rule states that one should never remain in place but march with others, running to one's goal on the steps of Christ. It urges that we engage ourselves resolutely in body and soul. Malcolm had in mind this running image—both of Jesus and of a responsive Christian action—when he later wrote his book of prayers, *Are You Running with Me, Jesus?* In the whole meaning of Taizé, there is a steady, joyful running movement toward Christ. Yes, it is understood that Christ runs to meet us. But we too can move toward him in our response to his will.

Christian prayer originates with the God who already knows what we need before we pray. Also, Christian action and good works are God acting in us. It follows that the Christian life is love of neighbor, as well as the love and obedience to Jesus. Whenever Jesus lives within a person, that person's life will have authentic effect on the world. The Taizé community insists that prayer is work, and work is prayer. Malcolm's worship with the Taizé community took place in a twelfth-century church. In the early morning, sunlight streamed through a stained-glass window, making a pool of color on the ancient stone floor. It began with blue and yellow, but soon red ran slowly along the sharp edge of the stone. In the evening when candles were lit and the brothers chanted a psalm, the essential plainness of the chapel was enriched by the soft, golden flames. "Let us abandon ourselves to the living Word of God, let us allow it to affect the intimate depths of our being in order that it may take possession not only of our spirit but also of our body," says the Rule of Taizé.

Malcolm especially admired the artistic ministry of Brother Eric, who once placed a black angel playing a saxophone in a stained-glass window of a church in Strasbourg. He used the theme of dehumanization in his artwork, inspiring Malcolm to see the deep impact art and spirituality could make on the soul.

Malcolm remembers one rainy morning when he was at work in the fields, digging to widen a narrow path. He slid in the mud, rain poured down his face and neck, and he felt sorry for himself. How could what he was doing hold any meaning for God or anyone else? Wouldn't he be better occupied working in a nice heated room in a library, doing his writing? Just then a young German brother came around the top of the hill, pushing a wheelbarrow filled with ashes, which would be placed in the mud to cement it. Malcolm knew that his father and brother had been killed by the Russians in World War II. At the end of the war, this German gentile traveled to Israel and learned Hebrew. In his room at Taizé hung one picture, that of Anne Frank. On this morning he was smiling in the rain, neither morose nor discouraged. "Malcolm, isn't this a wonderful day to offer to Jesus?" he asked.[25]

Malcolm met a monk and fell in love with him. For a short time, Malcolm stayed in Taizé as a member of this extraordinary religious commu-

---

25. Malcolm Boyd, "You and Me: Prayer Is Work, Work Is Prayer," *The Episcopal News Online*, Spring 2007.

Malcolm at Taizé.

nity focused upon welcoming young people into an ecumenical environment of prayer and worship. In one of our spiritual direction sessions, Malcolm looks up at his book shelf and says, "It's funny that the Rule of Taizé isn't up there. . . . It should be." Instead, Malcolm quotes a French mystic from Taizé: "One who has not lost his life has no life." Malcolm wrote about being there and working at Taizé.[26]

There he was in a European religious order, being formed in the deep monastic life of Christian faith. Sam Wylie, a visiting bishop from Michi-

---

26. For Malcolm's years at Taizé, see Boyd, *As I Live and Breathe: Stages of an Autobiography* (New York: Random House), 1969.

gan, a charismatic man, preached a great sermon in his perfect French while Malcolm, with his own imperfect French, struggled to understand. The epiphany that the bishop's sermon elicited in Malcolm was that it was time for him to go home. Malcolm agreed. Malcolm told me, "There are great powers in our life we don't fully realize. When they speak, we would do best to listen."

From France, Malcolm had no idea that he would go to a parish in the inner city of Indianapolis. Malcolm's friend from Union Seminary, a Japanese priest, preached and no one came because people remembered Pearl Harbor. Malcolm had an exchange with a black church when he was working in the Indianapolis parish and it turned into a disaster similar to the one his Japanese friend had experienced when Malcolm's white parishioners boycotted the worship service. Malcolm was trying out his sophisticated ideas on this sincere but backward parish.

Malcolm laughed when he said that the Indianapolis parish and he were both saved when he was called to be the Episcopal chaplain at Colorado State University. This salvation was short-lived because this is where Bishop Joseph Minnis, outraged at Malcolm's innovative ideas, surprisingly attacked his work. Malcolm remembers the attack as if it occurred yesterday: "You can't think of yourself as a beloved Son of God and at the same time go around with matted hair, dirty bodies, and black underwear. . . . Don't allow the puny minds of modern intellectuals rob you of the great truths."[27] Malcolm's courage in this situation made me realize the extraordinary life that was sitting in front of me.

I asked Malcolm if it was at Colorado State that he first challenged church structure? Malcolm answered that it really wasn't radical stuff he was doing on campus—setting up the coffeehouse (the Golden Grape) to feature poetry and dance. "It was harmless," Malcolm told me. And yet, these early practices contain the seeds of Malcolm's eventual reputation as a "rebel priest," challenging the established order in coffee shops and local theaters. At Colorado State, Malcolm began his practice as "the coffeehouse priest." *Time* magazine ran a photo of Malcolm in a coffeehouse. Malcolm ceased to be an organization man. Henceforth he would place the identity of Jesus ahead of institutional loyalty.

Malcolm was ahead of his time and yet this was punished in more provincial settings. For example, Bishop Minnis did not seem to want any new ideas about how to do ministry with young people. Instead, the

---

27. From Malcolm Boyd Archives, "Minister Sanctions Religion with a Cool Bongo Beat," *The Rocky Mountain News*, No legible date or page number.

Malcolm laughing.

bishop needed life to be orderly in some medieval, European way—just like it always had been. Having recently come from modern-day Europe, it was clear to Malcolm that the church needed to come up with new methods to articulate the spirituality and genius of Jesus. After seminary, Malcolm realized that he needed to unlearn some things. Malcolm, like other great spiritual figures, went on a pilgrimage to other countries to test what he had learned about God. Malcolm completed his theological training at Union Theological Seminary in New York, receiving a Master's in Sacred Theology (STM) degree. His theological training thus occurred at a cutting-edge seminary, which taught him how to think beyond stifling and outmoded ways of being the church.

Malcolm became so well known as a radical cleric that he laughs as he tells me a humorous story of mistaken identity. It is an ironic story about a Roman Catholic priest who goes into a bar and sits down. Immediately, upon recognizing the clerical attire, someone goes over and says to the Catholic priest, "Hello, Father Boyd." Malcolm chuckles.

Soon Malcolm ministry was so untenable that he accepted a new position. His new tenure at Wayne State as a chaplain was vital to Malcolm's ministry. At the beginning of his chaplaincy, Malcolm accepted an invitation to join a Prayer Pilgrimage—the Freedom Ride in the South. The journey would move from New Orleans to Detroit. When Malcolm accepted this invitation, I'm not sure he realized the extent to which his life would be forever changed. Now, he would be involved with a different identity that America could never reconcile, the black person. Subsequent to this invitation, Malcolm's identity became inextricably linked to black identity. After the Freedom Ride, Malcolm had to answer another question of identity, namely: how could he help liberate black identity if his own gay identity was still in the closet? Malcolm laughed when he told me he became black when he realized he had to retreat to a gay bar to find refuge from "the man," a reference to the powerful white culture. Malcolm went to the gay bar because he knew in his heart that when the stories broke that he was gay he would never be able to do that again.

Malcolm was ordained an Episcopal priest by Bishop Bloy in Los Angeles in 1955.

Bishop Paul Moore rescued Malcolm's position in the church and even provided financial assistance to bring Malcolm to Washington, D.C. Malcolm told me, "You need power despite fighting it." During this turbulent and fragile time for Malcolm, his most famous book came out, *Are You Running with Me, Jesus?*

While on a pilgrimage to the Holy Land and Rome for two weeks, Malcolm took time off from being controversial. He was part of a Roman Catholic retreat. Stopping in Cyprus, staying in a dormitory, Malcolm wrote the first prayer in *Are You Running with Me, Jesus?*

It's morning, Jesus. It's morning, and here's that light and sound all over again.[28]

At that time, Malcolm had no idea that he would write a book. Malcolm wrote more prayers upon returning to the United States. I asked Malcolm why he used the form of prayers as the content of his book? He replied that it reached a point where he couldn't pray any longer in Old English to an elderly white God "up there."

A young editor in a major New York publishing house, William Robert Miller, was passionate in his encouragement to Malcolm to write the book. Miller wrote *Goodbye Jehovah* and included a chapter about Malcolm. Miller had a mission once he read Malcolm's first draft. Upon publication, the book created an instant sensation. It was a major best-seller. Reflecting on this series of events, Malcolm concludes, "It's a wonder I survived such a roller coaster." Then the gay question made matters worse. Why did Malcolm have to be gay on top of everything else?

As Malcolm took me through this deeply turbulent part of his life, I thought about the many gay priests in the church. I asked Malcolm, "What advice would you give to a priest, to be authentic in this day and age?" Before Malcolm could answer my question, I gave more texture to my question. There are lucky young priests who discover themselves among communities and senior priests with vision, who are already thinking about how to be a Christian in a post-Christian world. There are other contexts in which young priests find themselves in which communities and senior priests are clueless about how to live in a post-Christian world.

Malcolm finally responds. He tells me that no structure is helpful in a young priest's formation if it is such that you have to fit into a defined box. Even if a senior priest wanted this, he or she is insanely busy and pressured in such a way that there is no time to form the box anyway. In the economic meltdown of 2008, the church may have been given an opportunity to do things differently. Given the fact that the Episcopal Church has traditionally contained many wealthier people, I asked Malcolm if the same opportunity to do things differently also lies with Episcopalians? Malcolm told me, indeed, Episcopalians have incredible opportunities in these days of economic difficulties. For example, Malcolm educated me about the changing status of being Episcopalian in Los Angeles. The dynastic weddings of importance used to be in the Episco-

---

28. Malcolm Boyd, *Are You Running With Me, Jesus?* (Cambridge, MA: Cowley Publishing, 2006), 3.

pal Church. Now they're Jewish. He questions the degree of Episcopal wealth today. Wealthy Episcopalians have departed and their children are not going to church. Like a sage, Malcolm instructed me to meditate on the following: what if the Episcopal bishops did an experiment and asked themselves in one of their House of Bishops meetings, "Are our own children Episcopalian? Are they still in church?" Answering those questions could reveal painful realities.

Here is where I think we discover Malcolm's genius—his ability to stay conscious of painful realities that point toward constructive change and better direction. There was a point where Malcolm walked away from fame in the seventies and eighties, especially after his best-selling book, *Are You Running with Me, Jesus?* Malcolm became so well known because of this book that strangers would walk up to him and ask, "Are you running with me Jesus?" Malcolm took refuge in being a writer because, he told me, as a writer you are the magician and mystic and people leave you alone. They leave you alone because they don't want to be a character in your narrative. Malcolm has pursued authenticity. Here is the paradox: he was moving into a world of vast misunderstanding and criticism by finding authenticity in the public eye of celebrity.

His fame was catching like wildfire, but he walked away from it. There was something in Malcolm's nature that made him capable of walking away from the extremes. It turns out that it wasn't in Malcolm's nature to be the hardened activist, hell-bent on destruction. In the eighties Malcolm seemed to completely withdraw from the limelight. Upon accepting an invitation from R. W. B. Lewis at Yale University to be a Resident Fellow in Calhoun College, and an invitation from Yale's chaplain William Sloan Coffin to be a visiting chaplain at Yale, Malcolm found this opportunity to become contemplative and find balance after a life of great turbulence. Lewis was Master of Calhoun College and professor of English and American Studies at Yale and recipient of the Pulitzer Prize for his biography of Edith Wharton. As Malcolm recalls this time period of his life, he writes me:

> Dick Lewis and his wife, Nancy, opened their lives to me and became the closest of friends. I was always fascinated by the fact Dick's father had been an Episcopal priest. My life at Yale gave me both a longed-for solitude as well as an immersion in a rich swath of contemporary culture when I wished to participate. This included becoming a friend of Norman Mailer. I was invited to write a weekly column for the *Yale Daily News*.

This led to a highly amusing incident. Two friends of mine were about to launch a new press syndicate. They pressed me to write a column for them. So they subscribed to the *Yale Daily News* in order to read my work as a way of determining if I were really columnist material. At that same time Garry Trudeau was starting a new comic strip called "Doonesbury" in the *Yale Daily News*. My friends discovered it. The rest is history.[29]

Having come out of the closet with his gay identity in the seventies, Malcolm found the desire to return to church work for about fifteen years. Malcolm told me, "I'm happy about this—that is, I went back to the church. Things came out okay and I was saved in many respects for having done so. For activism to last, you've got to reflect and pray." Maybe this was the best advice for my young associate priest, Troy Mendez. To last he would have to deepen his prayer life. Such insight comes from someone with great authority. Malcolm's insight is authoritative because he not only survived turbulent years, he flourished because of them, even into old age.

Life as a priest in the church made Malcolm a durable person. "What about the life of being a priest made it helpful or unhelpful?" I asked. I explained to Malcolm what I meant by the question. Usually, the unhelpful connotations of a priest are ritualistic Sunday mornings, the collar, the jovial priest who slaps you on back, and the Monte Python sketches of a priest's buffoonery. The helpful connotations are of a priest who is with you when you are dying; or the French worker-priest living with the poor. Malcolm was this latter kind of priest. When Malcolm departed Hollywood in 1951, everyone bowed their head (including the bartender) at a going away party for him at Ciro's.

For Malcolm, it was helpful to get out of the headlines because you are forced to play a role when in the headlines. Malcolm was tired of the caricature—the controversial Malcolm Boyd. Why wasn't there ever the headline: the noncontroversial Joe Smith? Media thrives only on controversy or making you controversial to keep people's attention. Bishop Jack Spong agrees when he says that he can hardly be mentioned in the press without the adjective "controversial" being attached to his name. "That word has almost become a part of my identity."[30]

---

29. Boyd, "Comments on the manuscript," e-mail message to author, December 8, 2009.

30. John Shelby Spong, *Why Christianity Must Change or Die* (San Francisco: HarperSanFrancisco, 1998), ix.

Malcolm with Shelley Winters and Norman Mailer.

In addition to making him more durable, Malcolm's priestly life helped him sort out the complications of gay identity. As a child, being "that" different in his generation meant that Malcolm was an enemy that needed to be killed. Any child growing up in such a frame of reference would need radical support to offset the culture's xenophobia. Final healing only occurred in Malcolm's life during those less public years of accepting the limitations and blessings of the church, and especially in meeting Mark. They have maintained an open, monogamous gay relationship for twenty-seven years.

In one sense, Malcolm told me, he could have turned out an alcoholic, utterly misunderstood and living in the hell of an ego-driven personality. So, I asked Malcolm, "When you died to the famous Malcolm Boyd in those turbulent years, did you find not only your life but also your longevity?" Malcolm responded that this was a complicated, but good question. In some ways, from the very beginning, he was led by spiritual forces to resist destructive patterns, never chose them, and walked away from them. There was a sense of the *imago dei* (the image of God) ever present in Malcolm that preserved his life or the life of others.

The Pestilence of Celebrity

Malcolm's own celebrity came from his spiritual classic *Are You Running with Me, Jesus?* This book is now recognized as one of the icons of the 1960s. Malcolm wrote the "You and I" column for the *AARP Magazine* for the decade 1990–2000. With 32 million readers, it had the largest circulation of any magazine in the United States. After writing best-selling books, Malcolm appeared on the nation's campuses, was leader in the civil rights and peace movements, and was interviewed more than 3,000 times in print and electronic media, including taping with Barbara Walters, David Frost, Phil Donohue, and Hugh Downs. Malcolm's memoir, which included his coming out as a gay priest, was entitled *Take Off the Masks*. It was published in 1978.

In the 1980s Malcolm served as president of the prestigious PEN center USA West, reviewed titles for the *Los Angeles Times Book Review*, and served on the parish staff of St. Augustine by-the-Sea, Santa Monica. Boston University now houses Malcolm's archive of letters and papers, which include even more personal observations. *Life* named him a member of the "Take Over Generation"; *Time* dubbed him "the coffeehouse priest"; *Mademoiselle* included him with Federico Fellini, Norman Mailer, James Baldwin, and Jules Feiffer as a "Disturber of the Peace." *The Atlanta Constitution* called him "a secular saint" and *Publisher's Weekly* wrote that "Malcolm Boyd is becoming an American institution."

Few people exhibit such celebrity coupled with social awareness. Malcolm's genius is contained in his resistance to caricature and stereotype. Such genius looks like an amphibian eking out a living between the desert and monsoon—someone capable of living in harsh environments, surviving among diverse environments and identities. By being an amphibian, Malcolm also becomes prophetic to provincial (narrow-minded) worldviews incapable of living alongside the worldview that God could have actually created gay humanity. Malcolm's pestilence was for the narrow minded, challenging them to a more profound hope beyond self-interest. With this genius, Malcolm becomes the apocalyptic figure on a white horse that makes this world consciousness of unnecessary hierarchies and false gods. Such consciousness is the necessary foundation that must be laid first in order that Malcolm can help bigots and xenophobes experience epiphanies that gays are human beings rather than abhorrent flesh to slaughter and hunt down. So, how was Malcolm able to bring on such epiphanies? I think it was through his celebrity. And yet, Malcolm riding on a white horse had to make his world conscious of its idols. One such idol is celebrity—something Malcolm is quick to dash against a stone. Although Malcolm was not famous yet, he found the courage to leave Hollywood and enter seminary. Instead of giving in to the creeping seductions to become famous, Malcolm tried hard to remain innocent and authentic. Malcolm writes me:

> The year was 1955. That fall I was to enter Union Theological Seminary in New York City to earn a graduate degree. I had just spent 1954–55 at Oxford, the Ecumenical Institute of the World Council of Churches in Switzerland, and random travel in Europe.
>
> I can't remember where I met this man whom I'll call William. A charming host on the international circuit, he reacted positively to my Hollywood background (we knew a number of the same people). Prior to my return to the U.S. to enter into seminary life again, he invited me for a week of rest and relaxation at his estate outside Paris. The invitation seemed entirely above board and natural. At the end of the week I'd fly to New York. William and his chauffeur met me at Orly and we drove to the nearby estate.
>
> Although I didn't recognize it at the time, I was soon to be caught up in an emerging mystery. I must confess that I was a combination of Billy Budd, a Boy Scout, and perhaps a young Marco Polo. I was quite innocent and simply thought a wealthy and philanthropic gentleman was offering me a week of rest before I began a Spartan existence as a student in Manhattan. However, rather quickly other elements emerged. I had no way of grasping or understanding them. Let me explain. Although I realized that I was a homosexual, I'd had no sexual experience up to this time. Homosexuality appeared to be a complex combination of leprosy and enormous danger. I had no idea how to cope with either. I imagine that I was per-

A youthful Elizabeth Taylor was a guest at a party in Malcolm's Hollywood home in 1949.

ceived as charming, attractive (but not overly), ambitious, sincere, and terribly interested in the life that beckoned to me. I was growing up but had not done so.

Clearly, William must have assumed I comprehended that he wished to have sex with me, and on his terms. Probably he wanted me to offer myself to his power by acknowledging him as my master. He was sophisticated and predatory while I was clueless. There was no one to act as interpreter. This situation caused me confusion and some dismay. It worsened when William changed from being warm and hospitable to being coldly abrupt and withdrawn. I didn't want to be there. An increasingly bad experience was becoming a nightmare. There was no one I could talk to or seek counsel.

Then another guest appeared. She was film star Joan Fontaine, who had become a celebrity with her role opposite Laurence Olivier in *Rebecca* and won the Best Actress Oscar for *Suspicion*. I can't imagine what she thought of me: a graduate theology student, self-absorbed, reflective, utterly serious and unsure of myself. I found her not only charming and lovely—an image fully realized—but also someone kind, open, genuinely offering friendship. Sensing my deep need, she was a warm human being instead of a remote or narcissistic screen goddess. We had an opportunity to talk at great length when William left us to lunch nearby at the Duke and Duchess of Windsor's country home. She told me that the Aly Khan kept insisting that she visit him in the south of France, but she didn't go.

It seems apparent that she confronted William and informed him that I must be left alone and allowed to leave quickly and safely. In fact, it seems apparent to me now that she saved my life. I was in way over my head and hadn't the vaguest idea what to do. I could easily have been wounded, seriously damaged. and my entire vocation and psyche dealt a serious blow. I do recall a last ugly, bitter conversation with William when I was, in effect, saying goodbye. He said he had the highest Episcopal Church connections in the U.S. with powerful bishops and would see that my attempts to work in the church would be blocked at every opportunity.

Needless to say, I never saw William again. Joan Fontaine kindly had a car pick me up and get me out of there. I got to London, caught a flight to New York, and in a few days was enrolled in Union Theological Seminary. After a couple of years I earned my STM degree, wrote my first two books, and soon went to serve my first parish, a small inner-city church in Indianapolis. In ensuing years I would grow and mature in my understanding of being gay and learn to link my sexuality to my spirituality. The last time I came across William's name was on a Christmas Day when I was on a plane flying from New York to Los Angeles. I was reading the *New York Times* when I saw his name. It was in his obituary.[31]

Hollywood gave Malcolm an education far better than Harvard could ever provide. It taught Malcolm how to enter a room, how to do an intimate scene—all serious stuff for any public figure. The geography of Malcolm's life contained the attention of celebrities and famous people. In many ways, I think Malcolm's formation in such a landscape gave him the swagger to become a "rebel priest." My work as Malcolm's biographer is to navigate such terrain. A key guiding star in understanding Malcolm's life is in his wisdom concerning what celebrity means. Malcolm sets the tone of what celebrity means in his description of Mary Pickford as a solitary goddess, seemingly adorned in white in the entertainment section of the Sunday newspaper.

How did Malcolm as a young priest meet Mary Pickford, a quintessential Hollywood celebrity? The linear answer is simply that Malcolm ended up working for Pickford in Hollywood. They seemed a strange combination: one a young man struggling with ambition and the other a celebrity whose ambition is comingled with her personality. Before he worked for Pickford, Malcolm writes, "I see Mary Pickford in a magazine photo. She's attired in white. Wears a large hat. Stands alone. Isolated. A small group of people nearby seems in a worshipful attitude. Pickford is the most famous woman in the world. I am twelve."[32] It was very strange for Malcolm to grow up and find himself constantly in Pickford's presence. Such encounters are one in a million because the worlds of celebrity and innocence rarely coincide; and more, to not just meet but to become intimate friends with celebrity. Malcolm illustrates, "I'm with [Mary Pickford] on a plane trip from Hollywood to tape an audition TV show for her husband Buddy Rogers. I've been up all night trying to sober up our writer who, I just found out, is an alcoholic. In the morning I'm tired. While seated in a limo headed for the airport with Mary and Buddy, Mary tells me 'Darling, I know you missed breakfast and must be hungry. So I took this pastry for you from our breakfast tray.' She reaches in her leather bag and hands it to me. I exclaim 'Mary, Look!

---

31. Malcolm Boyd, "Add to Celebrity," e-mail message to author, September 8, 2009.

32. From Malcolm Boyd Archive, Malcolm Boyd, Typed Reflection on Mary Pickford entitled "Goddess."

There's the Golden Gate Bridge!' She does. I toss the leather-scented pastry out the car window."33

Malcolm describes when he met Pickford in a monastery when he had grown older and become a seminarian. Malcolm had spent his last summer (before being ordained a priest) at Mt. Calvary with the prior, Father Karl Tiedemann, participating in the full ritual of worship and work, preparing for his spiritual journey as a priest. Before Malcolm had entered seminary, he had worked in the film and TV industry as president of the Television Producers Association of Hollywood and a partner with Mary Pickford in a production company called PRB, Inc. Mary was the "First Lady of Hollywood," the first great woman star, and was paired with Charlie Chaplin as the first world celebrity in the media age.

Mary visited Malcolm at Mt. Calvary one afternoon. She drove up to Mt. Calvary from Los Angeles to have tea with Malcolm and Father Tiedemann, who asked a Santa Barbara socialite to prepare the accoutrements of a "proper tea." In awe of Mary's reputation, the socialite wished to make an impression; she overdressed and wore too much jewelry. Mary wore a simple dress and no jewelry, and had her chauffeur wait in town, driving alone to the monastery. During the afternoon, Mary starred in a low-key drama. The socialite name-dropped other movie stars, Noel Coward, and even the royal family. An orphan in a storm, Mary sought solace. She found it in the person of Father Tiedemann. Caught by his steady gaze and warmed by his resonant voice, she engaged him in a discussion of spiritual matters. Sipping clear tea, Mary declined sweets. An "Oscar" winner, Mary deserved another for her performance that day as a beleaguered empress in a Byzantine drama. The hinterland socialite talked ever more stridently about dukes and queens. But Mary's voice grew eloquently still. Almost in a whisper, she spoke only of God.34

Hollywood's education was vital for Malcolm because I think it taught him the swagger needed to relativize others' bravado. In fact, Malcolm describes himself as the Cowardly Lion trapped in the vicious cycles of the Civil Rights Movement. And yet, as mentioned before, Malcolm's life seems anything but cowardly, although he nevertheless describes himself as cowardly, especially in coming out as a gay man. Malcolm mentioned three fears that he had to overcome: dogs, darkness, and public speaking. Such self-assessment is important in understanding how Malcolm's

---

33. Malcolm Boyd, "Goddess."
34. From the Malcolm Boyd Archive, Malcolm Boyd, "Remembering a Summer at Mount Calvary in 1953," A Holy Cross Publication.

Malcolm with Mary Pickford.

courage is deeply rooted in his ability to consciously examine his own weaknesses and strengths. Among these three fears, the one that seems most ironic in light of Malcolm's celebrity and priestly life is his fear of public speaking.

When Malcolm was in college, standing up and speaking in public took a great effort. Malcolm was afraid to stand up in a gathering and make a speech about anything. Once in middle school another student named Frederick Funk was running for head boy. Malcolm states, "Apparently I was his campaign manager. I had to stand up in a crowd and read a short speech about Fred. I was scared, blown away. Years later in college, I recall similar situations and the same kind of feelings."

However, when Malcolm started working in Hollywood after graduating from college, it became obvious that he needed, professionally, a public poise he did not yet possess. How to acquire it? Malcolm remembers, "I started out by arranging for invitations from clubs and organizations in small towns outside Los Angeles. I made sure I had a completed manuscript in my hands ready to read. I sweated when I stood up to speak. It was not only work, but agony. I persevered. Gradually I got better. Maybe it finally became a kind of fun thing to do. I spoke to all kinds of community groups north of Santa Barbara and south in Orange County. My fear dissipated. I learned how to get a laugh, relax an audience, even take control of a situation."

It was good Malcolm did this because, a few years later after being ordained a priest, he was a guest speaker at dozens—even hundreds—of college campuses throughout the U.S. He was in demand as a best-selling author and as a well-known advocate of civil rights and peace in Vietnam. Finally public speaking, even to a thousand or so people, became a simple and easy matter for him. Of course, as a priest, he was called on to give many, many sermons in churches. Malcolm concludes, "I was grateful that, along the way, I had learned how to address an audience and hold their attention, challenge them, convey significant and often controversial ideas."[35]

When Malcolm came to work in Hollywood, he arranged to be interviewed in out-of-the-way places where his reputation wasn't on the line. To counteract this public fear, Mary Pickford was good for Malcolm as she helped him navigate how to create TV and radio shows. By doing this he overcame the fears that often elicited sweating and great anxiety. Remarkably, Malcolm learned to speak without a manuscript. This was difficult because the prop of a script provided something to hide behind. Actually, Malcolm told me that a good preacher needs both a script and the freedom to do without it. "It is important to have the manuscript for a sermon," Malcolm says, "because a sermon is meant to be written for the longevity and ubiquity of the word." And yet, the sermon can't be delivered by simply reading it.

There is a ubiquitous urge to have celebrity, to be famous. In spirituality, however, such urges usually lead to "road-side bombs" that easily set off bad life trajectories and a disconnect from healthy well-being, and I dare say, a disconnect even from God. We discussed this spiritual disconnect in one of our sessions of spiritual direction which Malcolm recalls and writes me about:

> Dear Michael: Have been thinking about the book and its development. The four chapters are genius, in my opinion. Brilliant. Should bring your skill out at its best. It might make sense right now for you

---

35. Malcolm Boyd, "Fear of Public Speaking," e-mail message to author, November 11, 2010.

to move into the introduction which is so essential to the work and will establish the motifs. One of these is, of course, celebrity. That frightening, salacious, out-of-control global development that affects every area of life.

"Celebrity" and "church" are oil and water. The church not only has guilt complexes about celebrity (as perhaps about sex), but it tries to fit celebrity into traditional cultural categories. (It doesn't fit.) Celebrity is a major motif of your book. I think you need to tackle it in the introduction. This brings up questions. Why are you writing this book? Why are you dealing with these themes? What have been your feelings about Tutu's celebrity? Mine? How do you weave these things together? In the introduction you will probably want to introduce (briefly) the themes of the four chapters. Our spiritual direction needs to be defined in the introduction; this brings you into it directly and immediately.

The epilogue should wait until the finale, the finish, the end. In a sense it will write itself at that point.

When you deal with my celebrity, it seems necessary to go back to Hollywood and Mary Pickford. That total, global celebrity that shocks and startles the world, and brings up mixed reactions of guilt and anger and competition and awe. There's your introduction to celebrity with Tutu. Then there's my enigmatic, strange "return" to celebrity with my book and the images it created of the rebel priest. Then there's your involvement with me—on and on it moves like the Yangtze River. What sense can one make of all this? There's the brush of celebrity with Jesus (*Jesus Christ Superstar*—and you'll find my review of that in the *New York Times*) and again with the Beatles (We are more popular than Jesus now").[36]

Indeed, to navigate Malcolm's extraordinary life, you need to understand the complex life of celebrity that tempts many to be "God." What is extraordinary is how Malcolm consistently resisted this temptation and helped the many societies in which he led do the same. Malcolm was one of the few who could put on celebrity and take it off like a well-worn sweater. We see such detachment in many areas of Malcolm's life.

Like a spiritual sage sitting in the cold altitude of a mountain, Malcolm showed me how to wear this sweater. Why would he leave Hollywood and go to seminary? Malcolm writes, "I've departed Hollywood and am a seminary student in Berkeley, preparing for the Episcopal priesthood. Mary is invited by President Eisenhower to be the star of a national bond

---

36. Malcolm Boyd, "Introduction", e-mail message to author, 9-25-2011

drive and to visit a dozen major cities. San Francisco is one. I come over from Berkeley to stay a couple of days with her at the Fairmont while she does media events. Late one night Mary says she wants to take a cable car ride. We board a car atop Nob Hill. A passenger whispers to Mary, "Are you Mary Pickford?" "Yes, my good man, I am," she replies, giving him her best movie star smile. The cable car charges down the hill in rapid descent. The next night Mary and I play incognito from film stardom and go to dinner at a modest Italian neighborhood restaurant. Nobody recognizes Mary because it was inconceivable that Mary could be there. We order garlic bread. Before we know it we're rubbing what's left of garlic in our hair, laughing uproariously. Having fun. The gamine in Mary adored it. Once she employed a French maid for the sole purpose of having pillow fights with her."[37] How could Malcolm leave such a world and deliberately descend into the hell of the 1960s?

Why would a young white man risk his life by joining the Civil Rights Movement, even going on the dangerous Freedom Rides in the Jim Crow South? Malcolm recalls, "It's funny. . . . I grew up never for one moment imagining I might someday be one of those people who carry signs on, of all places, picket lines. I lived in my sheltered world, immunized against the suffering of the world. This is because I lived in the privileged white world of North America."[38] How does one reconcile these contradictory realities in Malcolm's life, from Hollywood to church, from white world to black? Why did he plunge into civil rights and mean it?

Not only does Malcolm's life demonstrate his detachment from celebrity by entering the Civil Rights Movement, one can also see this detachment occur in his confrontation with religion. Why would a priest rebel against his own church? Why did Malcolm have to be gay? Malcolm growls, "Can't you leave me alone, God?" And why, after all this is said and done does Malcolm return to celebrity status! When having difficulty praying to God, Malcolm decided to write what he calls "some screwy little book" that became a *New York Times* best-seller. To this day *Are You Running with Me, Jesus?* remains an ice-breaking work in literature. But why? So is there a pattern to such a life of no pattern? I think so.

Malcolm's life points us back to the guiding star of celebrity status and how one wears it. In family-systems theory, the one who constantly reveals the secrets in dysfunctional families is usually the one punished

---

37. Boyd, "Goddess."
38. Malcolm Boyd, *A Prophet in His Own Land: A Malcolm Boyd Reader*, ed. Bo Young and Dan Vera (Brooklyn, NY: White Crane Books, 2008), 114.

and yet later praised for stopping the patterns of abuse. When looking for God and discovering Malcolm, I discovered that Malcolm's celebrity life indeed reveals the secrets of dysfunctional societies and it is now time to celebrate his contribution to healing us all.

Malcolm's above encounter with celebrity entailed a more pristine world—the glamor of Mary Pickford and elegance of Hollywood at that time. Malcolm moved into a completely new territory of celebrity when he began impromptu appearances with the brilliant guitarist Charlie Byrd in the Showboat Lounge in Washington, D.C. Malcolm's own celebrity status was emerging as he moved from priest in the established church to priest beyond conventional settings. Not only that, Malcolm was emerging at the same time as new genres of celebrity. The following question is

hungry i

case in point. "Do you realize how important Charlie Byrd is?" A guitarist asked Malcolm this question to make him aware of his luck to be with one of the most famous jazz artists. Malcolm was beginning at the top. Why did he want to work with Malcolm? Working with prayers was somehow a delight for Byrd. He was such a serious artist, played jazz with a pick-up trio as comfortably as he played with a symphony orchestra. One of Malcolm's fondest memories of working with Byrd was during a three-hour Good Friday service in New York that Columbia Records recorded. Malcolm ended up on the front page with Byrd on the next day's *New York Times*.

For Malcolm, working with such a virtuoso wasn't easy, however. Charlie drove Malcolm crazy because Malcolm would show up early and Byrd would saunter in one minute before the performance. Malcolm longed to do his poetry with Byrd at the hungry i, but Byrd had an agent that charted his life and was signing up for gigs way in advance. Fortunately, Byrd had a relationship with Malcolm and was able to circumvent the red tape that would have prevented Byrd from playing with Malcolm. Hollywood in many ways taught Malcolm the courage to collaborate with Byrd—perhaps the only virtue Hollywood has to offer. It took courage and the prayerful curiosity of Byrd to work initially with Malcolm and Malcolm benefitted greatly from collaborating with the genius of a jazz artist like Byrd. Eventually, Malcolm would go on to read his poetry with other artists such as Oscar Brown Jr., who worked with Malcolm in Chicago. Malcolm's celebrity with other jazz artists like Vince Guaraldi even produced a Jazz Mass at Grace Cathedral in San Francisco.

Malcolm remembers a newspaper cartoon in which a child asked his dad, "Are we going to church or to the hungry i?" Malcolm's Christ-in-culture model of spirituality was indeed avant-garde for his time as he got people to listen to Jesus without the typical dichotomy of "I'm not religious but I'm spiritual." Malcolm even anticipates overcoming these false dichotomies by taking Jesus into bars and coffee shops.

Malcolm reflects deeply with me on this time of his life. In 1966 the hungry i was a San Francisco night club of seri-

Malcolm in a coffeehouse.

ous intent where Woody Allen and others appeared. Enrico Banducci, the manager of the hungry i, told *Time* that women's breasts weren't bringing in the crowds anymore, so he needed to move into some kind of controversy to attract more people. "I was not out to save souls," Banducci said. "I just thought it would be a good business marriage." And it was.[39] So, he called Malcolm to appear with Dick Gregory. The first time Malcolm had seen Gregory was in Detroit where everyone was at first laughing and then crying in a sudden switch of mood, paying tribute to Gregory's genius.

For example, Dick Gregory welcomed a particular audience he was sharing with Malcolm at the hungry i. Gregory went over to Malcolm and put a slice of bread on Malcolm's bar stool in case "the reverend" was in the mood for miracles. A *New York Times* article described the scene in which Malcolm read his prayers at the hungry i.[40] Wearing a wrinkled clerical suit, he stood at the lectern improvised from a music stand and read from his book of "pop" prayers, *Are You Running with Me, Jesus?* A three-man combo played a jazz processional, the lights dimmed, and a spotlight searched out a slight, diffident man in a clerical collar who had stepped on stage to say his prayers.

> It's morning, Jesus. It's morning, and here's that
> light and sound all over again
> I've got to move fast . . . get into the bathroom, wash
> up, grab a bite to eat, and run some more.
> Are you running with me, Jesus?[41]

Peter Yarrow of the Peter, Paul, and Mary trio softly played a guitar while Malcolm recited the above prayer.

Malcolm would be an unlikely night-club entertainer if he wore no clerical collar. Most of his hair is gone and what remains is graying. The glare of the spotlight makes him squint. He has something of a Bob Hope nose, an open face, and a boyish grin. He reads his prayers with considerable feeling but at the end of his act he is snappish when answering questions from hecklers. He does not suffer fools gladly even when they have paid $3.50 ($4 on Fridays and Saturdays) to pray with him.

Most audiences applauded between the prayers, and when they didn't Malcolm seemed concerned that the silence was due to false piety. But

---

39. Julius Duscha, "And Now Even Prayers Are Pop," *New York Times*, November 13, 1966.
40. Ibid.
41. Boyd, *Are You Running with Me, Jesus?*, 3.

once he finished praying, and sat on a bar stool to answer questions, the audience had no inhibitions.

"Hey father, do you think the Catholic Church is really in favor of peace in Vietnam?"

"Well, baby, I don't know what the Catholics think in Vietnam."

"Are you doing your job?"

"Completely. We've got to get with it. We need some armpit theology."

"What are your ulterior motives?"

"If you mean, do I want to sprinkle everyone with holy water?—no. The population explosion, black and white, hunger—these are my concerns."

Clergy who infiltrated the hungry i wrote to Malcolm. The Rev. James Clark Brown, of San Francisco's First Congregational Church, said in the press: "You were on, man. . . . It was the most effective and, for my money, gutty evangelism I've observed in a long time."

The Rev. H. T. Knight, assistant minister of St. Luke's Church in San Francisco, commented: "I had read the book, but the prayers moved me even more in the setting last night. What a fantastic opportunity to reach so many people who would never go near a church at the 'holy hour' Sunday morning."

These engagements were enormously successful for Malcolm, too. They led to seven minutes on the Huntley-Brinkley show, an interview with Johnny Carson, photos and articles in newspapers and magazines, increased sales of his book, a new record album made with guitarist Charlie Byrd, and offers galore.

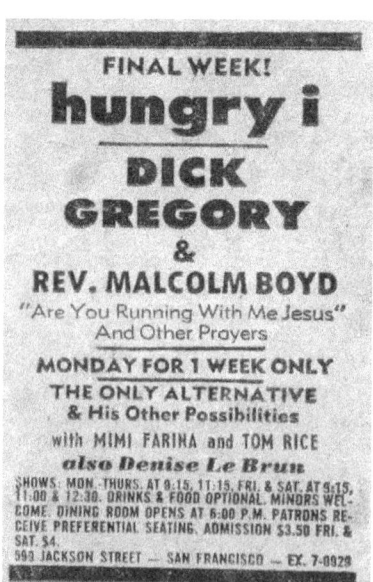

Malcolm didn't think his appearing at the hungry i would be so controversial. Well, it was. NBC, CBS, ABC, *Time*, and *Newsweek*—each had a night at the hungry i, to cover Malcolm and Dick Gregory. When I asked Malcolm about his stand-up routine, he told me that he did "a sophisticated theological thing" that seemed to go over surprisingly well with the audience. Malcolm read his prayers to the audience and opened it up to discussion.

For Malcolm, this was pure evangelism—on the people's turf. Perhaps this is why Malcolm developed the nickname, "the Espresso Priest."

I was curious about Malcolm's relationship with one of my favorite jazz musicians, Vince Guaraldi, best known for playing the theme music for the television show *Charlie Brown*. I was even more curious to find out that Malcolm performed with Guaraldi at Grace Cathedral on May 21 and 22, 1965. When we were discussing this in a spiritual direction session, all of a sudden, the producer of a documentary on Guaraldi called to interrupt us and I hear Malcolm ask me, "You want to go to the filming?" Well, it was a great blessing to this book for me to see Malcolm return to his element. I had the great fortune to see Malcolm's "sophisticated theological thing" firsthand. For many years, Malcolm did this "sophisticated theological thing" in coffee shops and night clubs. The filming was taking place at the Jazz Bakery on Easter afternoon, 2009, in Los Angeles. My wife, Raquel, and I went and greatly enjoyed ourselves. After the performance, Malcolm told us, "I love working creatively with people."[42]

The image of Malcolm sitting on a stool delivering his prayers in sequence to a jazz trio of professional musicians and flashing images was mesmerizing. I looked at Raquel next to me, and I saw tears rolling down her face as Malcolm's twist of phrase or uncanny combination of images would release my wife's emotions. So, indeed, Malcolm had a "sophisticated theological thing" he did extremely well. I saw why he became a celebrity.

I saw Malcolm in performance a second time at the Jazz Kitchen during the Episcopal Church's General Convention in Anaheim in July 2009. Again, I saw Malcolm's living genius in these performances—this time for church folk, the very ones who would have given him the most grief when he performed in coffeehouses and bars in the sixties and seventies. At General Convention so many church people responded positively to Malcolm that I think it meant something different to him in his mature stage of life. Malcolm told me, "In the oddest way this happens to be the most humbling thing that ever happens to you. This is hard for people to understand. But this can be addicting, yet again. Seeking the praise of church folk can be so dangerous." Yes, but Malcolm said that he's not an Oscar winner, or the president of Ford Motor Company.

Not having some tangible role of celebrity is an advantage. Malcolm has learned to want, and to want differently. He doesn't want the Nobel Prize,

---

42. For another example of such creative collaboration, see Malcolm's prayers and Pulitzer Prize–winner Paul Conrad's editorial cartoons in *When in the Course of Human Events* (New York: Sheed and Ward, 1973).

Malcolm giving poetry reading in the hungry i.

but he does want his life to have a significant impact for reconciliation and justice.

As Malcolm's life of celebrity happened, so did his spiritual formation continue. This is an odd combination considering that most celebrities are famous because of their ability to rise above the banalities of religion. Celebrities are able to rise above religion because they can surreptitiously demand their own glory and praise. They can be the objects of their own religion. Malcolm, however, is an exception. Are there others like Malcolm? I think the hungry i shows that there are—those celebrities capable of an amphibious life that moves in and out of glory. Where Malcolm demonstrates more prowess than others rests in his ability to put on celebrity and take it off. He doesn't simply move in and out of celebrity; rather, he shapes celebrity to benefit others. This is a rare breed. Malcolm describes those capable of doing this as mystics because they possess a profound detachment to the seductions of celebrity so as not to become its victim. In this sense, Malcolm's navigation of celebrity, the longevity of his career, and his ability to use celebrity to shine the camera on the ills of society, all point to Malcolm being one of a kind. Malcolm said to me in one of our spiritual direction sessions, "There is a little loneliness in all of this because you're asking: is there anybody else out there like me?" I have learned from Malcolm such important questions are only asked from a character capable of perseverance and longevity.

Malcolm's life was such that he could not help but think about appearance and image and how we all are seduced to believe the superficial. Mary Pickford and others influenced Malcolm to see the absurdity of celebrity even further. Should someone seek celebrity? If there is anyone on the sidelines longing to be famous, should we warn them of the dangers they seek? Shouldn't we put up the sign that warned Dante not to enter hell? The problem, Malcolm reminds me, is that seeking fame affects all of your relationships. When you're trying to be famous, it gets complicated. You can't help but destroy relationships.

Now arthritic, Malcolm can no longer cut his toenails. So, he recently went to have a pedicure. While waiting around, he read a *People* magazine containing articles about celebrities (and noncelebrities trying to be celebrities, Malcolm was quick to add). A lot of people are whores about celebrities, Malcolm told me. A decent person could be seated in a restaurant and if Marilyn Monroe enters the room, all of a sudden that decent person behaves like a whore. Celebrity does something to us. What is done is frequently bad. For example, at the time of my conversation with Malcolm on celebrity, Farrah Fawcett was dying of cancer. Instead of a normal community lamenting these tragic circumstances, the media made us dwell on Farrah Fawcett's son who had been caught driving under the influence. The curse of Farah Fawcett's celebrity was the feeding frenzy needed by the masses to be entertained by both the tragedies and the celebrations of celebrity life. Celebrity catches up with you. At the lowest point, you see celebrities behind bars still trying to believe in their own fame. Malcolm has heard of such imprisoned celebrities saying, "Don't you know who I am?" Malcolm mimics what the celebrity would say, "Order me a martini and a dinner and let us put this prison thing behind us." Celebrity is a virus that makes us delusional.

At the time of writing this last paragraph—July of 2009—Farah Fawcett died, causing a shock wave on CNN. And then a hurricane hit—Michael Jackson died. I asked Malcolm about the tragedy of Jackson's death. "Were you surprised?" I asked. Malcolm wasn't. It was as if Malcolm came out of the wisdom literature of Hebrew Scripture. There's nothing new under the sun for Malcolm. "There's nothing new for me," Malcolm said. Malcolm said that Jackson didn't have a childhood—that he had to be forty years old right out of the gate.

Michael Jackson's life represents a lack of authenticity and decades of hard work. He felt more at home on stage than off it. Malcolm saw the parallels to his own passion to be at home on the stage, for that hour on stage is community with the audience. Some people never had it. In Jackson's case, we witnessed the withdrawal and the pain, the absence of being human, and a reversion to childhood—public horror, perhaps merciful death. He tried to change his biological race.

The White Horse

Malcolm reminds me of the White Knight of the Apocalypse as he struggles with becoming a celebrity, the Civil Rights Movement, and becoming a gay priest. In many ways Malcolm beheld a white horse; and "its rider had a bow; a crown was given to him, and he came out conquering and to conquer" (Rev 6:1–2). The apocalyptic image of the White Knight conquering the nations of the world is misleading, however. Such an image is ambivalent in that white symbolizes holiness and yet the White Knight's appearance inevitably followed evil.

For many, Malcolm's appearance was just as ambivalent. How can a priest be gay? How can the same priest be a celebrity? And for many in the white institutional church, how can a priest be in the Civil Rights Movement? These questions reflected the difficulty of Malcolm's audience in recognizing Malcolm's good or evil persona. It was just as difficult for Malcolm who struggled to stay true to himself, even if others wanted him to put on a different mask on stage.

I also associate Malcolm with the White Knight who became known as Pestilence because of the ambivalence of the White Knight seemingly having a good name and yet causing so much destruction. Even among twenty-first-century theologians, it still proves difficult in appropriating interpretations of the White Knight's identity. It should be noted that this popular interpretation of the White Knight as Pestilence is generally espoused by those unfamiliar with the biblical text, which describes the White Knight more as Conquest than Pestilence. Though it is apocryphal, the interpretation of Pestilence remains most commonly used for the White Knight.

In the midst of all that we have seen so far in Malcolm's life, perhaps Malcolm's greatest struggle was in the dichotomy of being a priest and celebrity at the same time. After all, he knew his gay identity would inevitably emerge despite his own internal struggles of being in the closet. He also knew that black people would eventually obtain their civil rights under the law. What seemed to glue all of these struggles together was in Malcolm's own resolve to be authentic, if not humble in a Western world hellbent toward ego gratification.

Despite the ambivalence above, knowing that the White Knight was sent by God saved Malcolm. Malcolm was content to know that God could be frightening to some whose versions of reality resisted any interruptions. For Malcolm, these were those who found it difficult to understand how the "Negro" was also made in the image of God. To such people who could not accept God's image in black folks or gay folks, Malcolm was apocalyptic—he was the White Knight. Malcolm's acceptance of how he affected others was the key to his longevity and impact. Also key was Malcolm's awareness that God was calling him to see larger realities than himself. I think this enabled Malcolm to resist the many seductions and temptations that he faced in life. Perhaps there could be no greater temptation than his confrontation with celebrity.

On one hand, celebrity provides a platform from which a person can get access to the media for promoting their "cause," whatever the cause may be. We see celebrities frequently being the spokesperson for one thing or the other. On the other hand, many cannot balance themselves on the platform that celebrity provides. Usually, a celebrity is an accident waiting to happen. As Malcolm said in one of our spiritual direction sessions, the Judy Garlands of the world have an awful time winding down after performing. The law of diminishing returns wreaks havoc when usual addictions can no longer bring the celebrity back down to earth.

In the sense of balance, Malcolm was no ordinary spokesperson. What I mean is that he had to learn the ebb and flow of rising to the top and yet still be able to walk (not fall) to the bottom. Malcolm is unusual in this way. In large part it is in this kind of "inordinate" character and talent that inspired my apocalyptic vision of him through the four horsemen. Listening to the myriad stories of his own encounter with celebrity, I could not stop thinking about how consistent he remained entangled with celebrity—relinquishing celebrity status, moving from Hollywood to seminary, and achieving longevity that many "crash and burn" celebrities find impossible to achieve. The celebrity who lives a long life has figured out along the way how to give fame away and not be addicted to it. Perhaps one of the ways Malcolm learned to do this was through his life of prayer.

In the sense of prayer, Malcolm was also no ordinary celebrity. Most celebrities who pray use the same sound bites: "I want to give thanks to my Lord and Savior Jesus Christ for making that touchdown" or they point up with their index fingers as if God also has a heavenly box seat in the stadium. In the way Malcolm prayed, however, he was no ordinary spokesperson. An example of this is in how he prayed—matter-of-factly in *Are You Running with Me, Jesus?*

It's morning, Jesus. . . . What I really want to do is get back into bed, pull up the covers, and sleep. All I seem to want today is the big sleep, and here I've got to run all over again.[43]

Such real prayers ironically are shocking to many religious folks who need to change their voice to pray or use certain "God talk" and posture

---

43. Malcolm Boyd, *Are You Running With Me, Jesus?* (Cambridge, MA: Cowley Publishing, 2006), 3.

to recognize that they are in fact praying. The TV evangelists and megachurch celebrity preachers need, like a new suit or dress, to put on different personalities when they are before large crowds. And as we have seen with many celebrities, their life in private overcompensates in negative ways through sexual and drug addictions. In Malcolm's celebrity status, however, he focused on helping others to pray better in public. Praying better meant praying "really" and authentically—"What I really want to do is get back into bed, Jesus."

In short, Malcolm's celebrity status did not make him fall down and stay down due to celebrity and its moral dangers. I think it was because of his prayer life. Such a prayer life, not the phony prayers, but the real ones enabled Malcolm to get out of bed for at least nine decades. Such a prayer life increased the insight in Malcolm that celebrity itself is the problem. What I mean is that celebrity status enabled him to get media exposure for those things most people of his generation would not like to see, such as civil rights, gay identity, the Vietnam war, an anemic church, etc. Malcolm's celebrity was intrinsically problematic because his spotlight revealed internal struggle. Malcolm explains as he writes me:

> Hollywood was my first brush with celebrity. Being partnered with Mary Pickford was altogether beyond my imagination. I couldn't grasp it. Did Marco Polo feel this way in China? I was fascinated. Glamour was not unattractive. My reactions and feelings were interspersed with shock, a certain sadness (when fun was replaced by reality), and sheer incredulity on various occasions.
>
> Yes, my life was often Oz-like. I was a kid who had liked to go to movies. Now I was hobnobbing with stars and partaking of great luxury and privilege. However, I wanted more. Which is to say I wanted more meaning. My life needed to cut deeper and perhaps make a contribution. For an assortment of reasons—including feeling called by God to a spiritual vocation—I departed Hollywood and entered the Church Divinity School of the Pacific in 1951. Three years in the seminary represented a complete turnabout in my life. My focus changed. I was also terribly busy studying Old Testament, New Testament, Church History, Theology, all the elements that now comprised my daily existence. We seminarians formed our own community and developed a life among ourselves. Upon graduation I served an inner-city parish in Indianapolis and college chaplaincies in Colorado and Detroit.
>
> In 1965 a short book of contemporary prayers I had written was published. Quietly published, I should say. No one expected what is described as "success" to emanate from it. In fact, I insisted upon the

title "Are You Running with Me, Jesus?" The publisher wanted to call it "Prayers for the Post-Christian Era." I kept insisting. One day I found a memo written by one of the top bosses: "Let him call it whatever the hell he wants. We're losing money on this one. What a mistake we made."

There was no reaction to the book for several weeks. Then the tsunami hit. A part of it was the lead review, extraordinarily positive, in the *New York Times*. It welcomed the book with open arms. (It should be noted that, at the time, books with religious themes were seldom equivalent to a footnote). Before I could catch my breath, I was caught up in a celebrity and huge national success that literally took over my life.

What is celebrity? The dictionary says "A famous person. Notoriety or renown; fame." I didn't want to acknowledge it because I judged it, finding it lacking in everything I seemed to believe, such as depth and seriousness and social justice. So I was quite a snob about it. Too, I looked at nationally known clergy (who shall be nameless here) who were virtual household words, but who scored zero in my scorecard of authenticity. I placed myself in the judgment seat. As someone who worked in civil rights, I felt opposed to most of the status quo.

It was ironic that as my fame increased, it became automatic that I moved into a kind of mainstream acceptance. I appeared on national magazine covers and national TV shows. I suppose I became "familiar." I think I took for granted a 1971 *Look* magazine cover that I shared with Duke Ellington and Joan Baez, Walter Cronkite, Margaret Mead, and Sammy Davis Jr. I became "news" much of the time without having to think about it.

I suppose I ended up feeling more or less "entitled" to a new kind of experience with "fame." Yet, of course, I had to ask such questions as "who am I?" and "where am I going?" A year as a guest fellow at Yale allowed me a respite from the rat race and a friendship with Norman Mailer who was also a guest fellow at Calhoun College. But soon the fact this celebrity stuff was happening to me as an Episcopal priest caught up with me. Now I asked new questions: "what am I doing?" and "do I want it?" This led directly to dropping out of limelights and trying to refocus. A dozen years followed when I served as a parish priest in a Southern California parish.

Of course, I'd now experience a brand new bout with celebrity when someone would call me a "has-been." I realized the magnificent irony of this. While I was no longer "important" for some people, at the same time I became more "significant" for others. My first sermon at St. Augustine by-the-Sea in Santa Monica was a "coming out" one. I explained that I was a gay man and went on to discuss/explain various ramifications of that. I felt my entire life was becoming transformed in an ongoing kind of AA experience. Healing was clearly going on. So was an ever deeper journey into soul. I could only stand back, witness, pray, and offer thanks. I find this is still the case. I've learned life is never resolved with a smashing and self-written finality. Always it goes on, even into and past death. Healing and the urgent need of communication and acts of forgiveness and loving go on, well, forever.[44]

The White Knight is an ambiguous figure that creates polarities between good and evil. Left unchecked, such polarities run amok. In many ways Malcolm's life as a priest, celebrity, and provocateur caused such polarities. With Malcolm's identity as a gay, celebrity priest some went so far as to include him in categories of religious and political apostates—the Antichrist, or a representation of false prophets. The complexity of the White Knight is in whether he is evil or not. This was also the predicament of many who tried to understand Malcolm's encounter with celebrity and being gay.

The White Knight points to the violence, warfare, and persecution that will be part of the end of the age. Although it was not the end of Malcolm's age, Malcolm's impactful years were such that they also contained the volatile times of the civil rights era and the 1960s.

As we move toward the remaining Red, Black, and Green Knights, it is important to note that these other three knights are more conspicuous in their destructive forces. Given the unified way in which all four are introduced and described, it is likely that the White Knight really brings the opportunity of a new heaven and a new earth. Ambivalence surrounding Malcolm's life or outright hatred of Malcolm is the result of misinterpretation, similar to those militia who misinterpret the sayings of the Bible in order to achieve misguided ends. Such militia may even think they are doing Jesus a favor by killing others. For example, on May 31, 2009, Scott Roeder shot to death a late-term abortion provider, Dr. George Tiller, who ironically was serving as the church greeter in a Sunday morning worship service. Roeder reportedly subscribed to *Prayer and Action News,* a magazine that advocated "justifiable homicide" as a way of protesting abortion.[45]

---

44. Malcolm Boyd, "Celebrity, etc." e-mail message to author, February 4, 2011.

45. Read more: http://www.time.com/time/nation/article/0,8599,1902189,00.html#ixzz1Dnn8hIkm

Malcolm was deeply aware of all of our confusion around good and evil. Some cast the White Knight as civil war and internal strife. Others, as was held by evangelist Billy Graham, cast the White Knight as the Antichrist, or a representation of false prophets, citing differences between the white horse in Revelation 6 and Jesus on the white horse in Revelation 19.[46] For some, Malcolm can be identified as the rider on the white horse carrying the evil connotation of the Antichrist and its forces that seek to conquer the followers of Christ. And yet, others identified the White Knight as good. For example, Irenaeus, an influential Christian theologian of the second century, was among the first to interpret the White Knight as Christ himself, his white horse representing the successful spread of the gospel.[47] Various scholars have since supported this theory, citing this appearance in Revelation 19, of Christ mounted on a white horse, appearing as The Word of God. The color white also tends to represent righteousness in the Bible, and Christ is in other instances portrayed as a conqueror.

To sum up the first apocalyptic rider, the White Knight, is to conclude that there are ambivalent views of Malcolm's life, especially as they relate to Malcolm being a celebrity, gay priest. For some, Malcolm as the White Knight represents the lust for conquest. From such lust follows the remaining apocalyptic knights of war, famine, and death.

Those who view Malcolm's life in a negative light see a White Knight embodying the Antichrist who brings havoc and misery on the world as indicated by the second, third, and fourth knights. And yet others view the White Knight as Christ conquering secular forces through the power of the gospel (the good news). It is perhaps appropriate that near the end of the apocalyptic vision of the book of Revelation in the Bible, Jesus appears on a white horse proclaiming good news (gospel) in the midst of war, famine, and death. This gospel also goes throughout the earth in the four directions of the compass just as the remaining knights do through war, famine, and death.

Malcolm as a White Knight makes the best sense in terms of Malcolm's life because his message was peace despite the persecution that arose from the message—that God's peace could be just as real in coffee shops and bars as in churches on Sunday morning, that God's peace could be just as

---

46. Billy Graham, *Approaching Hoofbeats: The Four Horsemen of the Apocalypse* (New York: Avon Books, 1985).

47. Robert Mounce, *The Book of Revelation,* New International Commentary on the New Testament (Grand Rapids, MI: Eerdmans Publishing, 1997), 140.

valid in a "Negro" as in a Caucasian, and that God's "restless" peace could eventually emerge in a gay, celebrity priest like Malcolm

So Malcolm is mounted on a white horse. Although we tend to associate white with purity, Malcolm does not come forth in purity with an easy message. When approaching the four horsemen, it might be wisest to refrain from seeking our own self-fulfilling prophecies. Malcolm teaches us that we would do better to refrain from vapid conclusions that misrepresent God's revelation of love and peace. God's love and peace can appear scary and restless. With that in mind, we might do better to simply recognize the rider on the white horse as representing an authority that is still part of God's ultimate plan—albeit a strange one.

Malcolm's appearances in strange places like the "hungry i" and with Mary Pickford certainly caused strife as he came out in public as a gay priest. As we will see in the next chapter, such identity becomes complex in light of his secular witness as a civil rights leader and his religious identity as an Episcopal priest. Malcolm's complexity also comes from his celebrity status as he dealt with large publics without watering down his authenticity. For many, the combination of being a gay, celebrity priest was an abomination. The rider of the white horse (or the White Knight) fits Malcolm because his words frequently shocked and offended others who could not handle someone who seemed to be both good and evil. The White Knight causes such polarities.

In our next chapter we will see what results from the initial appearance of the White Knight. Among the civil wars concerning full inclusion of gay identity, interpretations swing between extremes as to whether gay people can be fully human, married, serve in the military, and even be Christian. Similar struggles were waged by African Americans and others in the 1960s. Malcolm's life demonstrated such pendulum swings.

Thus being the White Knight seems to represent at least three things for Malcolm: gay identity, celebrity, and civility among disparate people. The White Knight facilitates the arrival of the next three horsemen as Malcolm's apocalyptic identity now shifts horses. We turn now to the Red Horse of War. In the wake of the White Knight comes War, riding a large, wild red horse and wielding a tremendous sword symbolizing continuing war over the domination of the world, killing millions in his path with his sword. We learn that much of what shaped Malcolm's life as a gay, celebrity priest also prepared him for societal conflicts of his time in which many were killed, often in the name of God.

CHAPTER THREE

The Red Horse of War

> And there went out another horse that was red:
> and power was given to him that sat thereon to take peace
> from the earth, and that they should kill one another:
> and there was given unto him a great sword.
> (Revelation 6:4, KJV)

If you sit down and think about it, this is a strange prophesy. The Red Horse of War carries a rider with great power and yet with ambivalence. The power is known through the great sword and strength of his horse. And yet, John's Revelation shows power as displayed through Jesus as a Lamb sitting on a throne in heaven. What kind of power does the Lamb have? And what kind does the Red Knight wield? The ambivalence comes through knowing that he takes peace from the earth. Jesus even said, "Do not think that I have come to bring peace to the earth; I have not come to bring peace, but a sword" (Matt 10:34). In many respects, this chapter is about war, but not the kind that is typically debated in conversation. This is the kind of war that happens internally as well as externally. Few exhibit such consciousness as well as Malcolm. Even in the writing of this biography, Malcolm helped me struggle internally with all the buzz words of war like "race" and "gay." The struggle (internal war) was for authenticity and perhaps originality. He writes me:

> Dear Michael: These are notes following our good meeting yesterday. Where are you going to place two of the major pieces in the book: (1) the "race" part dealing with the 1961 Freedom Ride as well as the summer of 1965 (that huge event in my life) plus MLK; and (2) the "gay" part (from my earliest childhood throughout my life, that basic part of simply who I am), including your interview with Mark?

Whom else are you wishing/needing to interview other than Mark? Jon Bruno? I am just trying to get a focus on where you are right now and where you wish to go next (and ultimately). Maybe you have far more data on these matters than I realize. In other words, you may be far closer to home than I am aware.

Was the Yale information (from Boston) worth the effort? Can you use it or do you wish to? I just thought it might cast light on a curious part of my life in transition. Does it? If so, what does it say about me? I was surprised by the *Yale Daily News* columns and I'm not sure why. Was it a past part of my life I don't exactly understand? Do you?

Are you satisfied with the Hollywood material? (Did you ever use "Goddess"?) Isn't it strange that I'm back in Los Angeles??? (Why not NYC, Berlin, Buenos Aires OR Wichita, Kansas???????) Geography is so odd.

Are you taking a look at me as a writer?

The present major part of my life is aging. Do you have enough of that? I think we've covered the significant bases, don't you? (No one else ever wrote my biography before.) A major point is that you are not writing a conventional, stereotypical biography at all. That is a HUGE point. All best—M.[1]

In one of my spiritual direction sessions with Malcolm, he asked me to listen to a quote by Frederick Buechner that "in the faces of the people who need us most we discover what we most need."[2] I was struck by the discovery that Malcolm was sad about the notion of thinking about who needs him. I was astounded because Malcolm's life was dedicated to helping so many people in need, especially black people in the civil rights era and opponents of the Vietnam War. As we continued our spiritual direction session, we concluded that to reflect upon those who need us most is best discerned in answering the question: who am I? Malcolm made this discovery himself as he waded into the waters of the civil rights campaign.

> Malcolm prays, "The Lord is my shepherd, I shall not want." What are we supposed to do, Christ, when our worldly shepherds fail us, lie to us, betray us, and even lead us unto evil? Christ, what are we supposed to do?[3]

---

1. Malcolm Boyd, "Where are we now (existentially)," e-mail message to author, December 18, 2009.

2. Frederick Buechner, *The Longing for Home: Recollections and Reflections* (New York: HarperCollins, 1996), 158.

3. Malcolm Boyd and Paul Conrad, *When in the Course of Human Events* (New York: Sheed and Ward, 1973), 110–11.

"We don't stop at schools anymore..."

Malcolm told me that in the 1960s he struggled with questions of identity: Am I somebody? Have I made a mark? Malcolm writes:

> Do I know what life is—what love is? (Am I somebody?) Have I been loved—have I loved? (Am I somebody?) Have I made a mark at all: on a heart, on another life, on the earth, on a piece of paper, on a piece of wood? (Am I somebody?)

Malcolm is the red rider of war because he not only battles himself for authenticity, he also takes this war to some of the most difficult places in the world that are struggling for authentic freedom. Malcolm writes, "You found a crack in my defenses, Lord. What about me? I no longer belong to myself, but God says do not fear."[4] This is a war of authenticity because one can believe a complete lie and myth by thinking that someone needs me when all along I am really oppressing that person.

This chapter reminds Malcolm of apocalyptic moments, especially as he reflects on his role in the Civil Rights Movement. I brought up in our conversation the apocalyptic vision in Matthew 25 that the good didn't know their ultimate significance; and in trying to know one's ultimate significance, God could change the paradigm all together. In other words, I was agreeing with Malcolm that many think they are doing good or being authentic when all along they have constructed a false and oppressive worldview in which they measure self through low standards.

I learned from Malcolm the cliché that a person needs traction to go up the mountain—that we need to be thankful for the struggle to know ultimate meaning; otherwise, we can settle upon lesser goods, if not evil. What deepened our particular spiritual direction session was when we talked about paradigm shifts. What happens when God puts us in an ocean instead of at the foot of a mountain? I identify with the disciples on the shore with Jesus rather than on the mountain. For most of us, recognition of Jesus or the divine happens not on the mountain but in the mundane—in the fluidity of life. Sure, Jesus' transfiguration occurred through blinding light on top of a mountain, but we must always remember—we are not Jesus. Our encounter with transfiguration usually occurs in common places.

It's profound that the disciples couldn't recognize ultimate significance apart from the mundane. They needed Jesus to spit on the ground and apply dirt and spittle to heal a blind man's eyes. They needed bread and wine to remember the communion they had with Jesus. Ultimate significance relies upon the mundane—that's what the Incarnation is all about and what makes for the genius of Christianity. The world is loved so much that God wants to be like us. Such a theology is why Malcolm looks for God in the secular world and not in the institutional church. For Malcolm, the dressing up and the theater of the institutional church borders on the absurd. This was especially the case when Malcolm worked for the basic freedoms of black people in the South. When doing so, he discovered how the white institutional church was often more a part of the problem than a part of the solution.

---

4. Malcolm Boyd, *Focus: Rethinking the Meaning of Our Evangelism* (Harrisburg, PA: Morehouse Publishing, 2002).

Here I am in church again, Jesus.

I love it here, but, as you know, for some of the wrong reasons. I sometimes lose myself completely in the church service and forget the people outside whom you love. I sometimes withdraw far, far inside myself when I am inside church, but people looking at me can see only my pious expression and imagine I am loving you instead of myself.

Help us, who claim to be your special people. Don't let us feel privileged and selfish because you have called us to you. Teach us our responsibilities to you, and to all the people out there. Save us from the sin of loving religion instead of you.[5]

I talked with Malcolm about the scathing nature of this prayer. I asked Malcolm, "What about the little ones you offend?"

Malcolm responded, "It's perfectly okay to offend—Jesus did. We have to be honest."

In the hungry i Malcolm had to deal with the problem of offending Christians in institutional churches with his prayers and because the places where he hung out were, from their perspective, against heaven. Recalling all of this, I said to Malcolm that he had to deal with the problem of offending people a lot in his life.

Malcolm tells me, "It's simply meeting Jesus in the street where people are rather than in the church edifice." Malcolm says he could preach better sitting on a stool in a coffeehouse. What's good about this is that you're already halfway there. You're naked there in front of people who lack the hypocrisy of institutional churches. These people are not pretending to be holy. They know they are in need of something. They know they are vulnerable. In the church you don't have to be vulnerable. Religion these days is set up to make us formal and this can become the kiss of death.

When Malcolm visited a college campus in the Midwest for a speaking engagement, a fundamentalist man approached Malcolm, trying to figure him out. He asked Malcolm, "Have you been born again?" Malcolm said, "I can have three births in a good day and go five weeks without one." Malcolm laughs. "Is that speaking in parables? I don't know."

To many religious folks and institutional Christians, Malcolm was apocalyptic because he offended the formality of "God Talk." Malcolm's grammar of God was much different than those who thought God was only on the side of white people fleeing to the suburbs.

---

5. Boyd, *Are Your Running with Me, Jesus?*, 95.

"A White Man's Heaven Is a Black Man's Hell"

I heard this song many, many times when it was sung by young nationalists during civil rights demonstrations in the early sixties. Would today's black students sing it, too?

At least they might think it. For their experience of human life has been hemmed in by white power. I imagine they dream of getting away, even just once, from white judgments, ways of doing things, and ingrained attitudes toward black people.

This must be why an occasional black professor is such a welcome change from a white one. And a black administrator, a black judge, a black journalist, a black TV personality, a black priest, or a black mayor.

"A white man's heaven." It would be hell in its isolation, wouldn't it, Jesus?[6]

"You can't pray this in an institutional church," Malcolm concludes.
"But why not!?" I lament.

Malcolm proceeds to tell me his narrative of negotiating the war of the 1960s and how the institutional church often isolated him. Malcolm was an apocalyptic figure for many Christians. A woman said to Malcolm at the cathedral door in Wilmington, Delaware, "You Son of a bitch." Malcolm and I laugh as we try to analyze how such a remark was a term of endearment. Malcolm thinks that there was an authentic moment for this woman saying such a thing at church. During Malcolm's fame in the 1960s, not once was Malcolm invited to the College of Preachers at the Washington National Cathedral. Such extremes of Malcolm getting rejected by the College of Preachers and other major institutional church organizations reveals an ironic narrative to his life's work because through the Civil Rights Movement in the secular world, he found great acclaim.

In Indianapolis Malcolm was disturbed to see a little white boy jamming a knife into a board saying he wished it were a nigger. Malcolm told me this story in one of our spiritual direction sessions. When he told it to me, it was as if he were reliving the experience—making knifing movements with hands and showing the disgust of the little white boy on Malcolm's own face. Malcolm said this was a touchstone experience that led him into the Civil Rights Movement.

Although Malcolm was assigned to St. George's, he says he didn't know what made him go to Indianapolis, where he became rector of that

---

6. Boyd, *Are You Running with Me, Jesus?*, 46.

Malcolm's first church in Indianapolis (Malcolm lived in the rectory on the left).

parish. "I always pitied the people at St. George's for this 'firebrand idiot' [referring to himself] who parachuted down in their midst as a young priest. It was a wild time. In the rectory it leaked and had to have two tubs to catch all the rain. Today if a seminarian saw that rectory they wouldn't stay." But this was a wonderful time for Malcolm in which he could be experimental and try different forms of ministry. Most importantly, it was a community in which he learned deep compassion for the Civil Rights Movement.

As a young priest, this deep symptom of a racial war made Malcolm set up partnerships between his white church and a black church. Malcolm exchanged pulpits with a black priest. The black congregation treated Malcolm like royalty. With lament, Malcolm recalls that most of his white members stayed home when there was an exchange of pulpits.

After Indianapolis, Malcolm went to Colorado State University as chaplain. It was there that a letter came to Malcolm to join a civil rights "Prayer Pilgrimage" Freedom Ride. Malcolm laughs as he tells me of his dilemma in receiving this letter. "What you're open to will change you," he says. "I'm the Cowardly Lion who learned courage on the job."

> I've got to get into the left lane now, Jesus.
> All the energy of my life is suddenly focused on this sole objective. For the past few seconds my left turn signal has been blinking, but no one has let me into the lane on this crowded highway. Now the intersection where I must turn is only a few feet away.

Cars speed past. A sense of panic seizes me. Perhaps I'm somehow out of place here and can't compete. Is this such a deadly business as it seems, or do we all know we're playing a child's game? If I can't get into the lane, I'll be quite late. It's madness. The highway doesn't belong to anyone driving on it. Why must I fight for the small space I need, Jesus?[7]

In this biography, one of the identities of Malcolm as the purveyor of war comes from his days as a civil rights activist. Malcolm asked me to recognize—and pinpoint—the role of the white volunteers and followers in the Civil Rights Movement. A key highlight in Malcolm's life came in 1961 as a Freedom Rider.[8] However, this biography does not seek so much to provide a detailed description of such events as to display an authentic white, gay, and Christian identity known as Malcolm Boyd that emerged over many years to provide the world a sustained battle against racism. I am especially grateful to Malcolm in offering the reader and the archives of history a deeper vision of the early signs in Malcolm's life that set the trajectory for his courageous witness against American injustices. What we discover here is encouraging to many of us who discover that Malcolm is extraordinary in his ordinariness.

Wearing a priest's attire of a turquoise and burnt-orange chasuble, Malcolm celebrated a Peace Mass inside the Pentagon during the Vietnam War. The context of this worship service was such that there were a couple of quick readings and then a sermon. The theme of the sermon was: has salt lost its flavor? As this sermon was preached, a police officer's voice antiphonally asserted, "You're under arrest." Malcolm knew they would be arrested. Earlier Malcolm had sought the men's room because he knew they would be arrested or jailed and that they would have a long ride in a paddy wagon. There were two rows of urinals, fifty men making water. When they saw Malcolm and a student wearing clerical garb, the men put zippers up and the water stopped. Malcolm told me that they didn't want to deal with the guys in orange chasubles and well, queers. Malcolm and other protesters were taken to jail. Malcolm recalls being driven to prison and passing the area of the White House where at that time President Nixon hosted Billy Graham for dinner.

Years later, Malcolm tells me this story. Someone told Malcolm at General Convention 2009 of the Episcopal Church, "You called Billy

---

7. Boyd, *Are You Running with Me, Jesus?*, 64.

8. His role is documented in *Freedom Riders: 1961 and the Struggle for Racial Justice* by Raymond Arsenault (New York: Oxford University Press, 2006).

Graham a whore." These were sad times Malcolm said. But Malcolm couldn't help it as he was being dragged off to prison, knowing that Graham was drinking wine and dining with Nixon in the White House while, after his arrest, he was being transported in a paddy wagon to jail.

Weren't Malcolm's views welcomed in the Nixon White House as much as the more conservative views of Dr. Graham?

As if it were a scene from the Bible, the next night the arresting cop had been converted by Malcolm's actions—converted to the point of joining the Episcopal peace fellowship. I told Malcolm the cop's conversion should be a sign of hagiography (criteria for becoming a saint) because it's a miracle if an enemy repents.

How did a white boy growing up in a sheltered, wealthy household end up being this apocalyptic rider against war and racism? Malcolm responded to me that another crucial trigger, in addition to his days as a young priest in Indianapolis, was when Malcolm was invited to Louisiana State University (LSU), where he denounced apartheid and made other controversial remarks. The result was the cancellation of Malcolm's visit to LSU and of subsequent visits planned by Malcolm.

Malcolm was moved by the South African book *Cry, the Beloved Country*. It was when I heard Malcolm describe his love for this book that I asked: "Was this why you worked so hard and had a vocation to come

Malcolm's Pentagon arrest for "disturbing the peace" in Pentagon Peace Mass.

alongside black people?" Malcolm answers that Union Seminary formed him a great deal, especially in moving him into civil rights work and working mutually with black folk seeking equal rights with white folk. As I listened to Malcolm, my own writings on Dietrich Bonhoeffer, a famous German Christian martyr, came to mind. It was at Union Seminary, more specifically, Harlem, that Bonhoeffer learned about the plight of black people. This helped to shape Bonhoeffer's famous theological ethics in which to know God requires knowing God's dispositions toward empowerment of the poorest people. Union forms you if you let it, Malcolm says.

Malcolm prays, "How can we withdraw from the human heart, Lord?"[9]

Reinhold Neibuhr, one of the most famous American theologians in the United States, tutored Malcolm while they were both at Union Seminary. Malcolm said, "I'd go in and discuss my work with Niebuhr. He was a huge influence. And yet, most of the Union faculty was a huge influence." *Witness to a Generation*, writings from Union's pantheon of renowned theologians (1966), contains one of Malcolm's reflections called "Maintaining Humanness in the Freedom Movement."[10] Malcolm's days at Union Seminary prepared him well for the ongoing need to articulate meaningful prayers to Jesus. Upon graduation, he would no longer have the shelter of a seminary and theological giants like Niebuhr. Malcolm would now be on his own.

Years later when speaking to huge campuses and crowds, Malcolm was fatigued with celebrity and traveling. To get a respite, Malcolm walked the Golden Gate Bridge and had lunch. It was the middle of winter and he developed a terrible cold and just couldn't go to speak. To cancel was always difficult. Once in Cleveland, Malcolm felt the same fatigue and weariness. He told me at that time he had had it up to here (as he raised his hand up to his nose) with hectic schedules and the infighting, much less all the other racial wars being raised. He flew into the Cleveland rain (it always rains in Cleveland, Malcolm said). He found himself having to walk down into a church basement. Malcolm walked in the door and heard "Fuck you, motherfucker, who the shit do you think you are?" Malcolm said fuck you back. The alternative would have been to be Gandhi—another moment that Malcolm never forgot.

---

9. Boyd and Conrad, *When in the Course of Human Events*, 152–53.

10. Malcolm Boyd, "Maintaining Humanness in the Freedom Movement," in Wayne H. Cowan, ed., *Witness to a Generation: Significant Writings from Christianity and Crisis, 1941–1966* (Indianapolis: Bobbs-Merrill, 1966), 203.

Malcolm encouraged me to write about this difficult episode in Cleveland in which he pursued honest dialogue. Such dialogue was especially important as Malcolm wrote his dissertation on a Christian examination of the mass media that Doubleday published as Malcolm's first book, *Crisis in Communication* (1959). Those who struggled with Malcolm in Cleveland were activist types who happened to gather in a church basement.

I got involved in the civil rights struggle in 1961 when I became a Freedom Rider in the Deep South. I wanted to do something concrete and specific in order to bring about change. I didn't know much about racism except that I considered it a social abomination. Whether racism was rearing its ugly head in South Africa or Mississippi or

Another U.S. withdrawal

Chicago, I said quietly within myself "Enough!" What could I do to help bring about change?

Propitiously a letter arrived in my mailbox inviting me to be a member of a Freedom Ride consisting of black and white Episcopal priests, fellow clergy of mine. We would gather in New Orleans. Our task was to publicly oppose racial discrimination and, of course, to make a highly publicized public witness for racial openness.

I had no idea this undertaking would change my life. An initial token was when Martin Luther King Jr. provided us explicit directions. Their roots were in the concept of nonviolence. To my surprise we were given a startlingly fresh definition of it. "It's not a PR gimmick or a political tool," we were told. "It's the way you pick up a telephone to answer it." In other words, it is a way of life.

Bingo. It was instantly apparent to us that we were becoming involved in something that would be, well, revolutionary and different and astonishingly demanding. The experience of the Freedom Ride, with its strong sense of community and purpose, defined the course of my life for the next decade. I emerged a changed and different person. But the process was slow going because I needed to unlearn and learn many, many things.

For example, my education had not taught me basic truths I needed to know. School had provided me a classic, traditional educational smorgasbord that simply did not include race, blacks, the institution of slavery in the U.S., and segregation practiced in schools, churches, and seats of government. So, if I were serious about becoming a change agent, I had to start learning new facts and realities.

Examples of racism in South Africa helped me because they were more prevalent in our front pages than our own domestic situations. Courageous and astute books became significant signposts and helpers. Basically I learned that I had my own hard work to do. Wake up. Look around. Listen to the stories of others. Ask hard questions. Get out of old social ruts and seek new experiences with new people. If two plus two just didn't equal four, find out what was wrong here.

A key factor in my own experience was drawing closer to African-American men and women who had formerly remained invisible or distant or mere stereotypes in my life. For example, in 1955 I had been ordained an Episcopal priest. I'd served parishes and college chaplaincies in Indianapolis, Colorado, and Detroit. Now I asked if I could become a white assistant priest to an African-American priest in a black parish in Detroit. Later, moving to Washington, D.C., I repeated my request for a similar assignment there. My learning process picked up and accelerated.

Now I was in people's homes on an informal basis, hearing their stories, sharing experiences. Slowly I began to unravel and unlearn blurred and incorrect information as a precursor to a fresh approach.

The summer of 1965 proved to be my most painful and ultimately productive learning experience. I joined three young African-American men in SNCC (Student Nonviolent Coordinating Committee) to work in rural Mississippi and Alabama for black voter registration, which was virtually nonexistent. At the outset they told me: "You'll have to live as a nigger like we do."

This meant living with poor black families in shacks in the countryside. Sleeping on shack floors. One night we had to kill a snake that crawled through a hole in the floor. It meant being fed by poor blacks, sharing their sustenance. We lived that summer as if we were somewhere behind enemy lines, always avoiding dangerous public contacts (except that we had to fill the car tank with gas at filling stations), always striving to be as invisible as possible. However, three black men and a white guy with them clearly meant only one thing: "Outside Agitator." Our enemy? The entire white status quo, white media, white police, white churches, white power.

That summer I received the education I had been denied in middle school, high school, college, and seminary. I learned about the real existence of "the other America," its meticulously practiced dismissal of equal rights and opportunity. At summer's end I was in Atlanta for a night preparing to catch a flight to Detroit and resume my usual life. I found myself in a clean, polished motel room. It had a bathroom with a shower, a bed with clean sheets. I felt an interloper, an intruder. The next morning, on the flight, I struggled with basic questions of identity. Who was I? Where did I belong? What did it mean to be black or white, poor or cared for, free or not free, someone with rights or someone without rights?

As I've wrestled with such questions, I've been grateful that the life of Martin Luther King Jr. crossed my own. He was the great prophet in my experience. His words make such perfect sense: "(People) often hate each other because they fear each other; they fear each other because they do now know each other; they do not know each other because they cannot communicate; they cannot communicate because they are separated." I remember vividly a day in 1965 when Dr. King assembled blacks and whites to meet in Brown's Chapel in Selma, Alabama. I was among them. He walked into the room in shirtsleeves, looking tired and sweaty. He exhorted us to action. He seemed to be consumed by a fire that burned deep within him.

There was something of a young Moses about Dr. King as he taught and led us, struggling to make us want to reach the Promised Land that he saw. But he knew how long and hard that passage would be. The last time I was with him was in a nonviolent protest against the Vietnam War on February 6, 1968, in Washington, D.C. I took notice that his spirit had not flagged.

As we departed, one of those inexplicable coincidences that make perfect sense ensued. A carillon in the Arlington cemetery chimed the hymn which is a paean to unity and against the evils of separation, "In Christ There Is No East or West." It was a poetic goodbye. I had no way of knowing the occasion would mark my goodbye to him as well. His message remains our guide. Racism he defined as "total estrangement." The answer to it can be discovered only "in persistent trying, perpetual experimentation, persevering together." These remain the truest words I have ever heard on the subject.[11]

A War against Self and the Other

Malcolm remembers the morning of the Birmingham bombing. Malcolm, appearing in a white church, assumed that morning that after hearing the news, the church where he was preaching would deplore this tragedy in which four little girls were killed in their Sunday school class. So Malcolm started talking about this in a prophetic way, assuming they would agree. But they didn't. It was as if they thought white folks have the right to bomb their enemies.

> Malcolm prays, "They have mouths, but do not speak; They have ears, but do not hear; noses, but do not smell." Tear the scales off of our eyes, Lord. Make us hear and smell. Enable us to speak the truth, Lord.[12]

At what point do you know what is about you or what is about the context, Malcolm asked me. Malcolm answered for me: An important element is never to believe the hero stuff. That kind of thing is transitory. You can't believe in your own publicity or the "starlet mentality." Only experience can help someone with this. It's like the mystic who encouraged a disciple to move beyond praise and curse.

> One day a young monk called on Macarius the Egyptian and begged: "Abba, give me a word that I may be saved." Macarius ordered the monk to go to the local cemetery and curse the dead. A strange com-

---

11. Malcolm Boyd, "Racism as Total Estrangement," published online August 20, 2009, http://www.ladiocese.org/digital_faith/news/42.

12. Boyd and Conrad, *When in the Course of Human Events*, 42–43.

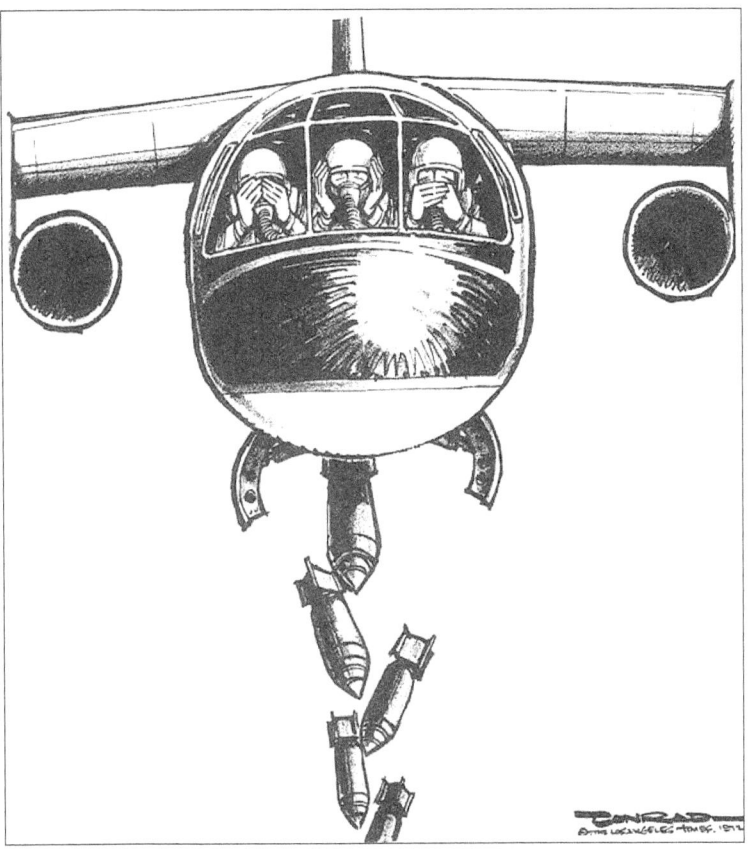

mand perhaps, but the monk did as he was told: he went out to the tombs and cursed the dead, throwing rocks to signal his disgust. When he returned, Macarius asked if the dead said anything back to him. "No," the monk answered. Macarius ordered him to go back and, this time, praise the dead. Again the monk did as he was told. Praises poured from his tongue. He called them "apostles," "saints," "righteous." Again he returned to Macarius, who again asked him what the dead said back. "Nothing," the monk replied. Macarius then gave the young monk a "word": "You know how you insulted them and they did not reply, and how you praised them and they did not speak; so you too, if you wish to be saved, must do the same and become a dead man. Like the dead, take no account of either the scorn of men or their praises, and you can be saved."[13]

---

13. *Selections from the Sayings of the Desert*, trans. Sister Benedicta Ward (Kalamazoo, MI: Cistercian Publication, 1975), 44.

Malcolm's own spiritual direction to me was similar to Marcarius's, extending all the way back into the fifth century. You're not fighting against racism to get a standing ovation. You can't take yourself too seriously because the war is crazy, those of your own kind will be against you.

Malcolm felt funny being introduced on an Easter Sunday. To his chagrin he received a standing ovation. When he told me this, he said that none of this has to do with the reality. I challenged him, saying those people were sincere; "they gave you a standing ovation because they knew in their hearts they wouldn't have had your courage. You deserved the adulation." Malcolm simply responded, "You go through the changes of being a hero to not getting a job." Malcolm digs up a quote from him in *Who's Who in America*: "The years have taught me the cost of getting involved in life. . . . the floor may give way without warning." Malcolm reads more about the swagger of standing up to power that he wrote and wonders about the "me" who wrote this.

Malcolm's chief virtue was courage. If Aristotle were still living, he would assign this as Malcolm's chief virtue as well. Courage in war caused the turning points for Malcolm. Malcolm has to look at self as he knows himself and then at the public Malcolm. Both exist but are not the same. Malcolm repeats that he feels like he is the Cowardly Lion who never really established courage in this racial war but who learned how to respond on the spot. He learned courage by exercising it rather than inheriting it. How do you inherit it? If you had a strong family, your father was strong, and you grew up in a structure, then you could be associated with courage. Malcolm got through school and Hollywood before his first bout with courage. So, the first example of courage was leaving Hollywood and going to seminary. This was a dying-to self and a living-to something creative. To be courageous implies a fear. I told Malcolm that I learned in the theology of Thomas Aquinas that you can't attain the virtue of courage without fear simultaneously being there all along.

> I'm scared, Jesus. You've asked me to do something I don't think I can do.
>
> I'm sure I wouldn't want to do it except that you asked me.
>
> But I don't feel strong enough, and you know that I lack the courage I'd need. Why did you ask me to do this? It seems to me that Paul could do this much, much more easily. Remember, I told you I'm afraid to stand up and be criticized, Jesus. I feel naked in front of everybody, and I can't hide any part of myself.[14]

---

14. Boyd, *Are Your Running with Me, Jesus?*, 7.

Classic Malcolm image in Look magazine.

Malcolm's three fears of dogs, darkness, and public speaking re-emerged in one of our spiritual direction sessions. (The reader will recall that when these fears were discussed earlier, we spoke mostly about the fear of public speaking.) In addressing Aquinas's virtue of courage, Malcolm focused this time on his fear of darkness. He began talking about his fear of the dark by describing his childhood when he was an only child and his family had servants and a chauffeur who taught him how to tie his shoes.

Malcolm thinks that all fears begin in childhood. We are molded forever by what happens then. As an only child, Malcolm remembers one day when he was alone in the house with a German woman who worked in the kitchen. She felt that Malcolm was irritating her in the kitchen. She was upset with Malcolm and decided to discipline him by locking him in a closet off the kitchen. It was pitch black in that tiny space as Malcolm heard the maid yell on the other side of the door, "A big white rat will eat you." Terrified, Malcolm screamed and beat on the door, but she would not let him out. Malcolm tells me, "I was afraid of the dark until I was well into my forties." Finally, in his forties, Malcolm practiced being alone in the dark. Friends were leaving for two weeks. They lived in a classic "haunted house" set back from a road in a forest-like area. It was all alone and quiet. At last, at forty, Malcolm thought: "I'd like to get over that fear." So, after Malcolm arrived, he simply didn't turn on any lights when darkness fell. Instead he wandered through the house, up into the "Dorian Gray"–like attic, down into the absolutely scary basement. Malcolm remembers, "My heart pounded. I was terrified. Yet I didn't turn on a single light. Slowly I grew more accustomed to the darkness. It seemed friendlier." Finally Malcolm was actually comfortable in it. "When my friends arrived to claim their house, and I departed, I realized that I was a changed person in certain ways. More at peace in and with myself. A stark fear, a cause of tension and alarm, had been erased. I felt considerably more at home in the vast universe."[15]

If he had a good family structure, wouldn't these fears have lasted only for a short while during a child's developmental stage?

The last of the three fears that needed to be overcome in Malcolm's life was the fear of dogs. Malcolm described how he did this when staying at an Orthodox monastery for Easter.

> A dog bit a man at the beach when I was a boy. My dysfunctional family, rapidly moving toward a divorce, had no more sense of dealing with this than anything else. An event over which I had no control healed me. In the 1950s I was visiting Istanbul. As a young American postseminarian and ordained deacon, I was invited to stay Holy Week in a Greek Orthodox seminary located on a remote island near the city.
>
> One day I took a walk alone. The air was brisk, the sun shining. Absorbed in my thoughts, I wasn't aware of surroundings until suddenly I looked up a hill directly in front of me and saw, to my horror, a pack of wild dogs. What in the world could I do? I was scared to death. There were at least a dozen of them, all poised to run down the hill and attack me. All the old fears of dogs welled up. Of course, I realized that my very fears were somehow communicated to the dogs unmistakably.
>
> This appeared to be survival time. There was no one to help me. I was on my own. This made me realize I had to handle the situation expertly and all by myself. I couldn't move faster or slower. It was imperative for me to keep going, keep moving, with an air and attitude of nonchalance and lightness.
>
> I did. Never glancing again at the dogs, I orchestrated myself along the path as if I were having the time of my life. I imagine I was even smiling in a moment of joy and happiness. The dogs stayed where they were. I left them in the distance as I returned to the seminary.

---

15. Malcolm Boyd, "Fears," e-mail message to author, November 12, 2010.

Never again was I afraid of dogs in the slightest. Since then I have had several dogs as beloved companions and close friends, major figures in my life.[16]

With courage Malcolm went to Taizé and then went to the inner-city of Indianapolis. Malcolm stood up to the Bishop of Colorado with courage. But where did the courage come from? Malcolm admitted that his courage changed him from being a frightened mixed-up young person into someone possessing quite a bit of courage. Coming out as a gay man was for Malcolm an extension of the courage he gained by standing up to the bishop. Did it take more courage to be the minority with black people in the South than it did to come out of the closet?

> Malcolm prays, "We do not see our signs; there is no longer any prophet, and there is none among us who knows how long." Too much innocent blood is on the hands of false prophets, isn't it, Lord? Enable us to see our signs, Christ.[17]

Most prophets don't get a standing ovation—at least in their own lifetime. Malcolm thought Martin Luther King Jr. was the best in all of this modern prophetic business. King had a great sense of balance. He walked in short sleeves, sweaty-tired in Selma. He didn't have to act. The prophetic gene was programmed so that King didn't have to expend unnecessary energy. I had just asked Malcolm about King's seemingly perfect appearance in public and yet having personal struggles in his home. Malcolm thought about this and then recounted a story when Malcolm called Coretta Scott King at her home. She quickly terminated the call. Think of the number of people who did that with her. Lack of privacy. Malcolm sat next to Coretta in Los Angeles with Mayor Tom Bradley and Junius Griffin of Motown. Malcolm was the keynoter for the occasion. Diana Ross was there—virtually everyone was there for awards for members of the black community from their peers. Malcolm looked at Coretta's life. She didn't ask to be Joan of Arc. Malcolm remembered when Coretta sang at Yale. Malcolm was there to support the movement because although she was known for her singing voice, Coretta was often criticized and even laughed at for her voice.

Malcolm points to his picture in one of the books on his shelf. In the photograph Malcolm is marching to protest. The irony was that King's

---

16. Ibid.
17. Boyd and Conrad, *When in the Course of Human Events*, 58–59.

daughter Bernice Albertine King (born March 28, 1963) said gays shouldn't claim civil rights and there was Malcolm putting his life on the line.

In 2004, Bernice King participated in a march in Atlanta against same-sex marriage. This action was in contrast to the advocacy of her mother and her older sister Yolanda Denise King, both long-time outspoken supporters of gay rights. Coretta quickly gave her public support to gay rights to minimize the effect of Bernice's participation in the march.

In 2006, King was with her mother when Coretta died in a hospital in Mexico. Bernice King is attributed with influencing her siblings to hold their mother's funeral at New Birth Missionary Baptist Church in Lithonia, Georgia, instead of Coretta's church home, Ebenezer Baptist Church. The King children allowed Coretta's body to lie in state at Ebenezer, where the funerals of their father and paternal grandparents were held. The decision to hold Coretta Scott King's funeral at a conservative congregation active in anti-gay work led to the protest of many civil rights activists, including Julian Bond, who did not attend in protest of the decision against Coretta's wishes.

The debate over Bishop Eddie Long, senior pastor of New Birth Missionary Baptist Church, is instructive because he is another prominent person who is against homosexuality. Many people came to know about the problems facing Long, in particular the problem of four young men claiming that Long coerced them into a sexual relationship. "They claim that Long used his status to seduce them with money, clothes, bling [jewelry], cars, foreign trips, access to celebrities and the like." For Long, the trouble was so intense that one of the plaintiffs claimed that he was fourteen when his relationship with Long started—bringing up issues of child abuse and statutory rape.[18]

What is instructive here is not the issue of Long's sexual orientation, but the possibility of hypocrisy and self-hatred. And if the charges are not true, he is still an anti-gay minister who has damaged many people. The Southern Poverty Law Center calls Bishop Long "one of the most virulently homophobic black leaders in the religiously based anti-gay movement." In one sermon, he says to gays and lesbians, "God says you deserve death!" The message of "hate the sin and the sinner" are strong words in a religion that is supposed to teach love, healing, and redemption.[19]

The moral here is that Long's misappropriation of the King legacy is shameful.

To add insult to injury, Bernice King and Long participated in a march to Dr. King's gravesite to support a national constitutional amendment banning gay marriage. In 2004, Long and others successfully pushed for a similar amendment to the Georgia state constitution.

Established in the racial storm that followed Rosa Parks's arrest in 1955 for refusing to give up her seat to a white man on a segregated bus in Montgomery, Alabama, the SCLC was shaped by Martin Luther King Jr. as a peaceful campaign for voting rights, housing fairness, and opposition to the Vietnam War. But critics say its mission has become blurred in recent years and divisions have emerged, in particular over its skeptical approach to gay rights. Among the potential flashpoints for Bernice King will be the debate on same-sex marriage. The president of the SCLC's Los

---

18. David Love, "The Eddie Long Scandal: Betraying the Memory of MLK," *The Huffington Post,* accessed September 29, 2010. http://www.huffingtonpost.com/david-a-love/the-bishop-has-no-clothes_b_743234.html

19. Ibid.

Malcolm and Rev. Henri Stines picketing against racism in front of the Lovett School, Atlanta, 1963.

Angeles branch was almost fired in a clash with the leadership over his support for gay marriage. Bernice King opposes it and has implied that her father would have too, once remarking: "I know deep down in my sanctified soul that he did not take a bullet for same-sex unions."[20] The war on racism is messy when comparing civil rights for all in America.

---

20. Andrew Clark, "Martin Luther King's Daughter Bernice Takes Up Mantle as US Civil Rights Leader," *The Guardian*, accessed November 1, 2009. www.guardian.co.uk/world/2009/nov/01/bernice-king-sclc-female-leader.

Malcolm tells me about picketing Lovett School in Atlanta when it wouldn't admit Martin Luther King III and other black students:

> It was a chilly, gray morning in Atlanta, Georgia. Outside the distinguished Lovett School, located on the banks of the Chattahoochee River in the northwest sector of the city, parents and maids were driving children to the school for the day's classes. As cars drew close to the Lovett driveway, the drivers were shocked to see three pickets walking up and down along the road. The pickets, wearing black suits and clerical collars, were Episcopal priests.
>
> We were protesting the Lovett School's policy of segregation. The church-related school had rejected the application of Martin Luther King III and subsequently turned down Episcopal applicants who were African American.
>
> On the picket line we carried the "Cape Town Placard," which was originally placed on the grounds of St. George's Anglican Cathedral in Cape Town, South Africa. The sign shows a crucifixion scene in which Christ's body is pierced by the words "Segregation" and "Separation" emblazoned on a barbed-wire fence that bisects his body and separates two kneeling figures of different color, one black and one white.
>
> I grew up never for one moment imagining I might someday be one of those people who carry signs on, of all places, a picket line. I lived in my sheltered world immunized against the suffering of the world. This is because I lived in the privileged white world of North America. But my belief in human justice, which the Christian gospel taught me, led to my walking on picket lines. And, on that chilly gray morning in Georgia, I was picketing a church-related school that turned down African-American applicants. The parents tried to look away, but the children in the cars didn't. They saw the signs we carried.
>
> They saw us. They understood what we were doing.
>
> Maybe one of them would be marching in a similar picket line someday, but I hoped it wouldn't be necessary. I hoped the problem would be solved long before they grew up, Jesus.[21]

Malcolm writes this beautiful prayer not knowing the irony to come. One of King's own children goes on record disavowing how civil rights for African Americans should be co-equal to civil rights for gay and lesbian people. There is deep irony in Bernice's resentment of extending the Civil Rights Movement to all people.

---

21. Malcolm's prayer in *Race and Prayer: Collected Voices, Many Dreams*, ed. Malcolm Boyd and Chester Talton (Harrisburg, PA: Morehouse Publishing, 2003), 199.

Malcolm prays, "Where there is liberty, Lord, it is your gift. Where there is justice, Lord, it is your gift. Teach us not to despise your gifts, Lord.[22]

Burning Cross

"What's wrong with an institutional church?" Malcolm asked in a manner to reframe my question. In a sage-like way, Malcolm responded with a story that happened in Sewanee, Tennessee. Malcolm was in a group of clergy, black and white, that sought and was refused service at a church-operated restaurant. Malcolm was standing outside the dining area with the Rev. Quinland Gordon, a black priest and colleague. An angry white man, a member of the group opposing racial integration of the restaurant, confronted Boyd and Gordon, both of whom were wearing white collars over their clerical garb. Pointing to Father Gordon, the man said: "I can see the collar is white, but the face is so dark I can't tell if it's a man."

Malcolm writes me:

> This is a terribly painful story to remember . . . (interesting when one unearths the past, no???). Here it is. It should be a permanent part of Sewanee's story during the civil rights era. Quin Gordon, at the end of his life, was named to head the Absalom Jones Foundation in Atlanta. You must be aware of this or, certainly, can check it. I believe the Episcopal Church withdrew its support and ended the project, and this was rather heartbreaking for Quin. It was a very big project for him and meant a great deal in terms of completion of ministry and "legacy." I remember almost nothing about it except that it was painful for him, a kind of "failure" of the church to support his work. I was with Quin (as his white assistant priest) at Church of the Atonement in Washington, D.C.[23]

At this stage in the Sewanee narrative, Malcolm describes how a cross was starting to burn outside a large window in the restaurant. A few concerned local residents, apprehensive of growing danger, ushered the visiting priests to safety. Driving down the hill away from the restaurant, a car following theirs speeded by, and shortly crashed on the road. Apparently it was driven by a man, a white cook, seeking to ambush them. They pulled his dead body from the car. It was like a Hollywood scene with cars crashing and someone getting killed. Then Father Bob Chapman,

---

22. Boyd and Conrad, *When in the Course of Human Events*, 40–41.
23. Malcolm Boyd, "Cook in Sewanee," e-mail message to author, November 2, 2010.

"... One nation, divisible, with liberty and justice for some."

another visiting black priest, said prayers over his body. Malcolm prayed along with his other visiting civil rights companions for the racist who died violently in darkness on the lonely road.

As Malcolm reflected further on the horrible episode at Sewanee, he writes me:

> Have just been reading *Freedom Riders: 1961 and the Struggle for Racial Justice (Pivotal Moments in American History)* by Raymond Arsenault, Oxford University Press, 2006.
>
> On pp. 432, 433, and 434 is the account of our Episcopal priests' Freedom Ride. There is more on p. 643. This is a major source of

information. Perhaps you already have it. It includes the account of how several of us moved from the Freedom Ride itself to the subsequent visit to Sewanee: " . . . the staunchly traditional undergraduate student body remained all white. Encouraged by the interracialism of the nearby Highlander Folk School, local seminarians had been pressing for a full desegregation of the campus for several years, but university and church officials had refused to confront the issue, including a strict color bar at a popular on-campus restaurant leased to a local segregationist. As soon as Boyd and the other pilgrims arrived on campus and discovered that the restaurant remained segregated, he announced plans for a sit-in and a hunger strike. By Friday morning, however, Boyd had received assurances from church and campus officials that all of the university's facilities would be desegregated in the near future. After the Presiding Episcopal Bishop of the United States, the Right Reverend Arthur C. Lichtenberger, issued a strong public statement endorsing the prayer pilgrimage and condemning racial discrimination, Boyd and his colleagues canceled the planned protests and departed for the (General) Convention in Detroit."[24]

Malcolm and I reflect on this incident in Sewanee in order for Malcolm to teach me about the malaise of the institutional church. Herein, the University of the South, an Episcopal Church institution, contains a shameful history illustrating how the church was complicit with racism. This story about the reluctant desegregation of the University of the South came to me early on in our spiritual direction sessions and when we began to think about the scope of this book, this discussion took even more gravitas. I'm glad that this book found a brave publisher like Davis Perkins who writes me, "I hope Church Publishing is brave enough!"[25] A church publisher would be unable to tell the impolite harsh truth about itself. Malcolm says he can't be "polite" about this history; in fact, he says, "To hell with polite history." No one is supposed to say what Malcolm just said about Sewanee, in which the University of the South and the School of Theology exists. No one should bring up the past because this is a powerful Anglican/Episcopal institution.

In addition, there is also the difficulty of forgiveness in the black community. Similar to the homophobic nature involved in the Eddie Long

---

24. Malcolm Boyd, "Material on 1961 Freedom Ride," e-mail message to author, December 28, 2009.

25. Davis Perkins, "Editorial Comments," e-mail message to author, October 26, 2010.

situation, there seemed to be a "don't ask, don't tell" policy among the black community during the civil rights period. In one of our spiritual direction sessions, Malcolm seemed reticent as he asked, "How do you reconcile authentic emotion with Christian forgiveness? What I mean is how do I reconcile Bayard Rustin in his own community?" Rustin was an African-American civil rights activist, and nonviolent activist who worked diligently for the Civil Rights Movement of the 1960s. He was known as the chief organizer of the 1963 March on Washington for Jobs and Freedom. He worked closely with Martin Luther King Jr. on the techniques of nonviolent resistance. Although Rustin was prominent in the Civil Rights Movement as a black activist, Rustin received very little historical credit. But why? The answer that seems to be on Malcolm's mind was simply that Rustin was also gay. In addition, Rustin became an advocate on behalf of gay and lesbian causes in the latter part of his career. Homosexuality was criminalized at the time, which made him a target of suspicion and may have compromised his effectiveness.

As Malcolm continued his reticent mood, he reflects on one of his radical books, *Free to Live and Free to Die*. "Something I wrote that is powerful and honest," says Malcolm, "is on the struggle around political funerals." Malcolm recites a cryptic excerpt from one of his writings, "It's because I don't want to give them their body you goddamn hearse. . . ." I ask Malcolm what this means. He tells me he would rather talk about another text he wrote. Malcolm rehearses with me more of the kind of pieces that he will recite at the Bakery, an LA coffeehouse: "O thou who are omnipotent forgive us our human life . . . we are despicable flesh . . . o flail and burn us . . . as we cringe at our feet." Malcolm struggles to read this in public because of the brooding tone, but he tells me that he doesn't want to compromise his artistry and imagination. The son of jazz great Vince Guaraldi asked Malcolm to read one of Malcolm's most provocative pieces. Malcolm expresses his struggle in saying that in *Free to Live and Free to Die,* [p. 20] I kept "fuck" but not "goddamn." Upon listening to Malcolm's reading, I laugh when I realize I won't be able to bring our nine-year-old, seven-year-old, and four-year-old to hear Malcolm. I also tell my wife, Raquel, and we laugh together.

There is a time to laugh, however, and a time to cry. Malcolm lived for a decade fighting in the civil rights campaign and sometimes fighting against his own fellow Christians. He lived radically in an orthodox way talking about sin and Jesus and yet his opponents saw him as the greatest of villains and agitators. Wasn't it difficult to be so actively hated? I asked Malcolm. The activist crowd Malcolm could understand very well. He

Malcolm (second from right) with other clergy and civil rights workers standing in front of a bombed African-American church in McComb, Mississippi, in early 1960s.

could envision them well represented on the canvas of history. The church, on the other hand, was a more painful glance into history when it comes to racism. Malcolm turns to me, as if preaching to the choir, "Why don't they know better? They're talking about Jesus who is the most inclusive but they have no inclusivity. If Jesus came to them on Sunday morning, they wouldn't let him in, he wouldn't even be allowed to go up the aisle to sit down in a pew." Although I spend more substantial time on Malcolm's confrontation with the church in the chapter "The Black Horse of Famine," it is important to mention at least one good example of church leadership.

Malcolm and Paul Moore

On many occasions, Malcolm mentioned how Bishop Paul Moore rescued his vocation in the church, especially from the potential destruction of other powerful people in the church who meant to prevent Malcolm from ever functioning as a priest. Even before Paul Moore was a bishop, he supported Malcolm's growth in the church. For example, while in Indianapolis in 1957–59, Malcolm began a long-running role as a member of the Moore extended family. At that time, Paul Moore was dean of Christ Church Cathedral in Indianapolis. These times included communal occasions like Thanksgiving and Christmas. Paul Moore served as Dean in Indianapolis until he was elected as a Suffragan Bishop in Washington, D.C., in 1964. Over the years Malcolm saw their nine children grow up. Malcolm had two favorites.

Adelia always seemed mature and balanced, serious and committed, warm and friendly, geared to social outreach and service. His other favorite was George. Even as a child he was enormously creative, likeable and outgoing, caught up in the actual passion of life. He played musical instruments, was in some sort of a student band, and possessed the good instincts of what would later make him a healthy citizen of the world.

Paul and Jenny's second eldest child (eldest son) was young Paul, who was a student at Yale while Malcolm was a guest fellow at Calhoun College there. Paul had a major role at the *Yale Daily News* when Malcolm wrote a column for the paper. Later, after he graduated, Paul was hospitalized in the Bay Area. Jenny and Malcolm were in Los Angeles. They flew to San Francisco to see him and stayed at the Mark Hopkins. Malcolm experienced many life experiences with the Moore family which more often than not provided Malcolm his own familial relationships.

On the day in 1970 Paul was in Manhattan being elected the next Episcopal Bishop of New York, Jenny came from Washington, D.C., to the city. At the time of Paul's election she was having lunch in an East Sixties French restaurant. A telephone call came for her. It was from George Dugan of the *New York Times*. "Mrs. Moore, it is my pleasure to tell you that your husband has just been elected the Bishop of New York."

"Thank you, Mr. Dugan," Jenny replied.

"Madam, I'm on deadline and want to know if there is any comment you'd like to make."

"No. No, Mr. Dugan. I think not."

"Well, Mrs. Moore, you and the bishop have nine children. I wonder is there any kind of response from them?"

Jenny paused. She replied: "Well, Mr. Dugan, I did see scrawled in toothpaste on one of the children's bathroom mirrors this morning the words 'Fuck New York.'" This was completely Jenny. It became one of her so-called classic comments. It was also deeply thoughtful, but also predictive of her internal struggles.

Malcolm noticed Jenny was highly agitated, subject to depression, and somehow out of control of her life. Her mood swings were severe. When she was departing San Francisco for Washington, D.C., and Malcolm was readying his return to Los Angeles, she did not want them to travel together to the airport. Jenny urgently wished to be absolutely alone with her feelings. Could she be quiet and maybe write a few letters? Malcolm worried about her. Yet a gift Malcolm could bestow was to cooperate by allowing her even for just a short time in an airport to be Garboesque. She told Malcolm she felt startlingly depressed and rather helpless.

Jenny's life became more difficult when illness struck. An estrangement with her husband Paul deepened. Jenny was asking many questions about the meanings and possibilities of being a woman during a radical time of looking at gender in altogether new ways. When Jenny's cancer appeared and then grew worse, Malcolm visited her in a hospice in Washington, D.C. Malcolm remembered telling her that he had never seen her look more strikingly beautiful. But she told him she lacked the strength to stand up and walk across the room.

Jenny was sophisticated, Malcolm remembers, accustomed to moving in any part of society she wished with ease and grace. Her sense of humor often came from a gut level. She got a kick out of this. Jenny adamantly refused the public aspects of playing the role "the bishop's wife." It was not her wont to attend any regular Sunday morning church service. This led to questions and misunderstanding: why wasn't the bishop's wife in church? Jenny would fight tooth and nail against being placed conveniently in any kind of defined position or social box.

Over the years, whenever Malcolm was in New York City, Malcolm stayed as a guest of Paul at his quarters at the Cathedral of St. John the Divine. This continued after Jenny's death and Paul's marriage to his second wife, Brenda.

During Malcolm's visits to the city, he'd sleep in an immense room on a floor above the main quarters. It contained three fireplaces. Hundreds of books filled seemingly endless shelves. The room itself was part of history. One night as Malcolm climbed into the bed, just as he turned off the light, he more or less addressed the ghosts in that vast space. "Goodnight," he muttered. "Please be kind."

The next morning Paul and Malcolm were together in the breakfast nook, attired in bathrobes, their feet in bedroom slippers. They sat silently as they read the *New York Times*, sipping hot coffee, munching buttered toast.

Paul grew up like a young prince, his family enormously wealthy. He had every advantage, attended the "best" schools, and was given a sense of deep privilege. From what he told Malcolm, his military service in World War II shook his life. He saw the agony and price of war at close range. He recalled how, on one occasion, he felt an acute need to participate in the Holy Eucharist. Once he hiked many miles through war-torn terrain to attend mass in the Anglican tradition. His reverence for such an experience was a deep part of his life. This led to his seeking ordination as an Episcopal priest and, later, his years of serving in a poor inner-city parish in Jersey City from 1949 to 1957.

As Paul rose in leadership circles, so did Malcolm. For example, during Paul Moore's time in Washington, as a bishop, Paul became a national advocate of civil rights and an opponent of the Vietnam War. He marched with Martin Luther King Jr. in Selma and elsewhere. Malcolm did the same. Paul's leadership was characterized as liberal activism. So was Malcolm's impact in certain circles. Throughout Paul's career he spoke out against homelessness and racism. So did Malcolm.

Perhaps the key difference in spheres of influence between Malcolm and Paul was in the institutional authority given to Paul and not Malcolm. With such authority, Paul was an effective advocate of the interests of cities, once calling the corporations abandoning New York "rats leaving a sinking ship."

Paul is also was the first Episcopal bishop to ordain an openly homosexual woman as a priest. In his book *Take a Bishop Like Me* (1979), he defended his position by arguing that many priests were homosexuals but few had the courage to acknowledge it. Malcolm had such courage.

Like Malcolm, Paul is not that easy to characterize. His "liberal activism" found contradictions when compared with his fierce liturgical and creedal traditionalism. He even described himself as "born again," referring to his renewed faith in Jesus as a boarding school student.

Malcolm had never had a closer friend than Paul. It was a natural, simple, uncomplicated bonding. They were absolutely relaxed together and there was complete trust in their friendship. Always Malcolm had enormous respect for Paul's public role, which he performed easily without a trace of ego or self-interest. He had a job to do, believed in it, and did it.

The two men corresponded regularly. Today, Malcolm misses such correspondence and feels as though those years with Paul were some of his best days corresponding. Obviously this was before the era of ephemeral e-mails with their lack of permanence or personality. Paul and Malcolm also shared intellectual companionship. For a couple of years they read the same Iris Murdoch novels at the same time, exchanging views and reactions.

Paul's sense of humor extended to himself. He had not an inch of pomp. Malcolm had never known anyone so essentially relaxed. Paul was at ease with, and within, himself. He wasn't thinking about a dozen other things when he was talking to you. He was with you all the way. Underneath everything, there was that rock solid faith of Paul Moore. He believed. He was a believer.

Following Paul's death, there had been speculation and gossip concerning his sexuality. It brings up the relation between different parts of one's life and, at the same time, the apparent need of some people to "define" others and even to place them in prescribed boxes that are meant to "explain" who they were. In Malcolm's opinion, human beings are far more complex than that. Since Paul had fathered nine children, Malcolm thinks one might presume he was bisexual. Malcolm found little or no gay lifestyle in his behavior. Certainly he was open to people in general with far more than usual surface hospitality. A part of this stemmed from his vocation as a priest and a bishop. The main purpose of his life was public service instead of selfish, individual achievement. Malcolm thinks countless people would testify to Paul's presence in their lives as a helper who knew how to listen and also to assist human need.

Paul did share with Malcolm a concern that Malcolm had felt about his own life. He never wanted to hurt anyone, he explained to Malcolm. Malcolm could identify rapidly because, frankly, neither did he. Yet inescapably, as part of the human condition, Malcolm knew that on he had on occasion hurt someone. Malcolm writes, "I am sorry. I did what I could by way of reparation, and learned how to take this to God for forgiveness and healing. So, I'm sure, did Paul."[26] In other words, both of them were extraordinarily sensitive about the inescapable dilemma of coming short of perfection in dealing with life. Paul had no bluster or arrogance in confronting this reality. Nor did he hide behind a false sense of superiority.

In Malcolm's opinion, Paul's spiritual life was immensely deepened by his honest grappling with life. He didn't hide from life or attempt to. Malcolm perceived a kind of saintliness in him, perceiving that he shared human experience, including sexual, as part of his own running with Jesus. Paul knew a great deal about loving in a time when numberless people

---

26. Malcolm Boyd, "New Paul Moore," e-mail message to author, October 12, 2010.

Bishop Paul Moore helping an elderly woman run in Saigon, 1970.

treated love as a cheap joke. Paul's strength as a disciple is found in the saga of his own sensitive, searching, and unyieldingly faithful discipleship.

Malcolm is candid but not caustic about his relationship with Bishop Paul Moore and his family. Jenny Moore remains one of the favorite people in Malcolm's life. So does Paul.

Around issues of social justice, Paul Moore was one of the best bishops ever in the Episcopal Church. I remember a speaking engagement that I had with him in Newark, New Jersey. He was a tall, confident man, with a gentle countenance. And yet, in the culture war about human sexuality, it's possible that Moore couldn't be brave about his own sexual orientation. When you come to sexuality, it's complicated, Malcolm said. Such complications point to how Malcolm's life remains apocalyptic in the sense of struggle and conflict. There are few solutions in life that do not require struggle.

The Red Knight of War

The Red Knight represents war, and for Malcolm, there were many. The imagery of the Red Knight also flows from the book of Revelation in the Bible. When the second seal is opened, a red horse appears, its rider holds a sword that symbolizes war. When the Lamb opened the second seal, and the second living creature said, "Come," its rider was given power to take peace from the earth and to make humanity slay each other. In this chapter we have encountered some of the wars that Malcolm fought as well as some of those that others thought he caused.

Similar to the White Knight, the Red Knight represents the war of conquest or pestilence. Where the Red Knight differs from the White Knight is in both the literal and spiritual wars that Malcolm fought. The latter is accentuated by the fact that Jesus also fought spiritual wars. For example, one of the distinguishing features of the Red Knight is that he is given a large sword. In Matthew 10:34 Jesus states "Think not that I am come to send peace on earth: I came not to send peace, but a sword" (KJV). Jesus' peace is much deeper than our understandings and often appears as conflict and war. Malcolm calls this a restless peace, which I think becomes Malcolm's genius as he faces the last Green Knight of Death.

The historical context of the book of Revelation was such that no revolution was possible that would free the Christians from Roman domination. It seemed hopeless for many of that time. Malcolm's times were similar in that many (e.g., black and gay) in the civil rights era had lost hope for legal equality. But there were some who were "crazy" enough to have visions and dreams—like the dream of little black and white children who would one day grow up to be judged by the content of their character rather than by the color of their skin. John's Revelation was that God would reveal that there will be a time when he will release a spirit of revolution and strife on the earth that will result in a great deal of bloodshed.

Malcolm's revolution in this chapter was to take religion to the streets and make it incarnate. Despite the fear that this would cause, Malcolm would have to discover newfound courage. He did this through the support of fellow Christians like Paul Moore and others. Those Christians who felt persecuted would see this as an encouragement to know that, though the revolution is not possible now, it is coming. God's plan will unfold at some point, and their faithfulness will be vindicated. Physical war and revolution, with its inherent destruction of basic public administration and services, results in a breakdown of society. Malcolm was never such an advocate for such war because the destruction and/or theft of food, staples, and crops would result in a tremendous famine and poverty. Spiritual warfare, on the other hand, results in a deeper, although restless peace that passes current understandings.

In this chapter, Malcolm is described as the apocalyptic rider of war. Many events in Malcolm's life represent the wars of Western culture from the 1950s until today. The red color of Malcolm's horse represents blood spilled on the battlefields of racism, homophobia, and international wars like Vietnam which was fought in the name of freedom and democracy. Malcolm carries a powerful sword that represents his courage to fight against racism and war, conformity, indifference, the misuse of religion, and a flagrant worship of false gods.

Hopefully, learning from Malcolm's life will enable many generations to come to a different technique in engaging warfare by making them privy to Malcolm's genius and divine words. Malcolm's battle is more than engagement with what apparently meets the human eye. Malcolm's wars were against the powers and principalities. "For our struggle is not against enemies of blood and flesh, but against the rulers, against the authorities, against the cosmic powers of this present darkness, against the spiritual forces of evil in the heavenly places" (Eph 6:12).

In this biography, Malcolm's identity as the purveyor of war comes from his days as a civil rights activist. We have much to learn from his engagement with the powers and principalities regarding civil rights. The key lesson is not to repeat the same mistakes of unjust legislation. Those who have benefited from some victories of the civil rights era also need to help those today whose civil rights are denied. We must do more than apologize for institutional structures caught in the perpetuation of injustice. Learning from the spiritual wars of Jesus and modern-day disciples like Martin Luther King Jr., Malcolm teaches us that injustice anywhere is a threat to justice everywhere.

Due to the immense destruction of War and Pestilence, Malcolm now rides the third horse called Famine. Famine rides upon a black, sickly horse—representing malaise and poverty.

CHAPTER FOUR

The Black Horse of Famine

And when he had opened the third seal, I heard the third beast say, "Come and see." And I beheld, and lo a black horse; and he that sat on him had a pair of balances in his hand. And I heard a voice in the midst of the four beasts say, "a measure of wheat for a penny, and three measures of barley for a penny; and see thou hurt not the oil and the wine."
(Revelation 6:5–6, KJV)

The Red Knight and now the Black Knight belong together in their destructive aftermath as they spread war and famine. We move now from war to famine. The third seal releases the Black Knight, whose rider had authority to create poverty and famine in the land. When the Lamb opens the third seal, the third living creature said, "Come," and the Black Knight appeared with scales in his hand.

Malcolm rides the black horse called Famine because the black color of the third horse represents for many the grim circumstances of famine. Although since the 1960s much work has been done to reimage blackness as necessary and even beautiful, Malcolm is still the black rider of famine because of his constant cries from the wilderness that institutional religion in the Western world no longer feeds people. He who sat on the black horse "had a pair of balances in hand." This sense of measuring strength and weakness is one of the major reasons I decided to write Malcolm's biography; again, because his spiritual direction seeks authenticity. As I approached Malcolm to be my spiritual director, I realized that I was approaching him out of a famine, my own. Malcolm constantly coaxed my consciousness to realize my own needs (strengths and weaknesses)—

my own context in which this book is also written. He writes to me with balances in hand as he describes himself in the third person:

> Dear Michael: You are writing a biography of Malcolm Boyd. You are the biographer. Unlike 99 percent of biographies, you are describing how you met Malcolm Boyd, what role he plays in your life, how you interact, indeed, what he represents for you. How he might have changed your life? This, then, brings up the subject of you. The reader needs to know you, have a genuine sense of you, grasp your identity and conflicts and problems and questions—and even where you seem to be going in your life. At the end, while you are still on the road of your journey, does the road split into two Robert Frost paths? What sense do they make to you? Is it possible this represents maturity and understanding?
>
> So, as you move into Malcolm Boyd's life and search its meanings, are you at the same time moving into your own life and searching its meanings? In fact, does this help your reader to do the same?
>
> I think one key factor about myself is that, while I take myself seriously (and, indeed, am very, very disciplined) at the same time I do not take myself seriously beyond a point. I laugh at myself. I see the absurdity. I have perspective. I always stand outside the system even as I inevitably make it work for me. The key is I am a person of faith. This opens up dimension. God is hugely in my life. I am not at all a literalist; I am poetic and a mystic, terribly vulnerable and quite strong because my strength is outside myself.
>
> Hold on. Keep doing your best work (which is required). Maintain your vision. Have a fine trip to South Africa. A brass band will await your return.[1]

In response to Malcolm's request for my authenticity, I think there are two major causes of the famine dwelt upon in this chapter. These two issues are also part of my own famine that led me to Malcolm. They are diversity and institutionalism.

The Church and Diversity

First, in facing the myriad issues of diversity confronting a postmodern and post-Christian world, I have been especially formed to articulate a theological as well as a social response. My problem, however, is that I

---

1. Malcolm Boyd, "Morning After Thoughts," e-mail message to author, November 6, 2009.

fail to find the niche in which to articulate both a theological and a social response without having to compromise my soul. This is where I am envious of Malcolm, who is quick to remind me of his long life and sojourn to get to the point of his own maturity. Much of the subtext for my spiritual direction sessions that lasted from 2008 through 2011 was my desire to do creative things for God. In this light, Malcolm forwards an e-mail trying to place me in touch with a filmmaker. He writes:

> This will introduce Andrew Thomas, my friend who is making a major film about jazz great Vince Guaraldi, and my friend writer-theologian Michael Battle, who is presently writing my biography.
>
> Recently Mark and I saw the 2-hour rough cut of Andrew's film *An Anatomy of Vince Guaraldi* which was shown in September at the Monterey Jazz Festival. A CD is out on a performance reading of my prayer-poems with Vince's music at the Jazz Bakery last April (with three great LA jazz performers). A DVD is in progress.
>
> What prompts this e-mail is how *An Anatomy of Vince Guaraldi* has stirred very deep recollection and feelings in me. On May 21, 1965, Grace Cathedral in San Francisco announced a "Vince Guaraldi–Malcolm Boyd Conference. Mr. Guaraldi is an internationally known composer and artist who works in the contemporary jazz idiom. Malcolm Boyd has been called by *Life* magazine one of the one hundred young people in the United States in the breakthrough generation for his ministry to coffeehouses and other urban groups." Vince Guaraldi had written a new Jazz Mass. He would play. I would be the preacher.
>
> The event attracted huge international media coverage. It's funny that I didn't realize the impact on my own life at the time. We were in the mid-60s. I was a young man in a hurry—strongly involved in civil rights, speaking on the nation's campuses, writing my best-selling prayers. *Are You Running with Me, Jesus?* had just been published and created a sensation. So the Jazz Mass passed by in a blur. I worked together with Vince a year later at the hungry i in San Francisco, but I was running as fast as I could in those days.
>
> Looking at the film of the Jazz Mass now, I am struck by the way the film shows me "giving my sermon" in Grace Cathedral. My face and body do not appear on the screen. The film holds tight on my script itself. As my voice is heard delivering the sermon, the camera slowly pans down my script, line by line, revealing meticulous editing along with penmanship. Extraordinary filmmaking, skillful and dramatic. I also realize the incredible impact of the Jazz Mass on my consciousness. More to the point, I can see its impact on Vince Guaraldi.

It seems to me it was in mysterious ways a peak mystical and creative influence in his own experience. An absolutely high-water mark of meaning. (Looking at the film, this seems self-explanatory.) After that we went our own ways.

For both of us, I think, we'd found a freshness, an innocence and simplicity, that would mark us indelibly. I look back at the event, collaborating with Vince, as a kind of magical moment. Two strangers met, exchanged a brief encounter on a great stage, and the gods seemed to smile or, at least, show friendliness. So repercussions can still be felt by many newcomers who are somehow still touched by—what shall I call it?—this happening.

Andrew and Michael, I'd like you to be in touch. Maybe Michael can see a rough cut of the film? We can all meet. All best—Malcolm.[2]

Malcolm's wisdom in our spiritual direction sessions was not to be star-struck, with bright lights in my eyes, since I was enticed by Malcolm's creative life. Talking about Jesus in creative ways, even with jazz musicians. I wanted to be like that—not an ordinary mainline church minister waiting for his pension.

So, why was I so obsessed with being a creative Christian? I think it was because it seemed to be the only way that I could contain my "misfit" nature of being a writer and a priest. I felt guilty, however. I was longing for creativity and creative positions in the church when all along I was positioned as priest-in-charge under special circumstances at the Church of Our Saviour. The juxtapositions of mainline churches and creativity always seemed to be difficult to reconcile. For example, I was constantly reminded of the *New York Times* writer who covered Malcolm at the hungry i: "Neither Father Boyd nor any of those who approve of his unorthodox methods believe that he succeeded in getting people out of the hungry i and into Grace Cathedral on Nob Hill. Realists among the clergy feel that the church represents a minority view in a culture no longer Christian and that the church's job is to join with other forces in society to preserve the dignity of life."[3]

It almost seems impossible to move the church from the hungry i to wealthy areas like Nob Hill. Particularly, in California I was socialized into the siloed nature of socioeconomic differences that seemed to sabotage the people of God from coming together simply on the basis of

---

2. Malcolm Boyd, "hi guys," e-mail message to author, October 19, 2009.

3. Julius Duscha, "And Now Even Prayers Are Pop," *New York Times*, November 13, 1966; ProQuest Historical Newspapers, *New York Times* (1851–2005), 345.

being the people of God. In other words, Christians seemed to lie when they said their primary identity is known in Christ when so many other human categorizations seemed to control the institutional church. For example, there used to be dynastic social groupings by means of the churches in San Marino, Beverly Hills, and Pasadena. It was the norm for an Episcopal bishop, a patriarchal rabbi, and a distinguished Roman Catholic prelate to form a cabal of power to bless the Californian elite. Malcolm states, "Society weddings used to be the control of the Episcopal Church. Well, dynasty is over. Those who are rich today do not use the rites of passage in the church like baptism, marriage, or even death."

I challenged Malcolm that there still appeared to be some need to use the church for perfunctory public blessing. Malcolm told me this may be the case, but the intensity and degree of this is substantially less today. Again, he reminded me, more and more people don't even want to be buried in the church. The stability of mainline religion has been disrupted.

The Anglican social class used to be a bridge and people walked on it. If you were poor and of "no account," you could join the Anglican Church and at least hope to befriend the powerful and elite. But Malcolm doesn't think this bridge exists now or if it does, it's tawdry or worn. People no longer need the high-class church. In addition to the church, the opera, the symphony, the county museum of art, and other cultural institutions support the social elite's ego through their display of wealth and culture. However, Malcolm concludes, "Today you get the homespun, tweedy-types that disguise their money and drive an old car." We live in fragmented times today. No longer do we see the signs of power and prestige that mainline churches like the Episcopal Church used to have. And yet, many such churches continue to behave as if such prestige still exists. Many such churches think people will naturally want to worship in an Episcopal looking building on Sunday mornings at 11:00 AM. The fragmentation is in the reality that those days are not today. Churches, especially in Western culture, cannot assume that people naturally want to "go to church."

Malcolm was the person with whom I could talk honestly about these problems of the institutional church. But there was something more that he helped me with—namely, how do I reconcile my own rise up the social ladder with my Christian identity? In other words, Malcolm helped me with my ambitions in the church and the world. To do so with anyone else felt like an oncoming Shakespearean tragedy. If I shared my ambitions with fellow priests or parishioners, my ambition would be held against me.

So, Malcolm endured my obsessions. He constantly reminded me through his long life and struggles to learn not to be somewhere other than where God had me. I certainly didn't want to be in a dying church. Whenever I was around Malcolm, I was emboldened in this desire. I didn't want to continue the dollhouse in which people pretended there was a God and used this as a pretext to build a social club full of like-minded people based upon socioeconomic status and race. I felt like one of Malcolm's characters, Father Art, in his work of fiction *The Fantasy Worlds of Peter Stone and Other Fables.* Malcolm begins this story as if he had me in mind, "Father Art had decided years ago to be avant-garde, yet had long felt it necessary to conceal his feelings."[4] Father Art had been called to a rich church full of white people. They were spoiled, terribly sophisticated, obsessed with their own sense of self-importance, and would be nearly impossible to reach. Father Art longed for the time he could openly express his avant-garde feelings. "Noting that students were simply disinterested in the church, he wanted to bring them back, and arouse their sleeping parents, by sharply relevant developments."[5]

The story then moves rapidly into the contest between death and life of institutional churches. Instead of giving sociological statistics of the institutional church's demise, Malcolm uses this story as an allegory of the fierce war in which institutional churches are becoming casualties. The story continues:

> On the first Sunday in advent, when Rolling Hills society walked into St. Cyprian's for divine worship, it experienced a head-on collision with the world of art. The night before, moving vans had transported a collection of art to the church. Abstract designs were at eye-level with steel executives. A jazz combo, imported from an avant-garde downtown hot spot, struck up the processional hymn. An acclaimed poet, internationally recognized for his gay lifestyle, read an excerpt from his work. The president of the Junior League did an interpretive dance, accompanied by an Indian student playing the sitar, for the offertory. Instead of the sermon, the Rolling Hills New Ideas Theatre presented a reading of the story of "Jerry and the Dog" from *The Zoo Story* as a sanctuary drama. High school students dressed in clown costumes acted as ushers, wearing buttons reading: "All the World's a Stage: Are You Playing Your Part?"[6]

---

4. Malcolm Boyd, *The Fantasy Worlds of Peter Stone and Other Fables* (New York: Harper & Row, 1969), 53.
5. Ibid., 49.
6. Ibid., 59.

Malcolm provides this succinct commentary, "Back in their homes, people did not discuss church that Sunday."

As I continued to read this story, I saw more and more of myself in this story. Father Art spent more and more time away from his church. He worked within the inner-city in relation to which his own church was seen as existing in some mythical and royal suburb. Father Art decided that his church must be forced further into a confrontation with social issues. He gave priority to black power. Father Art met a very black man who looked angry and refused the social amenities of politeness. The black man was intrigued by Father Art's strange naiveté and earnest resolve. Within a short time, Father Art was catapulted into a whole new world of ghetto blackness. He ate soul food. He heard soul music. Then Easter Sunday came.

It was like the huge stone was rolled away from the empty tomb as Father Art's parishioners opened their heavy bronze door. They wanted to flee but stood still, gazing at the life-size African-American Jesus, garbed in a black loincloth, hanging over the altar. A black choir was bussed in to sing; they sang the processional hymn "Swing Low, Sweet Chariot." The church bulletin announced that on Tuesday evenings at 8:30 there would be a fifteen-session course on African-American History and Culture, conducted by a well-known black militant. The Easter sermon was preached by a militant black preacher and freedom fighter, a Baptist, who was flown in from Birmingham, Alabama. The Easter collection would not go to the building fund but to the Negro College Fund. Sunday school was dismissed so that the children could be addressed by a young black nationalist out on bail following a recent civil disorder in the city. Paintings by black artists filled the sanctuary. Still, Father Art didn't get the controversy he had hoped for. His church responded with *noblesse oblige.*

"Seesawing between the two worlds, one in Rolling Hills and another in the black ghetto, he sometimes felt as if he were losing all sense of his own identity."[7] Before Malcolm met me, didn't he have me in mind when he constructed his character Father Art? Didn't Malcolm have in mind all institutional church leaders?

The story ends with Father Art opening a coffeehouse in the basement of his rich church. It would provide a touch of authentic scandal to make church folks express their true feelings. "Then Father Art could, for the first time, engage them as human beings in honest controversy."[8] Students

---

7. Ibid., 63.
8. Ibid., 70.

painted the church basement in a combination of religious and secular motifs. An espresso machine was sent from Italy. The coffeehouse was named "The Appian Way." On the opening night, underground films were shown and a young Cuban poet recited provocative verse. To Father Art's surprise, the coffeehouse became popular. The city's leading newspaper featured it. Church parents were proud of their kids' involvement with the coffeehouse. There was no expected controversy. So, Father Art took steps to seek a transfer, when, overnight it seemed, the whole situation changed. A student in The Appian Way was arrested by a police officer for smoking pot. The students said the cop planted marijuana on the young man. Debate raged within family circles. There were cries like "moral decency" and "police brutality," and The Appian Way made it in *Time, Newsweek,* and *Life.* Clergy around the country gave sermons alluding to "moral degeneracy" in this church and its associated coffeehouse "which seemed to be a dope den." Hollywood celebrities waded into the debate. And even the White House alluded to The Appian Way. This controversy was getting to Father Art. "A few days later, Father Art made his tragic and irremediable move. He grew a beard." As Father Art's beard grew bushier and heavier, so attendance at his church diminished in alarming proportions. The story ends with Father Art leaving. "Inside the site of the former coffeehouse, only tea could be served." Despite repeated washing and fumigation, the odor of espresso coffee, however, clung resolutely to that hallowed room.

The Church and Institutionalism

As I read through Father Art about the fictional demise of institutional churches, it is as if I were reading a narrative of the demographic shifts occurring between the global north and south. Established churches in the global north are dying away. In many cases among mainline Western Christian denominations like Episcopalians and Presbyterians, the rate of decline is rapid. Whereas, in the global south, the church is growing exponentially. For example, the median statistic for an Anglican is a 36-year-old Nigerian woman.[9]

The demise of the Western church has become one of the central concerns for many. As we increasingly see through global interdependency, tensions are high between the two global regions of north and south

---

9. For a comprehensive picture of the demographic shift in church, see Philip Jenkins, *The Next Christiandom: The Coming of Global Christianity* (New York: Oxford University Press, 2002).

partly because of the globalization of economic markets, and also (and something that should not be taken lightly) because of major religious shifts that are occurring in these regions. Philip Jenkins's book *The Next Christendom* is excellent in charting these demographic shifts—including the growing fact that Christianity is increasingly moving south and back to where it began.

The institutionalization of Western Christianity occurred during the post-Constantinian days of Rome, and soon after became an essential part of European culture. I remember in my own theological training wondering if there were any real difference between Christianity and Western culture. Since most of the people and events I studied were European in nature, I often felt like my own culture as an African American was neglected in terms of being a lens through which to see Christian faith. I also knew that the church always encountered ethnicity and culture. For example, as the early church grew, it knew itself to be a new faith that was partly Jewish and partly Greek. Shortly after the early church took its baby steps to move into the entire world, it grew exponentially throughout the Roman provinces and also east to China and India, north and west to Europe, and south to Africa.

Then Islam moved across Africa and western Asia and caused the church to eventually lose much of its potency in Africa and the Middle East. This created competition for Christianity especially in Africa and Asia. Christianity, however, through colonialism and modern missionaries came to define Western believers especially through European sensibilities. When the institutionalization of the church set in, especially through the secularization of Western Europe, this changed the face of Christendom. This was also the point that the Western church began to decline.

The shift of Christianity from the West to the South and East is happening for several reasons. On one hand, Western nations practice being the church in more materialistic ways (i.e., needing building or a set time to meet). On the other hand, Western populations are growing at a slower rate than developing nations. If such trends continue, Jenkins claims Christianity will inevitably become increasingly Southern in style and culture, and less Western over time. I have learned from Malcolm that such a future occurrence is not all that bad.

One of the first programs I have implemented where I am—in one of the largest parishes in the Diocese of Los Angeles—is an official Asian Ministries Program, for which I hired an Associate Priest for Asian Ministries, the Rev. Ada Nagata Wong. Her ministry and impact were immediate. She facilitated an Asian church's worship service to be conducted in our Grace Chapel. She also started a Cantonese service during our regular Sunday morning services.

Secondly, with help of Bishop Jon Bruno, I hired the Rev. Khushnud Azariah, the first woman ordained in Pakistan to serve as my Associate Priest for Children and Family Ministries. Rev. Khushnud comes to Church of Our Saviour with much expertise, a PhD in theology and master's degrees in child formation. In addition, she is married to the Anglican Archbishop of Pakistan. Rev. Khushnud and Rev. Ada are vital additions to the staff in many ways, as they both represent the future of ministry in the Pacific world of California.

California is rapidly approaching a developing-world sociology in which wealth is concentrated in a small minority. When this minority is identified with a prestigious and powerful church, creating an inclusive community for both the rich and the poor is a challenge. I have learned from Malcolm an authenticity to befriend both the wealthy and the poor, and to galvanize a mission in which both socioeconomic groups discover a larger and more primary identity of being Christians for others. My experience is such that I have had to work hard to communicate in the multiple worlds of fiscal and social conservatives, libertarians, and radical and moderate liberals.

My Need for Malcolm

Since this chapter is about a malnourished church, I must raise the initial question: What is the church? And what is community? The following response attempts to answer these two questions concerning the nature of the church and heterogeneous community.

First, my definition of the church (*ecclesia*—a feminine noun in Greek) is that she is basically a worldview—one in which primary identity is revealed. As Christians we say our primary identity is given in our baptism. All other identities (for example, male, female, rich, poor, American, El Salvadoran, black, white, or Asian) are ordered by our primary identity of being in Christ. Our primary citizenship reflects a whole other kingdom now revealed in our midst—the church. God has made us stewards of this church and kingdom, and stewardship is nothing more and nothing less than our caretaking of all that we have been given. To understand this, we must start from a position of humble gratitude—all that we have is given to us for safekeeping, to use for God's work in the world. In other words, when all is said and done, we reveal this church and kingdom of heaven through a legacy in which you are loved no matter who you are. Jesus teaches this ecclesiology in Matthew 25:31–40:

> When the Son of Man comes in his glory, and all the angels with him, then he will sit on the throne of his glory. All the nations will be gathered before him. . . . Then the king will say to those at his right hand, "Come, you that are blessed by my Father, inherit the kingdom prepared for you from the foundation of the world; for I was hungry and you gave me food, I was thirsty and you gave me something to drink, I was a stranger and you welcomed me, I was naked and you gave me clothing, I was sick and you took care of me, I was in prison and you visited me." Then the righteous will answer him, "Lord, when was it that we saw you hungry and gave you food, or thirsty and gave you something to drink? And when was it that we saw you a stranger and welcomed you, or naked and gave you clothing? And when was it that we saw you sick or in prison and visited you?" And the king will answer them, "Truly I tell you, just as you did it to one of the least of these who are members of my family, you did it to me."

The reality conveyed in this passage is predicated on a worldview in which we are taught in our baptism that we are first and foremost Christians. Faith without such a working reality is dead. Such a worldview leads us to the vital importance of heterogeneous community in which a person may not claim their primary identity as a Christian. Here is the beauty of Jesus—namely, he anticipates the conundrum of primary identity in conflict with heterogeneous community. The parable of the great judgment reveals different criteria for the Christian community than the one often practiced outside the church. The church is not for herself, but for others. This means that our primary identity is not meant to keep anyone out or to marginalize the "other." If fact, in Jesus' parable, the ones who are saved in the kingdom of heaven don't even know they are saved. They had to ask the king why they were saved. The king answers, "Truly I tell you, just as you did it to one of the least of these who are members of my family, you did it to me."

With gratitude and devotion to God and the ministries of the church, Christians should always invite others to enter a new reality—a miracle, really—where we all realize religion, socioeconomic status, race, gender, and all other identities are not meant to marginalize or keep others out, but—through Christ—to constantly seek to be ordered to keep everyone in. I call this new reality the church.

I have a keen interest in ecumenism and inter-religious dialogue. For example, two of my best friends in seminary have become respectively a bishop in the Romanian Orthodox Church and a patriarch in the Ethiopian Coptic Church. I have served on Theology and Worship Committees of the World Council of Churches. And more particularly to our Episcopal/Anglican Community, I served for four years on the Anglican and Roman Catholic Dialogue Commission. In terms of inter-religious dialogue, much of my PhD work in theology focused upon African Traditional Religions, which led to my synthesizing concept of "Ubuntu" that seeks to harmonize the world religions, particularly through cultural worldviews. In addition, my training in African theology and discourse places me in the heart of ecumenical and inter-religious debates.

The inclusion of gay and lesbian people in the church, their ordination and their consecration to the Episcopacy, continue to be controversial in the church and beyond. How the postmodern church deals with these issues is key to her next rite of passage. I was an author of the Episcopal Church's response to the Windsor Report, *To Set Our Hope on Christ*, which defended our course of action in electing Bishop Gene Robinson. I have published articles (for example, in *The Christian Century*) defending the identity of being gay and Christian.

Malcolm writes me:

> Dear Michael: Spent some time this morning reading again through your last draft of pp. You've done an excellent job of bringing so many things together. I've put it in the mail to you, my observations and suggestions and corrections.
>
> The introduction needs a rewrite largely because it will now be essentially about YOU instead of ME. Also it will not be a chapter but an introduction. Here you need to dig into your own life and experience. You need to ask: Who am I? Go back into African Notes, anything that will provide some answers about the YOU who met ME—why and how we met. This can be a classic work about Spiritual Direction which so frequently is sunk in banality when it is crucially needed. The introduction needs to be a stunner, a brilliant piece of work drawing deeply on your self-examination and self-knowledge.
>
> After we met and started working together, you found me in the four chapters. They have an immediacy. You might wish to mark up a copy of them—indicating places where you might ask me to get into storytelling....
>
> I trust you completely in all this. You have a pattern, a clear one. Now you need to flesh it out. I do see where I fit into each chapter log-

ically and intrinsically. You are "telling my story" in a completely new and fresh way that also links it with "everyone else's story." What is good about the four chapters is that each is so different from the others. (Absolutely necessary.) Keep the link(s) between us clearly and directly. So, at the end, hopefully you have come to a "Robert Frost Moment" when you choose or start to follow a path, or at least see one.

Mark is looking forward to his meeting with you at our home. . . .

Now we move into Serious Time. The terrain is clear. We need to move through it. All best—Malcolm.[10]

On the night when Bishop Bruno introduced me as the Priest-in-Charge Under Special Circumstances, parishioners walked out in protest. I was given an eighteen-month letter of agreement in which I had the option of being called as rector. My mission as rector was to coalesce the concept of parish. What attracted me to the church was its unusually diverse nature: church, parochial mission (in a different Hispanic neighborhood), A Child's Garden School, major community center, Godly Play (its foundational operations based at the church), and Transitional Housing Program. All of these identities were the parish of Church of Our Saviour.

At the end of eighteen tumultuous months, the conscious decision had to be made as to my being the new rector (tenured priest). To my surprise, the vestry called me to be their rector. This was a surprise because in many ways I was doing the hard work of interim ministry in which I made decisions to change personnel, worship content, schedules, and the pedagogy of Christian education. My style of engaging conflict is to be nonanxious in order for apparent irreconcilable differences to be seen for what they normally are—unconscious differences. What I mean is that many recalcitrant differences find reconciliation in the simple occurrence of each side being heard. When two sides fully recount their narratives to the other, usually a third (common) narrative forms that presents the possibility of reconciliation. I found myself practicing this nonstop, from working with the Altar Guild to listening to frustrations of Sunday school teachers.

In the midst of such intense ministry, questions surfaced. How have I achieved a balance between the claims of my ministry and the claims of my family or personal life? What have I found helpful or not helpful in achieving that balance? Malcolm has taught me a vital lesson. From Malcolm, I learned that a balanced life is a cumulative effect. What I mean is

---

10. Malcolm Boyd, "Up to date," e-mail message to author, October 23, 2009.

that unless I practice a balanced life in microcosm, it cannot be realized overall. So, I try to achieve a four-fold balance on a daily basis. Warning! The following process is not linear or a ranked order; rather, it is more cyclical. First, I must find time for quality prayer. Second, I must jog, swim, or do weight lifting. Third, I must find intellectual engagement. And fourth, I must practice my communal identity both as a family person and as a spiritual leader. I find that when I am not paying attention to these four aspects of my life on a daily basis, what accumulates is usually not healthy. What is most helpful is to take advantage of the ancient spiritual practices of the daily office for my prayer life and the use of a spiritual director like Malcolm. In terms of my intellectual life, I always seek to be in the midst of a writing project such as a book or article. This book came out of spiritual direction. My physical health is enhanced when I set certain goals, like two marathons a year. And if I'm simply attentive to the health of my family and church community, I can tell how to prioritize my daily time.

What kinds of things do I do to relax? I try to have a deep tissue massage at least twice a month. I read comic books. Deep sea fishing and scuba diving are keen interests. Since my mother is a piano teacher, I am committed to restarting my piano lessons. And my middle daughter wants me to learn guitar with her. My wife, Raquel Battle, and three children, Sage Battle (10-year-old daughter); Bliss Battle (7-year-old daughter); and Zion Battle (4-year-old son) all naturally create a biosphere in which I must discern balance and health. Although it may not feel like it on some occasions, my family provides a balance for me that prevents my going off the deep end like Marlon Brando's character in *Apocalypse Now*.

Malcolm's Advice

All institutions are about self-preservation Malcolm taught me and perhaps this is why he has been such an apocalyptic figure in relationship to what counts for religion today. Despite this apocalyptic tone, and appropriate to Malcolm's own character, there is an inherent optimism in this chapter. Like rigorous archeological digging, however, we may need to unlearn a lot of our own caricatures and stereotypes in order to see this optimism. We need only to let God be God in order to escape the famine of institutional religion.

At seventy-two, Malcolm faced mandatory retirement. Malcolm started out with writing workshops. As he has continued his writing and work in the Diocese of Los Angeles, one of the vocations he has realized is his role as spiritual director. "It's been about twelve years now doing it formally," Malcolm told me. Further, he writes:

> I just finished reading someone else's "autobiography" (pretty good) and was struck by these words at the end: "That was when I decided to write an autobiography. I felt I might be able to do it. Maybe this was the time. Maybe it would help me to discover something about myself, to add it all up. What I am—and why. How I got here."
>
> Now, you are doing this for me. I'm grateful. Don't lose the momentum. Keep your vision, your energy. It's the best way. Get those other chapters finished. Can't wait to read them.
>
> You're recognizing and dealing with my work with you in spiritual direction, but don't forget the dozen others I work with, and how important this part of my life-cum-ministry is. You need to ask me about this. I need to tell the story of this. I don't follow an "outline" or "plan." It is dialogue. I am "in" it as much as the other person. I've worked with some people for many years (they range from 22 to 75, are men and women, a vast range of differentiation). In some ways I believe it is the most significant part of my ministry of 55 years. It is not "counseling." It is spiritual direction. It requires authenticity, deepest involvement, excavating the past including childhood, answering "who am I?" also "where am I now?" and "where am I going?" You may want to talk to one spiritual directee who really got me going. He surprised/shocked me when he asked me to be his spiritual director. We've been at it for a good dozen years. Recently he moved away and I've had to step out of that picture. He gave me "on the job training."[11]

Malcolm was a perfect fit for me in spiritual direction because I needed his advice about how to navigate the institutional church. Of course I was not on the same scale as Malcolm as a best-selling author or celebrity priest, but he offered a life that dealt profoundly with how an unusual priest like myself who writes books and speaks to larger audiences outside of the church can still be in the institutional church. So, I asked Malcolm what made him change course from the institutional churchman trajectory that he was on. His answer was this. As a writer and priest Malcolm had to be honest to himself. This honesty became his pilgrimage as he eventually matched his public tenacity of speaking truth to power with his inner tenacity of, as Malcolm would say, taking off his

---

11. Malcolm Boyd, "New," e-mail message to author, November 23, 2009.

mask. Speaking to the world came easy to Malcolm, although his prophetic words landed him in a great deal of difficulty. For Malcolm, as he gained celebrity status, not to disclose his identity as a priest was dishonest; corollary to that, to be a significant writer you can't be a phony. Through this journey, I learned that Malcolm is a person of deep faith.

There were other reasons why his institutional career was derailed. Was the fork in the road for Malcolm his coming out as an openly gay priest? As I read Malcolm's autobiography, I wonder if his touchstone crisis of faith occurred when he entered a gay bar and saw someone who took his breath away, "a Moorish prince who had apparently just stepped out of one of those Turkish cigarette ads." As you will shortly read, this encounter doesn't end well, and yet I think it is a touchstone experience for Malcolm's own encounter with a famished church. Malcolm writes:

> He came home with me. I made love to him. He tried to respond, and at moments I felt a flooding outpouring of himself as he clutched me. But then he'd retreat into some bastion of hostility, looking at me with smoldering eyes.
>
> I wanted to talk to him. To explain . . . explain what? The only language I could trust was the language of my body, and I flung meanings at him that I barely understood myself. How could I make him understand?
>
> He rose from the bed like a pillar of amber, like an avenging angel—and noticed my clerical collar on top of the bureau. He picked it up with great delicacy. As I stood beside him, he looked at me. "You a priest?"
>
> "Yes."
>
> "Well, how about that!" His eyes suddenly burst into flame. "I don't want to make it with a priest."
>
> "Why? What's the matter with being a priest?"
>
> "I've got no time for the goddamn church. It hates God because God made people. You're a fucking priest in the goddamn church."
>
> I saw the fist coming toward me, felt a crash of pain . . .
>
> When I regained consciousness, I raised my head and looked around the apartment. Nothing was disturbed, nothing taken. But the room was empty.
>
> Then I saw it, crushed and twisted, lying on the floor—my clerical collar. I was drained.[12]

---

12. Boyd, *Take Off the Masks* (San Francisco: HarperSanFrancisco, 1993), 111.

As I read Malcolm's autobiography, this incident seemed to be another trigger that spurred his own need for integrity and authenticity. The difficulty would be in how such integrity and authenticity could be handled not only being a Christian priest among gay society but how he could be true to his identity in the church.

To some, Malcolm's coming out as a gay man was the honorable way to acknowledge Jesus and the image of God. For others, Malcolm's coming out as a priest was akin to blasphemy. I asked Malcolm about any guilt he felt by perhaps being too controversial for many Christians (even though they might be immature—similar to St. Paul warning more mature Christians not to eat meat if it causes a crisis of faith in more immature Christians [Romans 14:21; 1 Corinthians 8:13 and 10:25]. Malcolm ponders and smiles and says he needs to think more about this.

Becoming a Priest

There was an old dean, the "Red Dean," who became Malcolm's role model for the priesthood. He was remarkable. Dean Roberts, the dean of Denver's cathedral, probably made Malcolm go to seminary. Dean Roberts was a saint, was beyond reproach. He wasn't ambitious. He had a wife and son and daughter. And then tragedy hit. The son was killed in a head-on accident that also injured two others. Malcolm began to imprint on the Red Dean's holy orders whenever he could, especially when the dean's voice cried out, "I am the resurrection and the life." Malcolm confessed, "Actually that converted me." Malcolm said this with tears in his eyes. "Dean Robert was not a phony clergyperson."

Despite this inspiration for Malcolm, he had a turbulent experience navigating the institutional church in search of authentic leadership. I asked Malcolm how his vocation to the priesthood was initiated. Malcolm was invited to go to St Augustine by-the-Sea in the late 1970s. Here, he decided that his vocation was in the church. It is easy to see a famine in the church, especially for Malcolm. For example, when Malcolm began his holy orders looking for his specific placement, he preached for Bishop Bob Rusack. There was no discipleship for Malcolm as a young ordinand, desperately needing the guidance of a bishop. Malcolm wrote Bishop Rusack a handwritten note but never got a reply. Malcolm doesn't know why Bishop Rusack was so distant in response to his need for guidance. Subsequently, Malcolm had a turbulent time trying to fit into the established, institutional church.

Like Father Art in Malcolm's fictionalized narrative cited earlier, Malcolm could never fit easily into the established church. In many of our

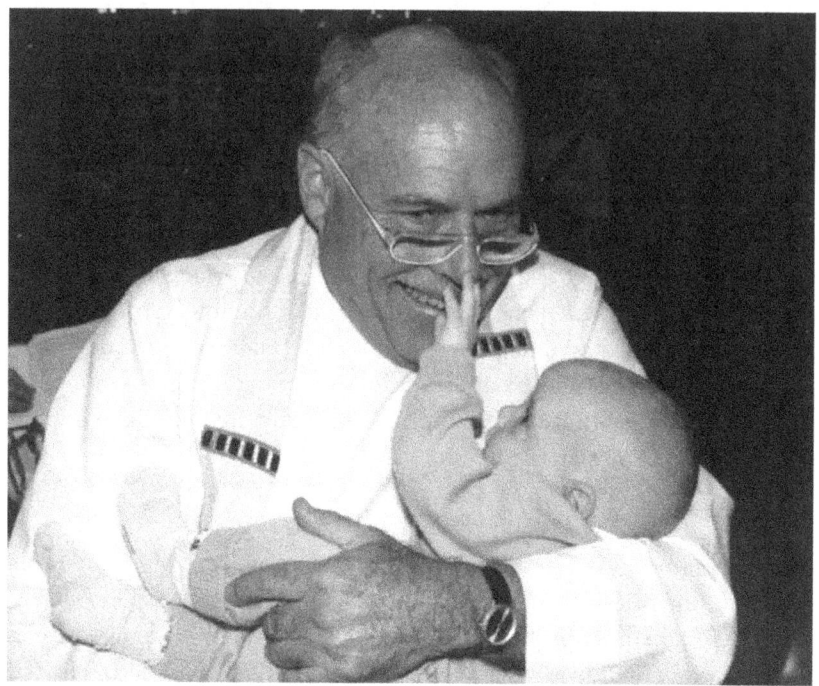

Malcolm baptizes Nicholas Barlow, November 5, 1989.

spiritual direction sessions, I shared my own common struggles of fitting into the institutional church as a black person trying to have a more public and far-reaching ministry. Malcolm's life encapsulated this impact for me, but I saw the cost to Malcolm for being an authentic priest that often bucked the socialization of the institutional church. "Wow," I thought. Malcolm's spiritual vocation as priest with a major public and far-reaching ministry moves from Hollywood to rural Alabama on the Freedom Rides pretty easily. Malcolm refused the false dichotomies between his vocation as a priest and his life as a public figure. Despite the socialization for him to become a priest over a small group of white people in a suburban community, Malcolm's vocation took him into uncharted territory.

So, how do we answer the preceding question: did Malcolm feel any guilt for being too controversial for more immature Christians—similar to St. Paul warning more mature Christians not to eat meat? Malcolm's ordination journey to the priesthood reflects his own maturation in which he constantly made allowances for those who could not accept him. Occasionally, he encountered the "Red Deans" or those who saw Malcolm's genius. These were the way stations that offered refreshment and drink in a long journey in the desert. Mostly, however, I think Malcolm resolved in his own life's journey not to blame anyone else for the famine of the church. Instead, he worked harder on his own life—to find nourishment and fulfillment. It was as if he listened to the prayer of his mentor Reinhold Niebuhr: "God grant me the serenity to accept the things I cannot change. Courage to change the things I can and the wisdom to know the difference." Now there are more bishops who are actually inspired by Malcolm. Unlike Bishop Rusack, Bishop Jon Bruno is now deeply engaged in Malcolm's life.

Malcolm's "coming out" as a gay man was extraordinarily difficult. "Coming out" was, at that time, a dangerous, highly complex public action. He had been in a fifteen-year relationship which had remained intimate and private. When he "came out" publicly, both partners agreed to leave their former relationship behind. Over the years theirs has remained a close friendship.

Soon Malcolm entered into a new relationship that lasted five years. He remembers it gratefully. His partner during that period is now deeply involved in a different relationship.

On May 16, 2004, Bishop Jon Bruno became the first sitting bishop to perform a public blessing of a gay union. He officiated at the blessing of Malcolm and Mark Thompson on the twentieth anniversary of their life partnership in the Cathedral Center of St. Paul in Los Angeles. Six bishops were present at the historic public event. Their relationship stays robust, spiritually oriented, and the central basic reality in both of their lives.

Once I learned about the pivotal role of Bishop Bruno, I interviewed him on June 11, 2010, at the bishop's residence in Pasadena. Going into the interview, I thought my primary context would be how Bishop Bruno found himself in lawsuits costing millions of dollars for the Diocese of Los Angeles because he had blessed Malcolm and Mark's union. The story leading up to Malcolm asking Jon to bless their union is humorous, as told by Bishop Bruno:

> Malcolm, Mark, Mary, and I went to dinner at Malcolm and Mark's house. Malcolm doesn't do the cooking. He did the set-up and clean-up. Mark did the cooking. We were all sitting around when Malcolm said to me "I want to talk to you," in a way that someone was in trouble. Mark and Mary went into the kitchen. Malcolm spent the next twenty minutes leading up to the question—"You know you don't have to do this. . . . I know this will put stress on you. . . ." Finally I said, "What in the world are you talking about?"

"Mark and I would like for you to bless our union."

It would be unconscionable not to. I had to do what was right and holy. I supported Malcolm. This goes back to bringing Malcolm to the Cathedral Center when he left St. Augustine.

Indeed, Bishop Bruno shared how his actions of blessing did spark the legal battles in his episcopate, but he made the interview go in a different direction by talking about how Malcolm was like a mystical sage in his life. Bishop Bruno made me see the providence in Malcolm's life and how he pushes others toward their higher calling.

"Three weeks after I did the blessing, those congregations broke away from the Diocese. The article broke in *The Advocate* and another magazine. I was on a motorcycle ride and returned home. Mary told me to call the office about something urgent."

Bishop Bruno told me, "There came a time in my own vocation as a bishop that I had to decide between articulating tolerance for the gay and lesbian communities or being an advocate for them. Malcolm moved me toward advocacy. We need to learn to live with pain. We need to learn to live with what is deemed a curse and turn it into a blessing. Malcolm was brought into the community to force us out of tolerance. The time for tolerance is past and we need to be advocates for what is holy. I'm sure the relationship Malcolm has with Mark is as holy as the relationship I have with Mary."

Malcolm was a major catalyst in Bishop Bruno's discernment to become the Episcopal Bishop of Los Angeles. I learned something even more from my interview with Bishop Bruno; namely, Malcolm sparked an authenticity. From the very beginning of Bishop Bruno's leadership, Malcolm had marked his change from tolerance to advocacy. A new integrity was born rather than the typical double standards of the church.

> Malcolm prays, "Dad is a phony, Jesus. Why do some of us have to be phony humans, Lord, and mistreat ourselves as if we were engines? But we're not, Christ. We're people. Can we learn how to treat ourselves that way?"[13]

I suggested to Bishop Bruno that he must have had a mystical relationship with Malcolm due to the unusual events of how Malcolm seemed to predict things that unfolded in his election. Malcolm called Jon and said that he should become Bishop of Los Angeles.

---

13. Boyd and Conrad, *When in the Course of Human Events*, 20–21.

The Black Horse of Famine 173

"...Son...!"   "...Dad...!"

"I was home," Bishop Bruno said "when I had just been cut from the list to be Bishop of Los Angeles. I was cooking dinner for Mary. I had come to grips that I wouldn't be the Bishop. The phone rang and I'll remember what was uttered on that phone for as long as I live."

Malcolm said, "I'm calling to say something to you. Although I should be keeping out of this, I'm compelled to say this to you because I believe God is asking me to tell you that you need to allow your name to stand for Bishop."

"Malcolm, they cut me from the list and I am perfectly happy where I am. God bless you, my brother, and I love you. Now, Mary just walked in the door and I have to finish dinner."

Bishop Bruno had the oil in pan and sautéed the veal when the phone rang again. Bishop Bruno picked up the phone and the voice said, "Jon, this is David Anderson [a more conservative Christian]. I've been thinking about it, but you need to allow yourself to stand for Bishop."

Bishop Bruno finished his veal piccato when Mary said, "Jon, you need to follow this discernment from others. Do you think God wants you to do it?" If two diverse people like David Anderson and Malcolm Boyd agree, there must be something divine occurring.

Malcolm was the catalyst for Jon to move forward in the discernment process to become a bishop. Jon learned from Malcolm's persuasion and his being a prophet that he didn't have to be polished, and the most educated, but only someone authentically capable of loving others as well as being loved.[14]

Angst and Religion

Much of the angst that took me to Malcolm in spiritual direction was whether or not I would or should be a bishop in the Anglican/Episcopal Church. After all, I had sat at the feet of one of the greatest Anglican archbishops of all time, Desmond Tutu—living with him for two years. I had studied with Archbishop Rowan Williams and even babysat his children. I had been the chaplain to the House of Bishops. There was a deep sense of melancholy, however, as I discerned becoming a bishop in the institutional church.

Much of my angst came from the death of the institutional church that Malcolm had long predicted. Malcolm tells the story of his own religious background to help place this trend in perspective.

Three of Malcolm's grandparents were Christians. The fourth, his maternal grandfather, was a Jew. During high school and college, however, Malcolm thought of Judaism as an alien faith, one utterly distant from his own experience. Judaism often seemed forbidding and even strange. What was kosher food? A bar mitzvah?

Malcolm's unfamiliarity with Jews was later mitigated when, during the Civil Rights Movement, he marched and went to jail with Jews. A rabbi with him said his participation was based on the teaching of the Torah that any and all suffering was his suffering, his concern. "Let justice roll down like waters!" the prophet Amos cried. This prophetic passage recalled Jesus' words: "I was a stranger and you took me in; naked and you clothed me. I was sick and you visited me; I was in prison and you came unto me."

---

14. Bishop Jon Bruno, interviewed by Michael Battle, June 11, 2010.

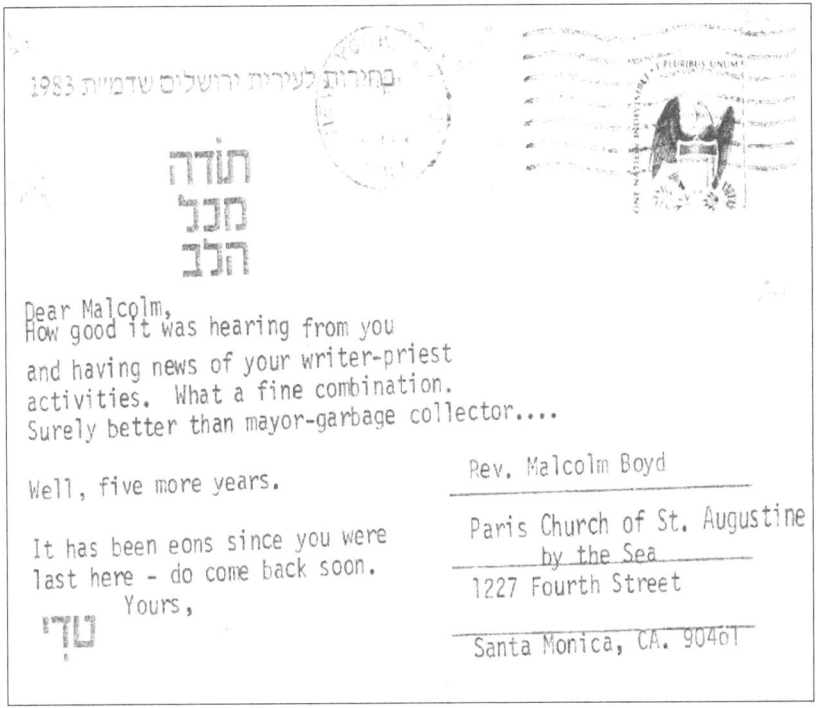

In the early 1960s Malcolm visited Israel for the first time. When in the early 1970s he was invited to live in Jerusalem for three months, it was a fresh experience to live by the Jewish clock: the Sabbath was Saturday, not Sunday. While in Israel, an interesting event occurred when Malcolm met a palm reader. Upon reading Malcolm's palm, she said, "You've changed your palm!" Evidently, Malcolm had the ability to change his fate. Malcolm said this was true as he recounted several rites of passage in his life: Hollywood, Indianapolis, Detroit, and Washington, D.C.

Living in Jerusalem Malcolm thought often of his Jewish grandfather. Malcolm's Jewish identity became more manifest in Jerusalem. At Christmas time, Malcolm went to hear Handel's *Judas Maccabeus* instead of the *Messiah*. Malcolm even got to know the mayor of Jerusalem, a social activist who sought solidarity with Palestinian garbage workers.

Late one night Malcolm stood silently before the Western Wall of the temple of Solomon. Malcolm was aware that his grandfather never had been able to visit this land or this place. A sense of kinship warmed his heart when he placed his forehead on a cold, ancient stone of the wall, offering thanks for his grandfather's life.

The Catholicism of his grandmother's friend was no less strange than the Judaism of his grandfather. Catholics were *different*, everyone knew.

Catholics couldn't come to Malcolm's services, and he couldn't attend theirs. Catholic priests couldn't marry. Nuns and monks wore funny-looking clothes.

So Malcolm always felt awkward when he went with his grandmother to visit the Catholic monsignor in the rectory next to the big cathedral. The monsignor and Malcolm's grandmother had been friends, like brother and sister when they grew up in the East, she said. Afterward they stayed in close touch through the years. He looked so stern in his long black robe with a silver cross around his neck. His hair was white, his back ramrod straight. But when he placed his hand on Malcolm's head, Malcolm felt he was kind.

One day Malcolm's grandmother sat him down and said she had to tell him something serious, even though he wasn't old enough to understand. But Malcolm must try. Malcolm's grandmother said she had passed lots of blood in her stool and thought she didn't have much time to live. Soon after that she went to a hospital.

After Malcolm's grandmother died, there was an Episcopal burial service for her. Malcolm couldn't believe his eyes when he looked up and saw the monsignor seated in the back row of the Episcopal chapel. Malcolm knew he wasn't *supposed* to be there. It was so strange that Malcolm never forgot it. It taught him that rules exist to be broken for love. The monsignor was a very important man, almost god-like to young Malcolm, and there he sat for Malcolm's grandmother in a chapel that wasn't Roman Catholic. Malcolm held his breath. Would God strike them with lightning? God didn't.

Through these vignettes I learned from Malcolm why institutional religion is struggling so mightily in the Western world. Good or bad theology is taught constantly in every church (religion) on the basis of its true beliefs (not just what it says in a creed) and actions. One Sunday Malcolm was invited to preach at a church in Chicago. Upon his arrival, he saw that three young acolytes had a fourth boy down on the floor of the sacristy. They were taking off his shoes. Malcolm inquired what was going on. It seems the fourth acolyte had walked into the church sanctuary, surrounding the altar, wearing his *ordinary* shoes. This was forbidden in that church. Acolytes were supposed to wear gold slippers.

What bad theology that was! It gave the impression that the sanctuary was somehow holy while the rest of the church was not. Worse, it conveyed the idea that when people set foot *outside* the church, and reentered their ordinary lives and concerns, it was *less* holy. Malcolm learned early on why institutional religion was on the decline because of these false dichotomies between the sacred and profane. It's no wonder mainline religions are barely staying alive in the Western world.

There are numerous statistics on the post-Christian era in which the Western world now resides. Especially, mainline churches are struggling to keep their doors open as white flight and gentrification is coming home to roost. I didn't want to be a bishop if it meant that I was to play the role of a hospice chaplain waiting patiently for an irrelevant church to pass away. Malcolm summed up my situation quickly. Malcolm said to me, "Michael, you know too much to become a bishop."

In one of our spiritual direction sessions, I asked Malcolm why he didn't have the ambitions of a Gene Robinson to become the first openly gay bishop? I had met Gene Robinson before he became a bishop. It was at a clergy conference in which he was very articulate and gregarious. I had heard that he wanted to be a bishop, having participated in prior bishop elections. Not many at the time thought he would have much of a chance of becoming a bishop given his honesty as an openly gay priest. And yet, Gene Robinson not only became a bishop, but as Muhammed Ali said, he "shook up the world." Gene Robinson wasn't the first gay bishop elected in the Anglican Communion. He was the first openly gay bishop—that is, he was the first not to hide his identity while serving in a leadership position in the institutional church.

As Malcolm and I talked more about the institutional church, I slowly realized that without Malcolm there would be no Gene Robinson. The framework to have an openly gay bishop would never have been established apart from the groundbreaking spirituality of Malcolm. Robinson states, "Malcolm Boyd is a giant in our movement. Countless people who do not know his name owe him a great debt of gratitude. He and a few other brave souls paved the way for the lives we now lead. . . . We too stand on the shoulders of our forebears in this movement. And early on in that line marches Malcolm Boyd. I stand on his shoulders. . . ."[15]

So, I began to wonder about Malcolm. He certainly had the chops to head the institutional church. Not many knew better than Malcolm how to diagnose such an institution and then prescribe treatment. He was the kind of leader the institutional church needed. So, why hadn't Malcolm exhibited such ambition to become a bishop? Even Gene Robinson confesses, "Malcolm Boyd is not only a 'prophet in his own land,' he is a pioneer. For me, he is a hero, and although he's not all that much older than

---

15. Malcolm Boyd, *A Prophet in His Own Land*, 14–15.

I, he is an elder in the gay community to whom I owe so much for what has become my life."[16] Malcolm writes me this haunting message:

> Dear Michael: You brought up a "comparison" with Gene Robinson. Perhaps others have done/do so, too. Frankly, I never have. I have no feelings for him other than unconditional love, total support, clear understanding. There is not the slightest element of competition here for me. I'd rather not "go there" at all if that's possible.
>
> In all my life I never wanted to be a bishop. It just never occurred to me. Mine was so clearly and basically a prophetic ministry and/or a creative ministry. I knew that I would never fit into a bureaucracy, a formal and pragmatic structure. Mine was altogether something else. Paul Moore saw this and acted on it very, very early. I was ushered into a continuing prophetic-creative role when invited to become poet/writer-in-residence in Los Angeles. Bishop Fred Borsch was hospitable and welcoming, Kristi Wallace was an angel who set up writers workshops and always paved the way, and Bishop Jon Bruno established my work as an integral part of the Diocese.[17]

Malcolm said it was a different time in his own discernment of the institutional church, and the times were a-changing so drastically concerning what was religious as opposed to spiritual and political. Plus, Malcolm didn't have the time to jump through the hoops and the hazing processes of the institutional church to become a bishop. Malcolm meant what he said in the hungry i—"Are you running with me, Jesus?"—taking religion out of the buildings and into the streets.

Interestingly enough, Malcolm describes himself as quite secular. He finds in the secular more spirituality and life and, in the church, a debilitating deadness. Malcolm clearly finds Jesus in daily life with people instead of in religious structures or behind stained glass. Malcolm's place was not going to be in the institutional structure of the church; it has never been. The irony, in all of this, however was that I was interviewing Malcolm in the Cathedral Center—the heart of the institution called the Diocese of Los Angeles.

There are more ironies of Malcolm's relationship to the institutional church, especially affecting the Episcopal Church. One such irony is how an Episcopal priest negates Sunday morning. Malcolm is deeply irritated

---

16. Bo Young and Dan Vera, eds., *A Prophet in His Own Land: A Malcolm Boyd Reader* (Brooklyn, NY: White Crane Books, 2008), 13.

17. Malcolm Boyd, "More Date," e-mail message to author, September 8, 2009.

by what he calls the culture of Sunday morning—there needs to be deep changes in vision of who the people of God are and where they reside. As I have learned about Malcolm's life, I discovered that he was deeply wounded by church folks (arguably more than others). There were lasting repercussions on Malcolm's institutional church life as he abandoned institutional church leadership for about twenty years. "The institutional church seems so unlike Jesus," Malcolm told me. Jesus was as inclusive as you get, and yet the church fights inclusiveness. Jesus is as much in the prisons as in the suburbs. Malcolm gazes past me as he states, "You go to this jail downtown with men eighteen to twenty-five, all black incidentally, and the church doesn't know they are there."

In my spiritual direction sessions, Malcolm insisted that I see how the church has become so bureaucratic that there are only a few institutional experiments of hope. This was especially appropriate given that the American secular society had developed an ear better attuned to hope, having elected as president the author of *The Audacity of Hope*. "But we're [the institutional church] beyond experiments," Malcolm told me.

Much of the problem of institutional religion was rehearsed two thousand years ago—even by Jesus himself. Religious folk were criticizing Jesus for not practicing religion correctly, and Jesus replies, "No one sews a piece of unshrunk cloth on an old cloak; otherwise, the patch pulls away from it, the new from the old, and a worse tear is made. And no one puts new wine into old wineskins; otherwise, the wine will burst the skins, and the wine is lost, and so are the skins; but one puts new wine into fresh wineskins" (Mark 2:21–22). Many people in the institutional church wanted Malcolm to burn at the stake.

Malcolm recalls an instance in which he first realized the severity of how others saw him. In seminary he had fallen in love with a foreign student. They lay together on a cot in the darkness of their room and peered out their dormitory window onto the night scene of a long courtyard below in the center of an urban campus. Lying on their bellies, close together, they scanned the trees and lights like secretive night owls, shielded by the night. Malcolm slid his arm over Laurent's shoulder and nuzzled his neck. Laurent responded with an arm across Malcolm's waist that moved down to his buttocks. They were at peace. The door locked in enveloping darkness. Only the vaguest outline of Laurent's face was visible to Malcolm. Everything else "was touch and a presence of flesh."

Yet, even then, Malcolm became afraid as he and Laurent heard footsteps and voices in the corridor of their room. As the footsteps faded down the hall, they both exhaled but only Malcolm had the urge to giggle like a child

Malcolm in seminary.

playing hide and seek. Laurent, on the other hand, lay there, motionless. When he spoke, it was a whisper.

"You see that circle the driveway makes in the middle of the courtyard?"

"Uh-huh." Malcolm responded. "Hearing his voice, I felt I was about to be told a tale from the deepest of the Black Forest."

Laurent said, "I thought I saw a big stake there, sunk deep in the ground right in the middle of the circle. Around the stake were straw and sticks of wood. Men stood about the courtyard, holding burning torches, the light shimmering on their polished helmets. Then, out the door beneath the chapel, came the procession, chanting."[18]

And yet, in the midst of such an apocalyptic scene in which it seemed as if Death was coming as the grim reaper, there remains hope and vision. Perhaps such hope and vision is a natural recurrence for a young seminary student. Malcolm writes me about this season of his life in seminary:

> I look out upon a vista. I can see all sides of everything, a remarkable purity. I can hear everything, understand. It is a moment in suspension. I am in awe, want to hold onto it, just let it remain and be.
>
> It is like absolute perfection in a seashell, a sunset, or a rose. Nothing is lacking. I'm in perfect balance. For a moment I possess perfect knowledge. There is nothing in the way. I can look to the left or right and see eternity. I'm not scared at all. I feel at home and comfortable.
>
> This isn't a passive, bucolic kind of scene. I gaze upon the firmament—the leviathan—huge, giant formations are in slow, easy motion. It is breathtaking. Everything is perfectly synchronized in highly complex action. There is a clear intelligence. I am amazed when the moment holds. I simply move in, and with, it. My vision seems limitless. I can see beyond past, present, and future. These terms possess no relevance. My experience is an outpouring of complete, total, endless revelation. It is more than I can fathom. I just let it be and also

---

18. Boyd, *Take Off the Masks*, 87–88.
19. Malcolm Boyd, "New," e-mail message to author, November 23, 2009.

myself.[19]

Such visioning haunts Malcolm as he thinks deeply about the history of the institutional church. Not all that long ago, he knows there was an inquisition in the church in which anyone could be burned at the stake. Even now, Malcolm knows he could be burned at the stake by so-called Christians who think they are doing the very will of God. Malcolm is the black apocalyptic horseman because he reveals the deep divisions in the church in which many sheep are aimless and starving for spiritual nourishment. You can't really fix institutional religion just like you can't put new wine in old wine skins. Malcolm carries this message in his bones.

To get at our systemic institutional problems, Malcolm had a kind of sophisticated humor that disarms the old religion. Malcolm asked me, "Is the institutional church some tame way for us to talk about ourselves?" If so, Malcolm implied, we don't talk very well. We need a fresh approach to talk about ourselves as religious folks. One way to do this that I learned from Malcolm is not to take ourselves too seriously and even to laugh at

Malcolm celebrating AIDS Mass in Santa Monica Episcopal Parish on May 5, 1985.

ourselves. In this spirit, I remember hearing Garrison Keillor tells a joke about Episcopalians on his radio show *Prairie Home Companion*. "Why don't Episcopalians have orgies? Because there are too many thank-you notes to write."

There's something funny about religious folks who think they have a sole purchase on the institutional church. Malcolm and I recall many and ludicrous examples of religious folks pontificating on ultimate solutions while all along having no real intentions to make the world a better place. Malcolm laughs with his own distinct cadence as he tells these stories.

> We're praying for repentance
> God:
> Take fire and burn away our guilt and our lying hypocrisies.
> Take water and wash away our brothers' and sisters' blood which
>   we have caused to be shed.
> Take hot sunlight and dry the tears of those we have hurt, and
>   heal their wounded souls, minds, and bodies. . . .
> Take our imperfect prayers and purify them, so that we mean
>   what we pray and are prepared to give ourselves to you along with
>   our words.[20]

Because of the need to resuscitate a malnourished and dying church, Malcolm's spirituality is anti-establishment. Prayer couldn't only be said on red carpet among stained glass. In Christopher L. Webber's book *Give Us Grace: An Anthology of Anglican Prayers,* there is an account of how Malcolm got rid of "thees" and "thous" in the practice of prayer. Malcolm wanted the real language of people heard in families, bars, and coffee shops.

Naturally, there was backlash to Malcolm's Christ in Culture model of spirituality. Such a model is one in which God is not against the varied and numerous human cultures that sustain us all. Instead of Christ being against culture (e.g., missionaries requiring African converts to up on ties and eat with forks), Malcolm's model of Christ in Culture is such that God sees various cultures as having essential worth on their own terms and need to be respected as such in combination with Christian faith. In much of Malcolm's own Western culture, he often talked to me about learning to be patient with those who find it hard that God can love our particular cultures. Malcolm mentions here right-wingers attacking his

---

20. Boyd, *Are You Running with Me, Jesus?,* 103.

prayers and published articles. "I have to learn how to love them and the contexts from which they come," Malcolm said.

Attacks on Malcolm were so frequent that he stopped responding to them. The paradox here, however, is that Malcolm's spirituality has itself been institutionalized too. *Are You Running with Me, Jesus?* came out and institutionalized Malcolm. And then Bishop Paul Moore invited Malcolm deeper into the institutional church. Now he is writer-in-residence of the Episcopal Diocese of Los Angeles.

For many years Malcolm represented white Christian presence against racism and war before he came out of the closet with his gay identity. Earlier, despite not being out of the closet, Malcolm didn't feel unique for his civil rights work since there were other stalwart white Christian protestors like Paul Moore, Jonathan Daniels, and others. Later, what complicated Malcolm's life was a gay contingent who rejected Malcolm in his embrace of the church—ironically, now that Malcolm was the institution. Now he was the enemy for not being radical enough.

Malcolm reflects that being older gives him a much deeper perspective on what it means to be institutionalized. I applaud Malcolm for staying in those tensions of being both attacked by segments of the gay community and the institutional church. Being hit from both sides, Malcolm still disarmed what I call a Monty Python–esque church—that institutional religion that takes itself so seriously but everyone else laughs at.

Malcolm's strength is resilience. Being a senior citizen is its own kind of revenge. When it comes to Malcolm's enemies, I remind him of his longevity and that he has outlasted his enemies, this exacting its own kind of revenge. It is to such longevity that we move to end this book and discover the last apocalyptic rider of the Pale Green Horse of Death.

Black Horse

The third horseman rides a black horse and is generally understood as Famine. The horseman carries a pair of balances or scales, indicating the way that bread would have been weighed during a famine. These scales were of the type used to measure commodities for sale. The stress on the economy caused by a lack of supply will generate tremendous inflation as the costs for food rises. As the costs rise, human institutions begin to fall.

The apocalyptic vision is such that the cost of a quart of wheat rises to the equivalent of a day's wages, twelve to twenty times its normal price. The biblical vision of Revelation deepens the concept of a desperate famine through the failure of more luxurious commodities such as oil and wine. During a time of famine, it is those staple foods that demand high prices, but the loss of oil or wine is the loss of hope. People are spending all of their resources on these, and there is no demand for luxuries. One can imagine this scene in many apocalyptic, futuristic movies in which people easily trade their gold and silver for just a bit to eat. In such a vision, there is no longer sustainable institutional life.

Of the four horsemen, the black horse and its rider are the only ones whose appearance is accompanied by this strange agricultural detail. The Black Knight will use his scale to equally distribute a day's wage among nations with force. The developed world (the global north) often takes the luxurious food for itself, leaving hardly enough basic sustenance for everyone else. Of course, this is unsustainable.

Before we move toward the final apocalyptic rider of death, Malcolm, in this fourth chapter, rides the black horse called Famine **because he seeks to feed a starving institutional church who could no longer feed its people.**

In this famine Malcolm takes his role seriously as an Episcopal priest trying to be relevant both within mainline religion and outside of it. Ironically, others mock Malcolm and cannot take his "unorthodox" ways of being the church very seriously. Or, they are so offended that they revert back to the second horseman of war. I explored Malcolm's times and places as a priest, especially in the unusual circumstances of Malcolm serving with Martin Luther King Jr.and in fighting against the Vietnam War, including an arrest inside the Pentagon while engaged in a Peace Mass in a corridor. What was unusual was how such events occurred through Malcolm's identity as an Episcopal priest. One would think the church would be proud of such priesthood, but as we see in this chapter, the institutional church acted often out of a worldview of scarcity rather than a worldview of abundance.

Malcolm's identity as a gay white man remains a stumbling block for many, especially those in institutional religion. Malcolm taught me that all institutions are about self-preservation and perhaps this why he has been such an apocalyptic figure in relationship to what counts for religion today.

Although Malcolm rides the black horse, his intention is not to destroy but instead create by bringing us in touch with the mystery of God's knowing and loving. This is why Malcolm is a great storyteller and spiritual director. Destruction from the Black Knight was really the projection onto Malcolm—whether such a projection was gay identity being inherently evil or that Malcolm's politics were suspect in light of the perception of the one confronting them. So, Malcolm as Black Knight carries the same unintended consequences as Malcolm as Red Knight. There was never any intention to destroy anyone—even Malcolm's enemies. Instead, Malcolm told stories with characters like Father Art, hoping that those in declining institutional churches could at least think differently and openly. Malcolm's genius is in how he helps us catch a glimpse of our truer reality and contexts. And then to hold them up to God to transform and redeem. God can be frightening, however, because it is much safer to live in our own political constructs of reality.

When I was in third grade, in Mrs. Harris's class, she asked the question, "Who was talking?" It was simply a rhetorical question . . . the kind that all third-grade public school teachers ask, not expecting a response from anyone. For some reason, I had to respond, shocking both Mrs. Harris and myself out of the rhetorical framework of teaching. I raised my hand and made my confession, thereby disrupting Mrs. Harris's normal teaching method. I had to confess that I was talking because I made a decision for my eight-year-old self that if God exists, I would have to behave as if God exists, and behave in way in which all of my life was fully transparent to God. "I did it, Mrs. Harris." I confessed. And this confession turned out to be my repentance from ever throwing my candy wrapper to the ground when no one was watching . . . helping elderly people across the street in the absence of being rewarded by others . . . that I would now have to match my behavior to the reality of God. But little did I realize that my third-grade confession would have to be said over and over.

Malcolm as the Black Knight forces us to relate to the political, not just for current contentious issues such as collapsing economies, wars on terrorism, sexuality, racism, and church authority, but for the constant and ongoing crises for the church and the world. Our practices are ongoing because we inevitably live in a finite world in which we are forced to construct political and institutional worldviews.

The current tensions between the right and left, the rich and poor, those of color and those called white, women and men, homosexual and heterosexual, are not solved from a consensus of ideas, for such a consensus will never occur, but from spiritual practices focused on the flourishing of diverse peoples. Malcolm reminds us that reconciliation is the slow, arduous work of the Christian vocation that claims to embody the succession and memory of Christ in the world. A Christ who is not against the world but in it. This work of being Christ-like is not a quick fix, as two millennia obviously demonstrate. This work often involves discomfort and dis-ease. This slow, arduous work looks like Paul's need to remember that we are new creation. Paul writes, "From now on, therefore, we regard [remember] no one from a human point of view [or, according to the flesh (*sarx*)] (2 Cor 5:16)." C. S. Lewis helps live into this spiritual coaching when he writes:

> It is a serious thing to live in a society of possible gods and goddesses, to remember that the dullest and most uninteresting person you can talk to may one day be a creature which, if you saw it now, you would be strongly tempted to worship, or else a horror and a corruption such as you now meet, if at all, only in a nightmare. All day long we are, in some degree, helping each other to one or other of these destinations. . . . There are no ordinary people. You have never talked to a mere mortal. Nations, cultures, arts, civilizations—these are mortal, and their life is to ours as the life of a gnat. But it is immortals whom we joke with, work with, marry, snub, and exploit—immortal horrors or everlasting splendors.[21]

When we take each other for granted, Malcolm reminds us that one of the crucial questions in light of the decline of the Western institutional church is how do we practice reconciliation when those that need to be reconciled keep changing (e.g., Native Americans, African Americans, Jews, Gay and Lesbians, etc.)? I think the Episcopal Presiding Bishop Frank Griswold gave the answer to this question in opening comments of the Spring 2002 House of Bishops Meeting at Camp Allen when he said, "The ultimate work of reconciliation has already been done by God. Our task is the living into, re-calling God's work of reconciliation."

Instead of settling upon static definitions of the church, Malcolm proposes that we actually inhabit our spiritual practices instead of simply talking about them. Christian faith needs to be in coffee shops and even bars. Our worry, of course, is how to inhabit such practices that lead toward living more faithfully into God rather than our negative projections that move us away from God. Malcolm's spiritual direction to a famished church is that we learn to move out of our buildings and static ways so that when past, present, and future conflicts arise, we may be equipped to negotiate such conflict openly and even discover resolution.

This worry of how to inhabit or practice our faith should make us vulnerable and open to each other as we seek to respond to God's call to live

---

21. C. S. Lewis, *The Weight of Glory* (New York: Macmillan, 1949), 14–15.

into the divine work of reconciliation already accomplished but not fully realized. Ranjit Mathews (who works with the HIV/AIDS ministry in Cape Town) helps me explain this unconscious accomplishment of reconciliation through an e-mail he sent to me from South Africa:

> All [people] dream: but not equally. Those who dream by night in the dusty recesses of their mind wake in the day to find that it was vanity: But the dreamers of the day are dangerous, for they may act their dream with open eyes, to make it possible.[22]

Our task in practicing our faith is similar to the odd image of those who dream during the day with eyes wide open. Practicing faith is similar to day dreamers because to want to be a person of faith requires a vision past the present moment of bloodlust and revenge. To practice faith in a well nourished church is to develop the habit of seeing beyond the natural instinct of retaliation. To want such faith is to be as odd as those who dream with eyes wide open.

When we dream, we need only to let God be God in order to escape the famine of institutional religion. This may mean, however, the death of certain forms of institutional religion. Instead of growing weary in the face of such a death, I have learned from Malcolm not to conclude from the demise of institutional religion that life is bleak and deterministic. Appropriate to Malcolm's own character, there is an inherent optimism or hope even when facing the last horseman called Death.

---

22. Ranjit Matthews works in the social ministries office at St. George's Anglican Cathedral, Cape Town, South Africa. This quote was sent to me along with a liturgy that was used for the World AIDS Day Ecumenical Service held at St. George's Cathedral.

CHAPTER FIVE

The Pale Green Horse of Death

> I looked and there was a pale green horse!
> Its rider's name was Death, and Hades followed with him;
> they were given authority over a fourth of the earth,
> to kill with sword, famine, and pestilence,
> and by the wild animals of the earth.
> (Revelation 6:8)

The last horseman that Malcolm resembles is the fourth horseman, who rides on a pale green horse explicitly named Death, someone Malcolm increasingly contemplated. I asked Malcolm, "Do you think about your own death? What do you think death is?"

He gave an interesting response, "Death is absence. It's like a crowd of people moving along a street one day. The next day, a person is missing—is absent."

When Malcolm told me this, I began to wonder again about Malcolm's internal sense of accomplishment in his own magnificent life. For someone who became great and did so much, it was eerie to realize that he could think that he wouldn't be missed. It was disconcerting to see in Malcolm any perception that he was an anonymous person in the crowd. Malcolm writes me:

> Is anyone out there in the dark? There is no sound, sign, or word. I am afraid. The scene is like one in a murder mystery or *film noir*. I feel unease. Also a closeness to someone silent, watching, very near. I need to communicate. Why do I wait for someone to walk out of the

darkness into my circle of light to greet me? Why don't I leave the bright room and walk into the dark space?

Perhaps someone there fears me. Maybe I am the mysterious one. For both of us a meeting may be difficult. Yet I want to talk, eat, laugh, share, communicate with this alien, this person.[1]

It was surreal when a reporter from the *LA Times* called to interview Malcolm for his obituary. Malcolm suggested a few things to the reporter. First, it would be helpful to read a couple of Malcolm's books—as Malcolm explains to the reporter, "After all you must be busy with other people who are actually dying."

The more that I have meditated on Malcolm's life, the more I realize that I shouldn't feel disconcerted that even a great person struggles with death, like Jacob wrestling with an angel. And yet, Malcolm always seems to be victorious in the wrestling match. Even his doctor shows the victory as he praises this eighty-six-year-old's health (see pages 191–92).

As I pray that Malcolm has many more years to bless God's creation, I also realize the sobriety that death brings to all of us. Being an octogenarian must come somewhat as a surprise to Malcolm, given his adventurous life. Surely, especially during his days behind enemy lines in the civil rights campaign, Malcolm didn't think his life of longevity would turn out the way it did. And surely, Malcolm did not imagine this period of deep reflection as an elder when he was navigating his lonely way "out of the closet." I distinctly remember reading the apocalyptic tone in Malcolm's descriptions in his very early autobiography, *Take Off the Masks*. And yet, here we are—Malcolm a senior statesman in the church and in the human movement of freedom. Somewhere along the line, Malcolm cheated death. But how?

A black school teacher, Vivian Evans, was driving with Malcolm at night in Detroit in 1963 when she turned to Malcolm and said, "You can't ride with me because the police will kill us both." She meant racial animosity. This was also the time that Malcolm was writing *Are You Running with Me, Jesus?* when Andrew Goodman, Michael Schwerner, and James Chaney were missing in Mississippi. These three civil rights workers were eventually found murdered. Chaney was a twenty-one-year-old black man from Meridian, Mississippi; Goodman, a twenty-year-old white Jewish anthropology student from New York; and Schwerner, a twenty-four-year-old white Jewish Congress of Racial Equality (CORE) organizer and for-

---

1. Malcolm Boyd, "New," e-mail message to author, November 23, 2009.

> January 13, 2010
>
> Rev. Malcolm Boyd
>
> *March 13*
>
> Dear Rev. Boyd,
>
> Enclosed are the laboratory tests from the recent visit you made to my office.
>
> At the time I saw you; you seem to be doing quite well at 86 years old. Your back pain was stable. You did have some complaints of acid reflux and also, some urination complaints. On your physical exam, your blood pressure was normal at 136/72.
>
> The laboratory tests I have enclosed for your review and they reveal a cholesterol level that is a little higher than ideal with the LDL cholesterol of 148 and the non-HDL cholesterol of 167. These are the so-called bad cholesterols. However, you have very excellent "good" cholesterol, the HDL of 57. The other aspect of risk related to atherosclerosis is a marker of inflammation, the high sensitive C-reactive protein, which is a little high at 2.8. Given that atherosclerosis is an inflammatory disease, we use this marker of inflammation to further stratify your risk. Given your slightly high LDL (bad) cholesterol and this marker of inflammation, it might be prudent to have you consider taking a low dose of one

mer social worker also from New York. For Malcolm, these three young men symbolized the risks of participating in the Civil Rights Movement in the South during what became known as "Freedom Summer," dedicated to voter registration.

Indeed, this was a dangerous time. Malcolm was working in a lower-class white area when the phone rang. Someone breathed into the phone and no voice was articulated. This happens six times through the night.

Malcolm rides and domesticates the Green Horse of Death because of his deep spirituality in which he grew to no longer fear death—even to embrace it. One way to learn from Malcolm about death is to drink in his wisdom about how death operates in Western culture. Twenty-eight percent of Americans don't want a religious burial; Malcolm told me this is a new trend. Perhaps this is due to living in a post-Christian age. In one of

> Rev. Malcolm Boyd
> January 13, 2010
> Page two
>
> of the statin (cholesterol lowering) medications. These medicines are well tolerated and by lowering your bad cholesterol, you can prevent any plaque over time from rupturing causing an acute heart attack. This has been well studied in people in your age group and does have benefits. I think it might be worthwhile having you consider taking a low dose of one of the statins at bedtime.
>
> The rest of your laboratory tests are unremarkable. You have no evidence of leukemia or anemia, no diabetes, kidney and liver function are normal.
>
> Your thyroid test does suggest that you maybe developing the beginnings of diminished thyroid production. This is not uncommon when you get older and it is something we need to follow-up on and perhaps you will need to consider going on some replacement dose of thyroid at some point in the future.
>
> Your prostate cancer-screening test, the PSA is nice and low at .98.
>
> Your vitamin D level, which is very important nowadays, is normal at 37.
>
> So basically what I am suggesting is that you take a low dose of one of the statin medications at bedtime and also, come back in about two to three months and follow-up on your cholesterols and also, on your thyroid test. When you do come back, please do not eat anything so that we can repeat your cholesterol panel in a fasting state.
>
> If you have any questions, please contact me.
>
> Sincerely yours,
>
> MD
>
> Enclosure

our spiritual direction sessions, Malcolm revealed his wisdom that there used to be finality around death in Western cultures that would drive complex economic and political systems. Such complexities range from how parents are no longer socialized to pass along inheritance to their children to how our healthcare system finds it difficult to know when a person should be allowed to die. We live in a new culture negotiating death. It's hard to say whether this new trend around death has gained a stronger foothold given the economic meltdown of 2008–2009.

Malcolm's insights about death do not stay on macro-economic levels. They also apply to local and personal levels where worldviews form. For example, Malcolm's grandfather was an Episcopal priest who had five children. Family dynamics developed in such a way that it became impossible for the family to stay together after the early death of both parents. In some sense, there was a death in Malcolm's nuclear family. Malcolm's father was raised by the matriarch in the family. However, he was a rebel and ran away. Years later he set up a business with his brother.

In 1929 during the Great Depression, Malcolm's father lost everything. Up until Malcolm was eight, there was a great deal of money in the household, but then a stark reality hit Malcolm's family, similar to the narrative told in the story of the prince and the pauper. Along with the change in their financial fortunes, the uncommon occurrence for that generation occurred when Malcolm's parents divorced. Malcolm tells the deeply moving story of his childhood in which his parents brought him into a room. Malcolm sat on his dad's lap. "Malcolm," his dad said, "Your mother and I are getting a divorce. Choose which one of us you want to live with." Such a choice kills childhood. When Malcolm recounted this story to me in his office some eighty years later, there were still tears in his eyes. There are all kinds of death. Perhaps the death of childhood hurts the most.

Cheating Death

As I reflect on Malcolm's life, his work as a civil rights activist, anti-war protestor, and gay man, I often wonder how he has lived so long. A gay man fighting for black people in the Alabama of the 1960s would surely put anyone's life in danger. As I research Malcolm's writing, I realize that I am not the only one wondering how Malcolm navigated death. He writes:

> I don't want to die the deaths, but I have to.
> Even a refusal to die then becomes itself another death. Can't death be sweet? Why does a death hurt so badly? I must be broken open again, feel the fresh air sweep against my selfish desire for isolation, hear voices when I simply cannot, and touch flesh when I want no flesh.
> I shall be pulled, screaming, outside the ghetto of myself. For I must die to this self in order to live for others.[2]

---

2. Malcolm's typewritten notes in his Boston University archive.

We learn here a deep secret from Malcolm—a key not only to cheating death but to how to live life. The secret is that no one should die alone. Having cheated death, Malcolm offers twenty-first-century people deep wisdom that cheating death is simply the ability to live an authentic life not only for self but for others. We cheat death when we disarm the pretense and duplicity that disallow the living to truly live. Malcolm's apocalyptic life is such that he cannot tolerate life full of pretense. Of course, Malcolm had many peers who were fellow prophets with similar disarming personalities. In *Free to Live, Free to Die,* Malcolm wrote to a prophet dying old:

> You had mellowed, they all said, before you died. I questioned what I know they meant by "mellowed": Softened to the point of atrophy. Sold out for final honors. Quit keeping up with new thoughts, and, indeed, thinking them.
>
> I saw and heard you the week before you died. You were as exasperating as ever to everything in me that wanted to be complacent. You rubbed me the wrong way when you bore down, ungraciously, I felt, and with unneeded force, on some highly sensitive areas in my life. You tenaciously caught hold of some issues we just don't talk about, and you talked about them until I honestly thought my nerves might give way.
>
> In other words, you were as independent, strong-willed, arbitrary, fierce, unrelenting, uncouth, and saintly as always. You made my blood flow faster, nettled my slumbering conscience, opened up my caved-in thoughts, and dragged me outside my wall-to-wall-carpeted ghetto into involvement again. Involvement with raw sunlight, raw ideas, and raw commitments. Damn it, I wanted you to leave me alone, and I deeply resented you and your coming. When you forced me to look honestly at myself and my world, you hurt me, embarrassed me, shook me, enlightened me.
>
> Yes, you had mellowed. Your old anger was more suffused by loving. But the embers of old fires still burned me when, seeking comfort and release, I came too close.[3]

This powerful reflection by Malcolm relates to all of our encounters with those who coax out of us a better life. Prophets do that. I remember saying to Malcolm, "But you don't see many prophets dying old." He

---

3. Malcolm Boyd, "To a Prophet Dying Old," in *Free to Live, Free to Die* (New York: Holt, Rinehart & Winston, 1967), 89–90.

said, "It depends on what you mean by 'prophet.'" When someone cheats death, I believe you encounter someone with a new life who no longer tolerates duplicity and habits that produce superficial character. In many ways, Malcolm is just like any stalwart character who learned through peace and justice activism to relativize his own life in order to fit into a grander and much more meaningful pattern. Malcolm, like most John the Baptists, invariably failed at small talk.

Malcolm told me on several occasions how in simple social settings, at dinner or in casual conversations, small talk inevitably would quickly move to more authentic conversation that many find difficult.

Death sobers you up. It makes you think about important and real things—small talk is no longer relevant. To begin with, nothing can be resolved regarding racial, religious, and sexual identity until we move beyond small talk and pretense. This is Malcolm's stroke of genius akin to other exemplars like Desmond Tutu and the Dali Lama. Like them, Malcolm reveals our false lives and makes us pay attention to the often painful reality of authenticity. In so doing, there is a death.

Flirting with Death

One summer, when he was a kid, Malcolm was playing baseball with his father when a sense of finality overwhelmed him. The finality was the awareness of how different he was—how much he didn't fit into mainstream America. Perhaps this sense of finality made him relate to black people as comrades, those with unacceptable differences like himself. It is indeed odd that a white man of Malcolm's generation became such an advocate for black people. The norm of the day was simply survival of the status quo in which white people in the United States were holding onto a dominant culture. Although this may still seem controversial to some readers of this book, I liken Malcolm's generation of white people to the majority of United States citizens today who fail to champion the cause of about twelve million undocumented workers who reside in the United States. This too is about survival as many Americans see "illegal immigrants" as threats to their wage scale and job security. Lest a younger generation of white people today think they would be like Malcolm, fighting on behalf of black people, think again. The vast majority of Americans have a worldview in which they too are trying to survive. Malcolm concludes, "The point is that you do have to survive in a world hostile to difference."

I think Malcolm became his exceptional self with the death of his childhood. He had to grow up too fast. To compensate for being an oddity, Malcolm learned to write, to have a talent, even to make people afraid of him on occasion because of this newfound talent. High school and college were painful. In high school Malcolm knew about boys who beat up other boys, especially those considered "sissies," and he tried to avoid that. Even though Malcolm says he had to survive, what about having a martyrdom complex? "I was strong,"

Malcolm as choir boy.

Malcolm says. "There was a sense of destiny and absurdity. When you're odd, there is a sense in which you need to say 'fuck it' on occasion." There were others who felt odd in the United States. Their way of rebelling was simply to leave. For example, Malcolm alludes to singer Marian Anderson, an African-American opera singer (1897–1993) who left the U.S. in order to discover color-blind people in Europe. More recently, I heard David Sedaris give a satirical picture of such colorblind Europeans when he described his own life as an American in France. Sedaris said that Europeans may have started out color-blind until a critical mass of "others" accumulated on their own shores.

Another humorist, Wanda Sykes, applies the insight that racial relationships become all the more complicated when sexual orientation enters the picture. In one of her stand-up comedy routines, she starts out saying, "Change is hard." Throughout her performance, this phrase becomes her mantra, "Change is hard." "A lot of changes," Sykes tells the audience.

> I got married in California. I had to publically come out. After the Proposition 8 fiasco in California I had to come out. I was hurt. That night was crazy. Black president—yea! Oh, Prop. 8 passed—O shit.[4] Now I'm a second-class citizen. What the fuck? I was up here and now I'm back down here. Actually, I was lower. As a black woman I could at least marry, but as a gay black woman that's even lower. It's harder being gay than being black. There's actually some things that are harder than being gay. I didn't have to come out black. I didn't have to sit my parents down and tell them about my "blackness." . . . Mom, Dad, I have to tell you something. . . . I hope ya'll still love me. . . . I'm just going to say it. . . . I'm black. "What did she say? . . . O lord Jesus, she didn't just say that she's black. . . . Anything but black, lord . . . give her cancer, lord. You been hanging around black people and they have been twisting your mind." "No, Mom I'm just black." "What did I do? Was it Soul Train? I knew I shouldn't let you watch Soul Train." I think the problem most people have with homosexuality is the religion and they think it's a choice. Being gay is not a choice. If you believe it's a choice, then you're believing straight people are straight because they chose not to be gay. I'm sure a lot of straight guys in here on several occasions probably thought, "You know. . . I think I'm gonna suck a

---

4. Proposition 8 (or the California Marriage Protection Act) was a ballot proposition and constitutional amendment passed in the November 2008 state elections. The measure added a new provision to the California Constitution which provides that "only marriage between a man and a woman" is valid or recognized in California.

dick today." [Sykes crosses arms and then says,] "Naaa, I choose not to." It's great being out . . . everything out on the table. I am what I am.[5]

The humor of Wanda Sykes reminds us of how hard Malcolm's life must have been. The change that Malcolm was bringing to the world must have felt apocalyptic as he rode onto the national stage with his Pale Green Horse of Death. Malcolm represented the death of the status quo. He represented the death of mainline religion. He made many kinds of oppressed people (for example, black, gay, poor, et al.) realize that they could not sit on their laurels and wait for the oppression to simply cease. He was a thorn in the side of the white elite who wanted Malcolm to have manners and not expose their interior machinations.

In kind, Malcolm departed (died to) those institutions and bureaucracies that failed to accept his humanity. Malcolm became like Jesus in the sense of embracing death. For example, Jesus was led into the wilderness by the Spirit. In this wasteland, Jesus faced the devil who wanted Jesus to cheat death. Jesus refused. When Jesus emerged from this desert, he reformulated the meaning of death when he approached his cousin, John the Baptist. Now, for Jesus, death would be seen as the lens through which one can now see the way to a meaningful life. Similar to Jimmy Stewart's character in *It's a Wonderful Life*, Jesus taught the world to appreciate the deeper mysteries of life by dying to selfish desires. In short, Jesus called this "baptism," which literally means a dying (drowning) to self and rising of life now known through God's Son. I realize that many people do not realize these more specific teachings around baptism in Christianity. But Malcolm does. Malcolm's desert was racism. The Spirit led him to become a Freedom Rider for justice.

The Freedom Ride

The days of the Freedom Rides brought attention to a lack of voting rights for black people. White and black volunteers enlisted in the civil rights struggle awakened Malcolm's sense of humanity, yet the Freedom Rides exposed him to the possibility of death. Malcolm was in dire situations in rural Alabama when he traveled with three young black men from the Student Nonviolent Coordinating Committee (SNCC). They slowly discovered that they were behind enemy lines. Unfortunately, the enemies were not who most people would imagine because these enemies were church members, the police, and people in the power structure.

---

5. Wanda Sykes, "I'ma Be Me," HBO Standup Comedy, Warner Theatre, Washington, D.C., taped live in August 2009.

Malcolm prays, "Why do we play games with human lives, Lord? If we got down to the nitty-gritty, God, business of practicing integrity in political ethics, and decency in treatment of the poor and dispossessed, we would serve you far better than looking pious in public, wouldn't we, Christ?"[6]

When Malcolm and his fellow civil rights activists' car broke down with a flat tire, a car drove up next to them with guns. Malcolm was in the car with all black men. Alfred Hitchcock's classic film *North by Northwest* comes to mind for Malcolm as he tells me, "It was frightening beyond belief."

There was a meeting at Brown Chapel, called by Martin Luther King Jr. Malcolm sat next to Jonathan Daniels during the meeting. Tragically, Jonathan Daniels was murdered shortly afterward. Malcolm writes about

---

6. Boyd and Conrad, *When in the Course of Human Events*, 76–77.

Jonathan Daniels in "To a Prophet Dying Young." He delivers this eulogy again, some fifty years later at a Vince Guaraldi jazz celebration on April 12, 2009. Malcolm recites his poetry to me:

You would never want me to wish you peace.

As Malcolm recites his poetry, I realize that it is really a mission statement for Malcolm. I asked Malcolm, "How did you escape being Jonathan Daniels? I mean, why weren't you martyred?"

Malcolm pauses and the memories flood in, "In 1965 it was crazy, I don't know how I got through 1965." Jonathan had been arrested on a civil rights charge, as Malcolm had been. They led Jonathan out of jail and a white supremacist shot him. "I didn't realize how vulnerable we all were," Malcolm said.

Malcolm told me he never really healed from the events of 1965. The wound was this: Malcolm had prepared himself for death and was still alive. How does anyone come down from such experiences? Malcolm's life in 1965 was a rite of passage in which he faced death, his own and others. And again, like Jesus, he reemerged with a deeper sense of life. Malcolm's days of activism were deeply informed by this summer of 1965 in which he learned the meaning and value of life through the danger of fighting for civil rights in the Jim Crow South. When Malcolm emerged out of this wilderness experience, it was as if he, like Jesus, formally began his ministry—at least, Malcolm's public leadership emerged. One of the crucial means of such leadership was Malcolm's ability to write. Malcolm's writing was indeed informed by his rich life of courage and risk on behalf of those who didn't have a voice to be heard. Malcolm became another voice crying in the wilderness for justice and peace. Malcolm's voice would not be silenced.

In part, this biography grows out of Malcolm's powerful voice, still crying out in the wilderness. With my writing this biography, Malcolm told me it was like oil in water with a black writer on a white subject, a heterosexual male in his forties studying a gay octogenarian.

In Detroit and Washington, D.C., in the early 1960s, Malcolm clearly recognized the "differentness" of his white identity as he worked in civil rights. He asked church authorities to place him as a white assisting priest in two black parishes, Grace Church in Detroit and the Church of the Atonement in the nation's capital. This brought him into regular, ordinary contact with African Americans in ways that superseded physical and psychological barriers of race.

Black friends and associates started to appear in Malcolm's day-to-day life. In 1964 Malcolm met Langston Hughes when both men were guests of the Karamu Playhouse, an interracial cultural center in Cleveland. After appearing on the program at Karamu, both participated in a joint reading of their work in a black community center. Malcolm read page proofs of his book *Are You Running with Me, Jesus?* Malcolm was deeply moved by Hughes's reactions to the prayers. He praised them and (to Malcolm's delight) called them "poems." This gave Malcolm an altogether fresh look at his own work.

"Langston's belief in my work gave me a brand-new sense of purpose and motivation," Malcolm told me. "The beauty he saw in my prayers or poems illuminated me. I found Langston one of the warmest, most charming and sensitive, most generous and gracious men I ever knew. He had an astonishing and completely natural sense of humor. Langston invented charisma as few people have ever been able to understand it, low-key, not obtrusive. Quickly I realized how much persecution he had suffered racially and politically. This became evident during a long radio interview we did together when listeners were invited to speak directly to us and ask questions. Some addressed to Langston were quite brutal. Our time together touched my life."

Different parts of Malcolm's life began to come together in unexpected ways. For example, Malcolm attended the funeral of the black martyr Medgar Evers in Jackson, Mississippi, after the civil rights leader was shot and killed at his home. Malcolm reflected on how Evers's home reminded him of his own. This brought home how vulnerable life can be. All of this reminded Malcolm how a black man in Mississippi could somehow be connected to white gay man. The interdependence of seemingly disparate cultures, races, and persons helped Malcolm see how he could make a difference in the Civil Rights Movement, even as a gay white man. For a long time Malcolm remembered vividly the tall grass surrounding Evers's house in which his killer had hid.

Months later, in a working-class suburb of Detroit, Malcolm rented a small house in which to finish writing *Are You Running with Me, Jesus?* He sat at a typewriter. Behind him a large window looked out upon a field of tall grass. The dangerous irony of different, yet similar landscapes surrounding the home of Megar Evers and his own did not escape Malcolm's attention. Apparently someone in close proximity to the house had seen Malcolm arrive accompanied by a black friend. This triggered an immediate reaction of racism. Over several days the phone calls never ceased. Finally Malcolm felt he had to depart the house and finish writing his book in his Detroit apartment across the street from Wayne State University, where he worked as a student chaplain.

I discovered that during this period Malcolm began to feel black. Despite these frightening days, Malcolm tried to continue his writing. So you were living dangerously, I asked Malcolm. Malcolm responds, "I always have."

I asked Malcolm about being closeted as a gay man during those years. What happens to a person's soul who is closeted? Isn't there something surreal when Jesus tells someone to go into a closet and shut the door? Malcolm responds that for some people there has never been any reality except the prison of a closet.

> I sit inside my jail, Jesus.
> I constructed it with my own hands, stone upon stone,
>   lock inside lock.
> Here I am a model prisoner of my own will.
> Here I am the slave of self.[7]

Writing and Death

Malcolm was once referred to in the *New York Times* as "a balding Holden Caulfield," who was the major character in J. D. Salinger's monumental book, *A Catcher in the Rye*. Malcolm writes me:

> Today's press announcement of the death of author J. D. Salinger at 91 brings up a memory for me. Of course, he is best known for his classic *The Catcher in the Rye* and the character of Holden Caulfield, its 16-year-old hero. My connection with them both is a *New York Times* review of one of my books a number of years ago. The reviewer described me as "a balding Holden Caulfield." What, I wondered, did he mean? In the closing lines of *The Catcher in the Rye*, Salinger wrote: "Don't ever tell anybody anything. If you do, you start missing everybody." Generations of readers have responded to Holden Caulfield's ability to see through the machinations of the adult world, according to *Los Angeles Times*' critic David Ulin, who commented on Salinger's ability "to look at the intersection of mystical and secular culture, at the satisfactions of the spirit and of the flesh."

---

7. Bo Lozoff, ed., *We're All Doing Time: A Guide to Getting Free* (Durham, NC: Prison-Ashram Project, 1985), 103.

It seems to me you may like to integrate Salinger/Caulfield into our own discussion of the spiritual and the secular. And, perhaps you can figure out why the *New York Times* called me "a balding Holden Caulfield." All best . . .

P.S. Do you think I am?[8]

In 2009, Salinger died. Malcolm told me in one of our spiritual direction sessions that all of the J. D. Salinger obituaries brought Holden into a bright spotlight for him. It is an interesting comparison between a balding Holden Caulfield and an aging Malcolm Boyd. Except for the comment in the *New York Times*, I wouldn't have thought of the comparison. I was intrigued. Why had the *Times* compared Holden and Malcolm? To find out, I revisited *A Catcher in the Rye*.

Relaxing with books.

Obviously, many readers identify with Holden as a hero, especially in the wake of Salinger's death. Literary critics and Salinger experts observed how the discontent of Holden resonated with the discontent experience by others from many different backgrounds. Holden's vivid way of expressing his discontent is perhaps the window into comparing him with Malcolm. Like Holden, Malcolm resonates powerfully with readers who come from backgrounds completely different from his. Both Malcolm and Holden invite those from different backgrounds to inhabit their point of views. Most interestingly, instead of disparaging their more prophetic (even caustic) natures, readers rally to understand and even empathize with Holden and Malcolm.

Malcolm told me, "As a writer, you wonder at a point if anyone cares about your writing." For example, the book that Malcolm edited with Bishop Chester Talton on *Race and Prayer* seemed to garner very little interest and support. Malcolm was concerned about the possible death of this book that you are reading. We strategized about our "hook" and how to attract readership. What's important for this book is buzz, one of those books you hear about and must read. The more we're honest, the better

---

8. Malcolm Boyd, "New Material," e-mail message to author, January 1, 2010.

the book, we thought. It's so easy to lie. You lie at the dinner table, you lie at the business meeting; do you also lie in church? When you lie long enough, the truth seems impossible.

One thing readers of both Malcolm and Salinger can appreciate: their honesty.

From his formation as a writer, I learned that Malcolm can be brutally honest. I remember the later stages of writing this biography in which Malcolm gave me feedback on my writing process. Malcolm indicates below that he was surprised by what I wrote about him—that it could be so powerful. As Malcolm's biographer, I took that in two ways. On one hand, Malcolm could be thinking that he never had this opportunity to think so deeply about his own life. On the other hand, he could be indirectly sending me the message that he didn't have much confidence at first that I could pull off this biography. Malcolm wrote me:

Dear Michael:

Yesterday I had quite an experience. I went through—quickly, not methodically—the drawer packed with my news clips, writings, the whole history of my life and ministry laid out before me. It evoked lots of feelings. It was terribly disturbing at times in opening up the past, suddenly and without preparation. I felt as if an autopsy were being performed on me. I had to relive so many things. Go back to old feelings, old challenges, old crises, my "old" self (or selves).

You started with "celebrity." It so clearly delineates my life, the perception of my life, and my place in my age. There is the initial celebrity of Hollywood and Pickford. But it gets really complicated when, suddenly, as a priest and writer I am thrust into it again in a completely different way. I had no idea how vast, how deep, the scope of celebrity went. My life has been as much a mystery to me as to anyone else. It's taken so many twists and turns. Yet the basic truths were there at the very beginning and have not seriously changed.

You couldn't actually write this book without this collection of old materials. It is indispensable. Also it saves us thousands of hours of conversations (and my memory isn't as good as the memory of all these documents and papers). It seems to me you may want to start writing several of the designated chapters at the same time. It is, indeed, A WORK in progress. But nothing is isolated. Everything is linked.

In a sense you have "all" the material now! Yet the portrait needs to be completed. The film completed. The book completed. You haven't pulled it all together yet. I don't think you'll probably need to go to Boston to visit my archive at Boston University. There aren't many people who really need to be interviewed. (There are very few people still living who actually know me at all.) Yet I think there are secrets and mysteries contained in all these documents and papers . . . Is it your task to turn it into a whole, to make sense of it, to link it to many other things including the 20th and 21st centuries???

I need to let go of this material now and simply turn it over to you. Your questions in relation to it will be most relevant to the book. I was surprised at every turn in reading what you wrote. It's powerful. I was somewhat astonished and, finally, had to let it go. I don't know what else to say. I realize my "life," my "career," has taken its own direction quite aside from myself.

We're meeting next on Thursday, Aug. 13 at 1 PM. Maybe it's time to organize our time together a bit differently. (Could the key word here be "organize"?) As you've mapped the project, have you also defined it? If there is "hidden treasure," WHAT and WHERE is it? Since this is a dialogue, where are YOU continuing to find your place in it?[9]

For Malcolm, such honesty goes back to being the gay boy that made Malcolm open to becoming a writer. Malcolm couldn't share the status quo as a boy, constantly finding himself utterly rejected. He was an outlaw and knew that. How does this compare to Holden? Well, both Holden and Malcolm are honest and see themselves as outsiders; both see the conventional world as "phony." They do their best to find truth even if such a task may seem impossible.

While Malcolm was at a high school with glamorous girls and star football players, he worked on the newspaper's editorials his junior year. They announced the staff for the senior year and Malcolm was not on it—it was catastrophic because there was nothing else for Malcolm to plug into except his writing. He wouldn't be the jock who could throw a seventy-yard touchdown pass. He wouldn't be a gregarious alpha-male who had learned to score touchdowns.

It was inevitable for Malcolm to eventually realize that he was "queer" or an outsider. In many ways I tried to engage Malcolm with how this realization may have felt like a death. I, as a heterosexual, imagine that a person who honestly confronts the knowledge of his or her gay identity also acknowledges a death of sorts to one's role in dominant culture. Malcolm agrees and said all he could do with his own realization of sexual orientation was to continue to write. Malcolm wasn't treated very well as his school's journalist, but he did have a margin of restitution because he was

---

9. Malcolm Boyd, "Da Book," e-mail message to author, August 4, 2009.

Malcolm with too many books.

the *Denver Post's* correspondent for his high school. Malcolm's byline frequently appeared in the *Post* and he won honorable mention in one of the journalistic essay contests. Mary E. Lowe was the faculty person at Malcolm's high school in which he submitted another essay. Malcolm gave Miss Lowe his paper, but she said his writing was inadequate because she didn't smell the sweat and didn't see the blood in his writing (which was on the theme of the American Revolutionary War). This was one of those do-or-die situations for Malcolm. "I rewrote the whole paper," Malcolm told me. He submitted the paper fifteen minutes before the deadline. Well, he ended up winning the contest. Winning the contest motivated Malcolm to keep writing. One can even say that such motivation for writing stayed with Malcolm all of his life.

What was it about writing that kept Malcolm motivated? Perhaps a writer cheats death in some way through writing. Maybe, a writer finds in writing a vehicle to float on the river Styx through Hades to the other side. This may also be the bridge from which comparison between Holden and Malcolm makes sense because both characters fought to break out of their hells—their deaths. To this end Malcolm became more appreciative of his writing teachers. Male pride prevented appreciation at the time for Miss Lowe, but "she is a saint of our time," Malcolm said with a gleam in his eye.

There were other major influences on Malcolm's writing. One was a professor at Union Theological Seminary who spent a lot of time with Malcolm and cautioned him, as a writer, "You can't have four ideas on a single page."

Malcolm's life as writer is prolific. Malcolm explored many genres, from playwright to poet. He wrote powerful short pieces like his *Christian*

Century articles in 1964. He was a columnist ("Blind No More") in the national African-American newspaper *The Pittsburgh Courier*. Malcolm also wrote several memoirs. One that stands out in his mind is: *As I Live and Breathe: Stages of an Autobiography*. Another is his gay coming-out book, *Take Off the Masks*. Malcolm performed his plays night after night in Detroit coffeehouses. In one play, Malcolm was a black shoe shine boy. It wasn't subtle, he told me. It was called *Boy* and, in it, Malcolm shined a white man's shoes. *Study in Color* was more sophisticated and still stands up to Malcolm's high scrutiny.

Recounting how his writings and performances affected many people, Malcolm tells me about one of his 1965 performances one evening scheduled for 8:30. He and the entourage sped along the highway toward their destination, but the odds seemed to be against them. It was 7:30, they weren't within miles of town, and four cops were trailing them.

Those headlights shining back there on the dark, menacing, swamp-lined highway seemed out of a romantic old Bogart movie. Yet they realized with clammy discomfort that they were indeed as real as any other part of their incongruous situation. They were in Mississippi, and it was July 1965.

Under the sponsorship of the Student Nonviolent Coordinating Committee, Malcolm was touring Mississippi, Alabama, and eastern Arkansas giving readings from the works of black writers and from his own plays on racial themes. He performed for rural black audiences in freedom houses, churches, and community centers. Four young African-American men, the Freedom Singers, traveled with Malcolm. Their audiences were as integral to their programs as the actors were. They were all part of the Deep South cycle, the Mississippi drama, and the Alabama Passion Play.

Miraculously, there was a performance that night as scheduled. An audience waited in a haggard, flea-bitten cavern that was the "Negro theater." The owner was white. He had been told by local civil rights workers that their performance would be a "cultural event" without racial connotations. So, instead of the usual B-film, Malcolm and his audience were present that night inside the seedy hall which, with its ancient red plush seats, seemed to be a huge mouth from which all the shiny clean teeth had been extracted, leaving only empty space and blood-red cushy holes.

Malcolm was on stage before the all-black (with the exception of the white owner) audience. The Freedom Singers had sung four selections. The weary, weary crowd had begun to respond to them . . . "Oh, freedom." "This . . . little light of mine." "Whadya want?" "Freedom."

"When?" "NOW." The theater owner was becoming visibly agitated. He stood up, walked to the back of the theater where he used a phone, and remained standing there, smoking intently, observing the rest of the performance with the air of a Madrid censor in Franco's Spain. Time was short and working against us. "We're here for freedom," Malcolm explained. Malcolm told something of what it meant to be a white man in the freedom movement of African Americans; one had the seesaw experience of being called, in one moment, "a white nigger," and in the next, "a white devil." There were laughs. Suddenly, everyone in the theater seemed to acknowledged a relationship. The theater owner was fighting it, but Malcolm experienced it, too.

"How many of you know the name Richard Wright?" Malcolm asked. A few hands were raised. "It's important for us to know black writers . . . Richard Wright, for example. . . to understand what is their experience and what they are saying." Malcolm read from Wright's short story "The Man Who Went to Chicago."

After another freedom song, Malcolm asked: "How many of you know who Ralph Ellison is?" Hardly any hands came up. Malcolm told them about Ellison. Malcolm said it seemed important for Mississippi to know about Harlem, and for Harlem to know about Mississippi, and Malcolm read the Harlem funeral scene from Ellison's book *Invisible Man*. A pin, had it been dropped, would instantly have been heard inside that old theater.

Soon Malcolm donned a black mask to perform his one-act play *Boy*. One of the Freedom Singers put on a white mask. The audience had to work hard to try to make difficult adjustments. What right had a white person ("white nigger" or "white devil") to become an African American? How could a white person possibly know how an African American feels?

The audience roared in response to the lines. The theater owner tried to stop the performance, but the people decided it would be completed. Cries rose and filled the theater, then ceased as abruptly as they had begun. The man on the stage slowly stood up. He was human and white, white and human, and he had been playing an African American. The applause in that old Mississippi theater rose in a giant roar and sounded like Broadway or London.

The theater owner was clapping his hands in a staccato movement against the people's applause, and he shouted in counterpoint to the roar: "The performance is *over*, you must *leave* immediately, quickly, *get out*." But it could not be stopped. The crowd and performers clasped hands. "We Shall Overcome." The words were shouted, the music starkly simple. Inside that Mississippi theater it was a hymn, a creed, a shared public statement of intention and solidarity.10

Malcolm has taught me a lot about writing. Writing is lonely. Malcolm writes in the morning around 6 AM and writes in a disciplined way. Malcolm says, "You have to summon the inspiration. The best writing was really in the disciplined way, not when one feels inspired." After his morning writing, he may then use the late afternoon for editing. Of course, there are those seasons of more intensive writing for two or three weeks when a deadline looms large. You can't live like this for an infinitely prolonged period without a break.

Malcolm frequently integrated his writing with music. When I attended Malcolm's performance of his prayers, accompanied by jazz music at Los Angeles' Jazz Bakery on Easter 2009, I learned this firsthand. Writing and performing with musicians have keen similarities in terms of the "high" experience from being with an audience. Both writing and performing provide a "high." Although the writer does his or her craft often in isolation, those who are successful form an audience in which they feel the triumphs and failures. The good writer knows when the character in the story takes a life of her own. Such knowledge comes from the intuition of knowing the audience for whom the character is coming alive.

Four days after Malcolm's performance that my wife and I attended, I had a spiritual direction session with Malcolm, following our weekly pattern of meeting on Thursdays at 1:00 PM at the Cathedral Center.

I remember in this particular spiritual direction session talking to Malcolm about listening to music as a normal habit in my own writing process. "Do you feel as though music does something to you?" Malcolm asks. I told Malcolm I was raised by a mother who was a professional musician. When I was four years old, I was carted off to hear a symphony orchestra play Poulenc, or I would be subject to my mother's piano recitals that seemed at the time to last for eternity. My whole family is musical, from my father who could sing like Pavarotti to my two sisters, one with a master's degree in music, to the other winning beauty pageants with her voice, to my distant cousin, opera star Kathleen Battle. As I searched for my own musical talent, I would always joke that I carry the recessive gene for music, and that my three children would take over the

---

10. "A Performance," from Malcolm's archive. Malcolm gave this to me with his handwritten note, "These are 'Short Stories'—anecdotes, bits of memory that you might wish to place here and there as illustrations."

musical lineage. Increasingly, however, I have discovered that writing is my way of making music.

Malcolm recounted to me that after the two shows at the Jazz Bakery, he felt quite drained. "How do you come down from intense performance?" Malcolm asked. If you're always doing these kinds of intense performances, many people no longer know how to regulate normal life and they get into drugs or alcohol. Many lack the maturity to stand outside of their celebrity experiences and see them for what they really are. When they become conscious about celebrity, they are only drained further.

Coming down from an intense experience is not only a problem with musical performers. This happens as well with clergy. After a significant sermon, I can't easily come down. Malcolm gains this wisdom from his own period of life of celebrity. Often times Malcolm would experience intense speaking engagements with several thousand students as an audience. He would then be taken to a motel room to sleep and then have to fly back home. Then do it all over again. When you meet new people, you need a reservoir of energy. Constantly there was yet another impersonal motel room, then another dinner in Malcolm's honor that a committee had been working on all year. And one has to come down the night before.

Not all of Malcolm's performances were successful or at least seemed to be. A black Episcopal priest invited Malcolm once to a school where student attendance was required, which is a different ballgame. There seemed to be endless situations in which students raged against the machine for being required to be there to hear him. The students were unruly but Malcolm refused to entertain them; in fact, he extended an invitation to leave for those students who wanted. Half of the students left. Now, communication could occur with students who chose to stay. It all worked out in the end because Malcolm said, "A deeper communication on the issues of the day occurred with more of an intimate small group." Malcolm could have "performed," but didn't. He responded to the hopelessness of forced religion and offered the caged bird freedom. Malcolm probably did something irrevocable to that school. A system of forced religion probably died that day.

Adiaphora

Few of us take advantage of our elders' wisdom. One of the key aspects of Malcolm's wisdom is that he has a better perspective than most about what is essential in life. To get at what I mean and why Malcolm's life is so important to all of us, I need to talk theologically for a moment. *Adiaphora* comes from the Greek (ἀδιάφορα "indifferent things"). It is a concept used in Stoic philosophy to indicate things outside of moral law. *Adiaphora* is a helpful concept in the culture wars concerning sexual orientation and identity. For example, sexual orientation is neither morally mandated nor morally forbidden. Scripture passages used by the early church were focused upon discrete acts of perversion mostly in the disproportionate power structures between men and women or between men and boys. These scripture passages were not talking about committed, monogamous relationships between the same sexes. Somewhere along the way, the church and world has decided to make sexual orientation a line in the sand by which people should declare which god they will serve. Malcolm's life is helpful to showing how the needless war over sexual orientation and identity can be avoided.

Adiaphora in Christianity refers to matters not regarded as essential to faith, but nevertheless as permissible for Christians or in church. This relates to matters of death in that *adiaphora* signals the death of everything that is not essential. It wakes a person up to their "bucket lists" and what really matters in life. What is specifically considered *adiaphora* depends on the specific theology in view. New Testament examples of *adiaphora* are often cited from St. Paul's First Epistle to the Corinthians. Some of this epistle was written in response to a question from the Corinthian Christians regarding whether it was permissible for a Christian to eat food offered to idols. In response, St. Paul replied:

> Food will not bring us close to God. We are no worse off if we do not eat, and no better if we do. But take care that this liberty of yours does not somehow become a stumbling block to the weak. (1 Cor 8:8–9)

The *adiaphora* (eating food offered to idols) is based upon the motive and end of the doer. In this sense there are no *indifferent* things.

The issue of what constituted *adiaphora* became a major dispute concerning whether a Christian could be a homosexual. Here the question becomes: Should the church split over a gay bishop? Is being gay an essential category of faith by which salvation is known? How you answer this question depends on your understanding of *adiaphora*—what are those things essential to faith?

Perhaps clarifying the meaning of *adiaphora* is what Malcolm has taught me most in spiritual direction. He has taught me to delve into essential matters—God's kingdom, kindness, family, integrity. Hopefully, this book has also taught the reader to apply the meaning of *adiaphora* to your own life. What is essential to why you are on this planet? Where Malcolm is vital in answering this spiritual question is in how he doesn't let us stay in the self-indulgent tangents of the culture wars. The Episcopal Church had an image of being an elitist church. I asked Malcolm to respond to all of this. Malcolm states, "It's strange. Yesterday I was alone and rummaged through my own life preparing for a screening of Ingmar Bergman's film *Wild Strawberries,* a painful movie, very reflective, a look backward at one's life."

Malcolm remembered being a boy in Manhattan again with his parents. "I was thinking, reflecting about them. They were clear, like a cinematic scope." Painful memories of childhood emerged. This act of remembering became more and more unpleasant as he rapidly moved through his life.

Malcolm's coming of age occurred in middle school. The emotional burden of concealing his sexual orientation took a great toll on someone young like Malcolm. As Malcolm grew older, reaching out to anyone by sharing his sexuality was crazy because in a sense Malcolm wasn't in a drawing room but in an alley. There was no safety in public honesty concerning his sexuality. He could only reach out to those who shared his context and struggles, and, as a result, an element of lower self-esteem set in. This was painful, confusing. If you're looking for love and someone says you have no right to love or that God hates faggots, then the soul is confused as to what indeed is *adiaphora*—what is nonessential or essential to faith. Here, I began to think about the pivotal scene in Malcolm's life when he fell deeply in love for the first time with a European monk, whom he thought he'd never see again. At the time, Malcolm was in Europe attending a conference with other promising young theologians. "It's everyone's right to find love," Malcolm told me.

As both Malcolm and I were looking back over his life, I asked Malcolm whether the European monk was sort of like Dante's Beatrice. "We're all who we are," Malcolm responded. This was a way of not answering my question, I thought. I did gain the insight that this monk was vulnerable with Malcolm and that it was the first romance of Malcolm's life. There was a period when they could be together, when the monk came to study at an American seminary. It was like heaven until they realized that they could not remain together. Malcolm put it this way, "The bill had to be paid, and the realization was that there was no future. It was heartbreaking."

I asked Malcolm, "Perhaps this is the ultimate way any of us learn what is essential in life—our hearts have to break first." Interestingly enough, it was while in this state of brokenness that Malcolm becomes famous through his writings, which allowed him to look for love in different ways. Malcolm doesn't know if most find love. "Love is a matter of perspective isn't it?" Malcolm didn't feel as though he was loved as a child although he's sure his mother loved him. As we have this conversation, something comes to Malcolm's mind. Malcolm has a hard time finding one of his own books on the shelf and turns to me and says, "Don't write this many books."

Malcolm finds the book he is looking for and reads an excerpt. Malcolm reads, "I loved you in a fresh urgent world. I can do this when you are with me. . . . I had to invent a new world."

As Malcolm reads, tears well up in his eyes. I realize that he is not just reading a book he wrote; instead, he is reliving an episode in his life. This was a day of melancholy for Malcolm as he recalls, "It is foolish to speak of wholeness. Everyone is fragmented." Later I discover the full quote and the deeper context.

> I loved you in a desperate, fresh, urgent way once. You know this. You remade my world, as if it had been clay. I could live in the new world you let me see. But I could do this only when I was with you. When I could not be with you, that world was just a dream for me. Do you understand this?
>
> When we could no longer be together, and it was necessary for us to become separated (worlds away), I couldn't walk back into the old world I knew. I couldn't function in the one you had shown (given?) me.
>
> So there had to be a new one. This is what I have never been able to share with you or tell you about. That new world. And what can I say about it now that will really describe it, or myself in it?
>
> The new world held a number of fulfillments for me. It was a terrain I had to discover and explore by myself. I had no maps and often no sense of direction. I trusted certain people who hurt me when they betrayed this trust. (Of course, I must have hurt and betrayed them, too.) Yet I knew there must be risks in everything, especially in relationships.
>
> We lived, holding one another in an arrested state of being. I could only assume the crises and decisions, the sadnesses and fulfillments, within your life and never know them. But I wanted to know them. It was the desire for this knowing which I had to relinquish. I finally did.
>
> I love you. What that means, now, for us, I cannot be sure. It is just that I speak to you from my heart. What is my heart? It is where I feel the most tender things, where my life is touched by an ultimate sensitivity. Here, in my heart, I love you. I feel your life tenderly. I am rawly sensitive to your existence. I am not whole without you, so have never been whole.

It is foolish, though, to speak of wholeness. Everyone I know is somehow fragmented, a creature of memory, fulfilled and not fulfilled, torn into pieces of time and suddenly, in short moments, glued together. So I am not feeling sorry for myself. In fact, I am aware how, if our lives had not been separated, there would not have been this strange wholeness of which I am now speaking.

It is just that there would have seemed to be more wholeness. There would, indeed, have been *more* wholeness. So there it is.[11]

Mark Thompson

Malcolm brings me to where he thinks there is "something essential" and something that defies death-in-life? This *adiaphora* is known in his relationship with Mark. It's ironic that I learn about Malcolm's relationship with Mark through Malcolm's deep reflection on his own writing. This is ironic since Mark is also a writer. Malcolm writes me:

> Dear Michael: I felt I should reread both *As I Live and Breathe* and *Take Off the Masks* over the weekend as a way of working with you. The first is excellent, especially on details. Well written and (especially) edited. The second is not so good on those terms, but migawd [my God], how stunningly honest it is. (Was I being naive or vulnerable, or both?)
>
> R. W. B. Lewis's foreword to *As I Live and Breathe* is perhaps the nicest thing ever written about me. My year at Yale (1968–69) is significant. Kindly offered because of "fame" or then-celebrity, it gave me a chance to escape celebrity (disappear behind ivy-covered walls) and enter a time of reflection and reexamination. Norman Mailer and I became friends there. I wrote my weekly column for the *Yale Daily News*.
>
> Reading these pages again, I realize how seriously I was apparently attracted to the monastic life in 1953 (when I spent the summer at the Mt. Calvary Retreat House of the Order of the Holy Cross in Santa Barbara) and 1959 when I visited Taizé. There is an undercurrent here which may be revealing.
>
> Before I met Mark in the early '80s, I experienced (as you know) a time of emotional upheaval and wondering where did I "belong." After I met Mark and when we were "dating," I wrote him this letter which I just discovered in an old book. (Nothing like an old book in our lives, is there?) It might be relevant:

---

11. Malcolm Boyd, *Book of Days* (New York: Random House, 1968), January, 2–3.

Dear Mark,

I missed you very much Friday night, darling, and didn't know exactly what to do with my feelings, so got smashed quite pleasantly. Luckily I was at Robert and David's where I was spending the night, so, after beating them at three consecutive games of UNO (which I don't remember), I fell into bed and slept until mid-Sat. morning, which was healthy and good.

Then, I drove downtown, parked, and walked and walked and walked and walked and walked, and walked, and walked.

The child in me played, sang, danced, celebrated being in the city. I had cappuccino at "the place," Vitamin C drink in the Latino market, found you flowers at a great florist's, bought new shoes (at a very nice sale). It was a wonderful day . . . sun shining, a cool breeze, lots of clouds. Found your card (which you'll find by the flowers near the fireplace) at a pleasant Japanese shop. Went to the roof of the new Otani hotel for a while, lovely waterfalls. (Would like to take you there for a long, quiet, sensuous brunch some Saturday.) Actually, I did everything downtown, even ate a chocolate cookie, climbed up stone stairways, found secret corridors in great buildings, looked at beautiful new buildings reflected in each other's shafts . . . lovely . . . .

I am delighted you had a great vacation in San Francisco, including that great party at which you were so justly honored by friends, peers, associates, et al. Welcome back to the city of the angels. Everybody here is an angel, even including

yours truly,
m.

That's it for now. All best—Malcolm[12]

On the morning of one of our spiritual direction sessions, Malcolm told me that Mark had a violent reaction that morning to some medication. What can you say in the face of a loved one who suffers? This is an extremely deep question because it points to Malcolm's most honest and full relationship with his partner, Mark, who has had HIV/AIDS for nearly thirty years. Malcolm sends me one of his pre-release columns for Episcopal News Online.

Mark, my partner of twenty-six years, has had AIDS these past three decades. Originally from San Francisco, he is of the generation who

---

12. Malcolm Boyd, "New," e-mail message to author, December 14, 2009.

caught the disease before it was politically identified. Lucky for him, his timing was propitious for AIDS medications which permitted life to continue instead of being terminated early. Mark's fifty-ninth birthday will occur next August.

As a result of Mark's health span, I have unexpectedly lived with AIDS, too, during these twenty-six years. I've learned it is an up-and-down condition. In other words, there are good days and bad days. Certainly there are psychological factors. Sometimes the medicines prescribed (the meds) create new problems of their own. These may require altogether new treatment. Difficult side effects like vomiting and diarrhea appear. Fatigue is a big factor. In my opinion, Mark has often appeared somewhat saintly under adversity, combining his natural good humor with patience and sheer guts.

Yes, there are certain moments when I find myself quite lost. What can I do? (For God's sake, what am I supposed to do?) Over the long haul I've learned to be helpful, a good listener, get myself out of the driver's seat, and have as much faith as I can. Once I remember Mark was explaining to me how he felt, and it wasn't very good. "If I can't tell you about it, Malcolm, whom can I tell?" Precisely.

Both of our lives have slowed down. We don't rush as much as we used to do. Acceptance is the big word here. Everyone needs to practice acceptance in a wide variety of ways. We simply don't have any kind of absolute control over life, including the living of our own. Every day brings a new mystery, a fresh set of situations and problems. In my opinion this ushers in fresh adventures. Isn't it best to remain open to these?

Mark prays a lot. So do I. He is Buddhist. We don't talk much about religion outside of routine church gossip, which can be fun and amusing. Mark has played a significant role in the formation and workings of SOS, the Society of Spouses. Under the leadership of Mary Bruno, its membership comprises spouses of clergy in the Diocese of Los Angeles. Formerly this would have comprised women married to male clergy. Now, of course, it includes men married to female clergy. Also it comprises same-sex spouses of gay and lesbian clergy.

Sometimes Mark is Mom of our household, at other moments he is Pop or whatever the equivalent of that is. At other times I am either Mom or Pop. We share everything, including close friends, paying bills, visiting museums, finding exciting new films, suggesting new ventures and avenues, and even a late afternoon dry martini in front of our fireplace. Our senses of humor are highly compatible. However, I've noticed that we tend to read quite different kinds of books. One ritual we share is buying the Sunday edition of the *New York Times* when it appears on sale at Gelson's market around 2 PM on Saturday afternoon. For a couple of hours we are glued to the *Times*, absolutely absorbed in its contents, ranging from Maureen Dowd's column to the Arts section, from Travel to Books.

Speaking of books, Mark and I are both writers. Simply being a writer is complicated. Having two writers in one family is even more so. Always when I've written something new, my immediate need is for Mark to read it and tell me exactly what he thinks of it. The same seems to happen whenever Mark has written something new. I feel he is inevitably on target in his analysis or criticism of my work. Mark and I are not competitive, period. We've never been. On the other hand, we're extremely supportive of one another.

We met quite by chance. It's kind of a miracle that we met at all. Our backgrounds and lives had been altogether different. We dated for a couple of years. Mark felt we shouldn't rush into anything. I agreed. So our gradual coming together became a natural process. We sealed our troth in a favorite restaurant when I gave him a ring. It seemed the most logical thing in the world.

But where would we live? We found our dream house and worked two decades fixing it up. A highly interesting aspect of our relationship is that we are thirty years apart in age. This has worked out well because Mark, the younger partner, is essentially an old soul. On the other hand, I never had a genuine childhood, so probably am having mine now. We met when Mark, who was a writer and editor for *The Advocate* in the Bay Area, flew down to LA to interview a renowned gay couple, writer Christopher Isherwood and his partner artist, Don Bachardy, for the magazine. They were thirty years apart in age also. We've always felt a close sense of kinship with them.

The future? Who knows? Both Mark and I live very much in today. In the moment at hand. AIDS has taught us to do that. I am deeply grateful for this great lesson.[13]

In their life together, Malcolm's and Mark's work include books, film-making, poetry, photography, journalism, education and religious re-visioning. While each became a pioneer in the gay liberation struggle in their own right, Malcolm and Mark believe their intergenerational rela-

---

13. Malcolm Boyd, "Living 26 Years with AIDS," pre-release for Episcopal News Online, March 1, 2011.

tionship of twenty-seven years is a crucial aspect of their witness to "gay spirituality."

Mark worked for twenty years as an author, editor, and photographer. He was involved in various capacities for the national gay and lesbian news magazine, *The Advocate*. Before ending that vocation, he published his acclaimed volume *A Long Road to Freedom: The Advocate History of the Gay and Lesbian Movement*. A subsequent work was his acclaimed trilogy—*Gay Spirit, Gay Soul,* and *Gay Body*—which he completed in 1997. He also published *Leatherfolk: Radical Sex, People, Politics and Practice* in 1991.

Mark and Malcolm were both invited on Sunday, September 13, 2009, to the Gay Academic Union celebration in Berkeley to honor Mark's work of photography, "Fellow Travelers: Liberation Portraits." Malcolm graciously gives me the transcript of his remarks for the evening.

> Twenty-five years. Twenty-five years is a long time, a big chunk out of one's life. It is how long Mark Thompson and I have been together as lovers, mates, spouses, and partners. What an adventure. Two writers, two gay men, one from Manhattan, the other from Northern California. One an Episcopal priest for 55 years, the other the author of the bible of gay spirituality, *Gay Spirit.*
>
> The concept of an archive has always been one of great interest to me. Boston University asked me for mine in May 1970. I've loved that experience. Boston pioneered the idea of the living archive. In other words, ask for the archival material while the person is living. Don't wait until families and others burn and destroy what is left of someone's legacy because they fear it and label it as incriminating.
>
> At Boston I've been grateful to share space with a fascinating assortment of people ranging from Martin Luther King Jr. to Bette Davis. My own archive is actually situated next to that of Irene Mayer Selznick, the daughter of L. B. Mayer, wife of David Selznick, and producer of *A Streetcar Named Desire*. So, on snowy nights in Boston, I suppose Irene and I—in a sense, in our adjoining archives—might be construed as snuggling and gently sleeping together.
>
> But really, Mark and I snuggle and sleep together every night in our romantic, beautiful home in Silver Lake. Two writers together! Can you imagine?
>
> I've been present for all Mark's books. The exciting, groundbreaking *Gay Spirit* in 1987. Thank you, Mark, for asking me to write a piece for it. Then, seven years later, *Gay Soul* came along in 1994. I found it exciting to be a part of the concept and execution. In 1991, *Leatherfolk,*

Malcolm and Mark.

a highly influential book, appeared. In 1997 Mark completed his trilogy with perhaps his most original work up to then, *Gay Body*. Somewhere along the line, his massive book *Long Road to Freedom* peeked out at the daylight in 1994.

So we've been busy, Mark and I, in our sleepy Southern California cottage. I wouldn't have missed any of it for the world. What's next? I have no idea except to wait for the next moment. We've always done that. But, of course, Mark's new book, *Advocate Days and Other Stories,* is at the printer and will be in our hands in the next few days.

How can I explain the man I love? I can't. Yet he's really quite uncomplicated, a naturally gentle soul, a promising, hardworking

American boy who became a beautiful man. The bottom line is: Dear, I love you very much. And I love being with you in an archive.[14]

I interviewed Mark on a cool day in Los Angeles, on December 3, 2009. This was the first time that I had visited Malcolm's home, indeed a beautiful cottage set in a vertical labyrinth in which the pilgrim seeks a home on a hill. From the street, no one would know there was such a heavenly abode. Mark made me fresh tea as I set up my video equipment to record our conversation. The first thing he does is make a joke as I awkwardly put together video recorders and electrical cords. "I hope this all works," I say.

Mark says, "Don't worry; I'll smile anyway even if the camera doesn't work."

As he graciously gives me his new book, *Advocate Days and Other Stories,* he comments on his trip with Malcolm to a seminary. "One of the last pieces in the memoir is certainly one you will want to read. It's called: *On Being a Preacher's Wife."* We both laugh.

I read a review of Mark's new book. The reviewer's first reaction, after reading Mark's "savory snippets from a life well lived, is—more, please." The first section of this memoir focuses on Mark's work as a reporter and editor for *The Advocate,* where Mark served as an eyewitness to the early days of serious gay journalism. Much of the second half of the book is comprised of remembrances of gay heroes and legends—Paul Monette, James Broughton, Ethyl Eichelberger, Harry Hay, and John Burnside. The longest chapter, and one of the most personal, is about Mark's bout with HIV/AIDS and his counseling with an infected teenager. Mark's collection ends with three pieces celebrating his union with Malcolm, a match made in heaven that has ennobled their life on earth. Conversational in tone, these affecting essays record the humble passage through contemporary gay history of a remarkable writer and thinker, whose earlier trilogy, mentioned previously—*Gay Spirit, Gay Soul,* and *Gay Body*— remains essential reading.[15]

As I began my interview with Mark, he, already in the form of a superb interviewer, began our conversation without my having to start. "What was it like being an openly gay man and the spouse, not just of an

---

14. Malcolm's typewritten notes for remarks at reception, Gay Academic Union, Berkeley, CA, September 13, 2009.

15. See "Book Marks," by Richard Labonte, who reviews *Advocate Days and Other Stories* accessed in my interview with Mark Thompson. www.markthompsongayspirit.com/advocateMore.

Episcopal clergy, but a famous one? I not only had to deal with the issues of the church, because I'm not an Episcopalian, but I also had to deal with Malcolm's celebrity."

I asked Mark to talk about himself and then would bring that self into relationship with Malcolm. I asked Mark about his growing up and his coming of age as a gay man. He tells me he grew up in Northern California in one of the most beautiful places in the world on the Big Sur beaches in Carmel. It was an artsy community with retired movie stars.

Mark spent his childhood years in Pacific Grove. "I had a quiet childhood," he said. Mark had a normal childhood. On Sundays he was trotted off to a Methodist Church. There was a Methodist Church on every block because of the history of church missions in that region of the country. Mark said, "I loved Jesus but didn't feel destined to be a Christian."

There was a strong Buddhist community in the area where Mark grew up. Mark makes me recall that a strong Japanese community brought Buddhism to California after the World War II. In the late 1960s the famous Buddhist Tassajara Retreat Center, Tassajara, was established near where Mark grew up. "For whatever reasons, Michael, I went in the direction of Zen Buddhism," Mark told me.

In 1970 Mark went to the local junior college and got into journalism. Similar to Malcolm's childhood, Mark worked on the school's newspaper. After two years Mark moved to San Francisco State to finish his college degree in journalism. During the summer he would frequently visit the Buddhist center. Mark had a great respect for other religions, but settled upon Zen Buddhism. Years later when Mark was reading the biography of Alan Watts, an Episcopal priest and Zen Buddhist, Mark learned how to bring religions together through such reading.

When Mark finished his journalism degree, he got a call from the famous magazine *The Advocate* to see if he would come and work there. *The Advocate* was the most important gay publication. Mark said, "I told them sure, I would. I was delighted to work for my own people. It was 1975. I met Harvey Milk." As we will shortly see, Milk was a major force in gay civil rights. There was a demographic shift at this time. Many gays were coming out because of the Stonewall riots, which were a series of spontaneous riots against police at the Stonewall Inn in Greenwich Village, New York, on June 28, 1969. But gay people still had to migrate to places like Boston, Lower Manhattan, West Hollywood, or Silver Lake (Los Angeles area). The Los Angeles area was pivotal in gay history—the MCC, *The Advocate*, and the Mattachine Society, which was the first gay political action group that was founded in 1950 by Harry Hay, who also clandestinely started the gay movement on Cove Street in Silver Lake. Although San Francisco receives most of the credit for the gay community, Los Angeles was the bedrock for founding the movement.

All of the San Francisco area, especially the Castro Area, attracted many gay people because the economic times were right for rent and job opportunities. A writer likened San Francisco at that time to a refugee camp.

As the gay movement formed, many contributed mightily to society as artists, political leaders, ritual makers, healers, and advocates for civil rights.

"I'm not surprised that the church attracts so many gay people because of our natural gifts," Mark said.

Gay people have always been around contributing to society. But there was a dark period in which gay and lesbian people struggled to emerge. With suicide and negative socialization, it is amazing how the gay movement has persevered.

"Mark, how did you survive this negative socialization that labeled you as evil or an aberrant to society?" I asked.

"Well, there was always hiddenness in society when I grew up in the 1950s and 1960s. But my younger brother was gay." Mark describes his gregarious, athletic younger brother who fit so well into society. Mark and Kirk were candid with one another. They also grew up in an artist colony. Mark had many positive role models; for example, Ralph Geddes and François Martin, world-famous puppeteers with 800 string-and-rod puppets.

One day Mark's dad, the town plumber, called him to meet in the garage. Mark said, "Oh no, not in the garage, that's where parents make you have certain kinds of conversations back then." Mark was seventeen and active in school in art and drama. "I hear you've been hanging out with that theater-set downtown," Mark's dad said. "Now, nothing bad has happened, has it?"

"No, dad."

"Well, I have some other work for you to do."

Mark's dad said Ralph and Francois, an openly gay couple, needed an assistant. Mark went to work with them in a theater. Everyone loved going there. This was Mark's apprenticeship into the gay world. It was Mark's dad's way of supporting Mark.

Mark said this was vital for him to be supported by his dad. "I couldn't throw the damn baseball." Mark's dad supported him for what he could do. "I wasn't necessarily the walking wounded." Mark learned to see his identity of being gay as a gift. It gave him a unique perspective to support others. He followed the Civil Rights Movement and feminist movements because of his early days of growing up in an intensely beautiful place that suggested that God is beyond the human fights. "In Monterey, I learned to see God in beauty. I learned to see the world as a living body. All of us are guests in creation. So let us live like this—so let us be nice to one another," Mark said.

Mark gave me good content in understanding his sense of self and the context of his formative years. The relationships that helped him navigate a difficult society and his growing up in activism and his spiritual formation were profound. Before moving to the subject of Malcolm, I reminded Mark that World AIDS Day was the day after our interview, December 4, 2009. "A big holiday or day of observance in this house," Mark said.

"Would you like to say anything about current situations of HIV/AIDS," I asked

"I certainly would. And thanks for asking," Mark said.

Mark recalled the murder of Harvey Milk, one of the first openly gay political candidates. After Milk won the election as the first openly gay man to public office in California, it was a major shock when he was killed. As gay men were flooding into San Francisco, people began to hear about a "flu." More and more people were disappearing. By 1981, a clear problem was identified as Gay Related Immune Deficiency (GRID), the first time any disease was named as a stigma against people. Then the number of people dying rose exponentially. There were no social services; it was devastating.

"One of my boyfriends at the time got sick," Mark said.

A call came in 1984 to move *The Advocate* to Los Angeles. By then San Francisco was devastated. It didn't seem like the world gave a damn. Mark wasn't sure he had the virus. It wasn't until 1987 that a test was available.

"We had to put up with crap like you could get AIDS from someone's tears," Mark said. AIDS patients wouldn't be touched. Those treating AIDS patients dressed up like astronauts in fear that they would catch this dreaded disease. These were virulent, frightening days.

Mark came to Los Angeles in February of 1984 to interview writer Christopher Isherwood and his partner, artist Don Bachardy. Mark was a huge fan of both men. "I wanted to talk to them about their spiritual life," Mark said. They were deep into meditation, Vendantism. They respected Mark's seriousness.

Mark was deeply attracted to their philosophy but never liked to talk much about his own convictions when interviewing others. Mark thanked Isherwood for such a real interview. Isherwood said it was because Mark was asking such serious questions. But Mark said that generally he doesn't get so subjectively involved in the questioning because there is a Hindu axiom: "If you do have an authentic, interior life, hide that fact as if your mother is a whore." Those who have the biggest mouths should be the most informed by this wisdom.

Well, that interview went well. As Mark was driving around the Los Angeles area, he realized that he had to leave San Francisco. "You know that those in Northern California hate LA. It's from birth. I thought I was going to Satan's den. But I had to move out of the nest because my friends were dying."

Mark eventually moved and didn't know anyone except his friend Don Kilhefner, who founded the Gay and Lesbian Center. Don also knew Malcolm, who was on a book tour. Don gave Mark a pink slip to say hello to Malcolm, who was staying in the same hotel as Mark.

Mark said, "Malcolm Boyd?! You mean the priest? I have to say hello to him?" Mark had seen Malcolm a few years before on the David Frost TV program. "During school days at 4:30 PM, I always rushed home to see David Frost's show. I loved the clip board. Frost was the ideal journalist. I wanted to be just like him." On this particular episode, Ravi Shankar was the guest playing with a Western artist, Yehudi Menuhin, the famous Hungarian violinist. The music album they were promoting was *East Meets West*, one of Mark's favorite albums. This was something to run home and

Mark (on left) with Malcolm in portrait by Don Bachardy.

see, but when Mark turned on the TV, there was a priest, promoting a book. "My beloved Ravi was bumped by a priest?" Mark laughed. "I never imagined seven years later I would meet him on that fateful night because of Don."

When Mark met Malcolm, they talked for three hours. Mark was struck by how deep Malcolm was. "Malcolm was very handsome—and I was not into older men. All of my partners were younger men." The age difference between Malcolm and Mark is thirty years. "I was in my early thirties and Malcolm in his early sixties."

A month or two later, Mark moved to LA. Malcolm called to go out to dinner. This was in 1984. They have been together since then.

They practiced safe sex right from the start just as a precaution. In 1987 Mark found that he had AIDS, and with very low T-cells, he had probably had it for a long time. For almost half of Mark's life he has had the virus. He has seen countless friends die, including three lovers. Two of his AIDS doctors are dead. And in 1995, Mark with tears in his eyes said, "My brother Kirk died—literally in my arms." There was nothing that could be done for him so the means were provided for Kirk to die without more suffering. Mark says, "This was one of the loneliest days of my life."

"Do you see any providence for why you are still alive?"

"Yes, so I can be here talking with you. And being with Malcolm. Sometimes we joke who will die first, Malcolm as the old man or me with AIDS."

Mark tells me that the medications have slowed the process way, way down. I push Mark to name the miraculous in his life, like Jimmy Stewart in *It's a Wonderful Life*. Have you developed a vocation in light of your suffering?

"I am still the same studious person I was as a little boy. I think the meta-reason for me being here is to bear witness of reconciliation in this holy war."

Mark gave me his seventh book in the effort to give witness to the awful divide between gays and heterosexuals. It's making young people turn to suicide and drugs. Then Mark jokes, "I think the real providence was in how I was called to be a preacher's wife." Mark reminds me that humor is a key gift to many gay people, so much a gift that there is a genre of gay humor, camp humor. Indeed, such providence gave us the language to talk about the unique and stable commitment that Mark and Malcolm have sustained for twenty-seven years. This made me recall one of the beautiful stories that Malcolm told me in spiritual direction. Malcolm told me that he realized he was married when Mark told him to take out the trash.

I ask Mark, "Tell me about the famous story of taking out the trash."

"It was early in our relationship. It was a Saturday, when we were first dating, at my apartment. We didn't immediately move in together. I said, no way José. First of all you're thirty years older, you're a priest, and you've never met my parents. We're going to have a proper courtship and do this right. Malcolm was reluctant at first but now says that that was the best thing we could have done. We soon settled into a domestic routine when we did move in together."

Malcolm described the situation: at first, Mark always took out the garbage, like the helpful Boy Scout he once was. Once their relationship turned into commitment, all of the transitions of a typical marriage set in. One day, a typical day of Malcolm reading the newspaper on the couch, Malcolm was shocked by Mark. Shocked, mostly because Malcolm had taken for granted the get out of jail free card for not having to take out the garbage during their honeymoon period. Malcolm got the message when Mark said, "Malcolm, it's your turn to take out the garbage!"

When we concluded our interview, Mark wanted to tell me that Malcolm has indeed received the word of the Divine. "I don't know when or how," Mark said. Malcolm is authentically gay, because he has never been with a woman. Perhaps this creates the portal to receive this word of the Divine. Being gay is not about sexuality, that's a misnomer. Gay and straight people are alike in what they do in bed; it's in the other parts of life that makes gays different and how they perceive things. According to Mark, Malcolm is not pretentious like many puffed-up clergy; he is filled with a Divine Holy Spirit.

I asked Mark if it was hard to live with such an intense person. The metaphor I offered was that New York is a great place to visit but many don't want to live there because of the intensity. Is there any truth in this comparison between you and Malcolm?

Mark said, "We do get along. We have a lot in common. We're both writers and so we have a lot to talk about. I'm a Leo and he's a Gemini so that works out well. I'm kind of bossy and cut to the chase. When Malcolm is depressed and says he's going to die, I say lighten up . . . you're not going to die today."

"It sounds like an age difference."

"Yes, but I'm an old soul."

"One of our problems is worldview. I met an African bishop who met Gene Robinson. The African bishop wanted to know who washes the dishes in a gay relationship."

"Oh, my God," Mark said.

"The problem of the African worldview is that to be single is just as much an anomaly as it is to be gay. Without children, you can't go to heaven according to ancestor rites." I wanted to engage Mark into the strange African worldview and how he could help us think beyond the culture wars.

"One of the cutting-edge paradigms for gay and lesbian people is from the two spirit tradition. The world of multiple genders that comes from ancient cultures provides a means beyond our wars. I'm surprised that dualisms exist in African cultures. In Africa they are still executing gays—how dare the president of Uganda, that criminal monster—he should be put on trial. You don't go and kill your own young people. I'm sorry, but this is willful ignorance when within your own culture there are ways of thinking beyond violence. We're living in a fear-based world of scarcity. It saddens me to see civil wars and plagues. When people are afraid, they have a tendency to project their fears on others. This explains racism. We project the dark on others. Gay people are now the dark people."

I ask Mark if Malcolm's institutional religion makes all of this worse. I press Mark, "This is medieval—all this religious stuff. Doesn't religion exacerbate all that we are talking about?"

Mark said, "No. We need a transcendent vessel to take us beyond our wars and binaries. Spiritual ritual helps us connect to the divine. I like that about Malcolm."

Malcolm realizes now why Mark and he are role models today—after all, they have been in a committed relationship for twenty-seven years. "Jesus!" Malcolm responds as he realizes this with me.

"How did they manage without breaking up?" I asked.

Malcolm told me that he learned to correct his own perceptions. Not to be so judgmental of others. And also boundaries come from life experience. Perhaps the vision to see or one's perceptions are corrected only through the crucible of life experience. This is a crucible because we all live in the angst that we too will die. The ultimate boundary being death. This brings us back to *adiaphora*—what indeed is essential.

Needed Deaths

Malcolm's life work has always been to present authentic language about God and humanity—language that does not stereotype "the atheist," "the black man," "the white man," or "the Negro." Such fixed stereotypical worldviews are often unhelpful. Malcolm states, "The Israeli who does not want a two-state system with Palestine is often used as a straw man argument. Usually in these kinds of arguments the need is to simplify so that you don't have to deal with all the ambiguities. We do this with the Hollywood star, the politician, the bishop."

I ask, "So your life represents someone who has resisted the stereotypes?"

The answer to this question is precisely this book. When the reader learns about Malcolm's life, you learn about an apocalyptic horseman who scares others away from the comfortable, simplistic stereotypes we make of each other, God, and the world. I think the following speaks for itself for how Malcolm's life transcends stereotypes:

FOR IMMEDIATE RELEASE

Two octogenarian religious leaders are engaged in a spiritual smackdown with competing CDs this holiday season.

Pope Benedict XVI, 82, and popular gay Episcopal priest and author Canon Malcolm Boyd, 86, have both moved from religious tracts to recording tracks with music-and-prayer releases.

Vatican Radio has licensed recordings of the Pope which will be blended with recitals by the Choir of the Philharmonic Academy in Rome, and distributed by Geffen Records, owned by Universal Music Group.

Canon Malcolm Boyd also has a new release this season of provocative readings from his spiritual classic *Are You Running with Me, Jesus?* performed live with a jazz combo that includes famed guitarist Johnnie Valentino, Scott Page-Pagter on keyboards, and Marina Bambino on percussion, straight from her recent tours with Macy Gray and the Isley Brothers. The limited edition release is available through Loose Canon Records, www.loosecanonrecords.com. Canon Boyd and the music combo performed the prayers with jazz as part of the 76th Triennial General Convention of the Episcopal Church in Anaheim, CA, last July 14th to a sold-out crowd, following their two full-house Easter performances at the famed Jazz Bakery in Los Angeles.

"Happily, I'm able to get my CD directly to audiences through unconventional distribution chains that don't require the help of an international mega-corporation," chuckles the avuncular gay elder. "Unlike the Pope, I don't have to support a fatigued brand or deal with his crushing overhead. Do you have any idea what it takes to heat the Basilica?!"

Though the Pope has remained mute on the recording rivalry, in recent days he has made gestures encouraging antsy Anglicans to "hop the fence" as the Episcopalian Church continues to embrace the broadest possible constituency of God's children.

Canon Boyd has performed his prayers with such musical greats as Charlie Byrd, Vince Guaraldi, and Oscar Brown Jr., in venues ranging from the National Cathedral in Washington, D.C., to the hungry i nightclub in San Francisco. He acknowledges that ritual Vatican pomp can "really bring in the crowds, especially at Christmas—but it's ministering 'in the street' that truly introduces a sense of the sacred into our everyday lives."

"Besides," he adds with a twinkle, "good jazz music is nothing to sneeze at!"[16]

Malcolm remembers reading the newspapers in which he was typecast "the controversial priest Malcolm Boyd," "the nightclub priest," "the activist," and "the ex-Hollywood cleric." Malcolm muses, "Why didn't they ever run a story like the noncontroversial priest, Harry Brown?" Those like Malcolm who stand on the outside of things are capable of these insights. They help us ask ourselves how we are stereotyping a nation state, the church, or the rebel priest.

Malcolm could easily stereotype the church, but he resists. Malcolm should be one of the first to be bitter about the church; especially being hurt so badly by "well-meaning" Christians who resented Malcolm's civil rights work, frank language about God, and his eventual revelation of being a gay priest.

It seems strange on the surface that someone could be hurt by the church. After all, Jesus' image of the church is a fold of sheep. Earlier I mentioned how Malcolm was really hurt by the comments made by then Bishop Minnis of Colorado, when he said in reference to Malcolm that he had matted hair, smelled badly and wore black underwear. Malcolm took on the Bishop of Colorado knowing that he wouldn't have a job.

Malcolm says he doesn't stereotype the church; he says he knows better. He knows the good people. He had lunch with a fifty-year-old priest who has spent five years at the same church and has almost nothing bad to say about it or its congregation.

So what is the church's identity if it is not a stereotype? I brought this question to Malcolm. He responded that the identity of the church is ambiguous because the church can only offer epiphanies of true identity

---

16. Malcolm Boyd, "FW: Pope and Priest Have Dueling CDs," e-mail message to author, December 1, 2009.

that cannot be stereotyped, just as people like Paul Moore or Dean Roberts of St. John's Cathedral in Denver cannot be stereotyped.

With deep integrity Malcolm is trying to say that he is not angry with the church, and remains an active priest after fifty-five years. The church for many in the gay community still represents an angry constituency; some would even say a self-righteous institution.

Death of the Civil Rights Era

Malcolm recalls when the Watts riots started. Upon hearing the news, Malcolm flew to Los Angeles. Malcolm remembered hearing the stewardess on his flight saying, "When you finish your cocktails, you can see the fires of the Watts riot on the right." Later, Malcolm found himself handing out bread and milk and interviewing people. He remembers standing in a circle with the National Guard and seeing the fires—remembers seeing LA burn.

When Malcolm came out to see Watts, he had a strange experience with how the church was handling the situation, especially the Episcopal Church. Instead of giving an official statement, Bishop Bloy was silent. He stayed in his home with the mail piling up in front of his door. The *LA Times* wanted a quote from the bishop but got none, so Malcolm and the Rev. Morris Samuel, another Episcopal priest, provided one of their own.

Given the seething anger at the time, the Watts riots were no surprise for Malcolm and others. We see this deep anger in Malcolm's encounter with a young black man in his book *Free to Live, Free to Die*. Malcolm notes to me that this seething anger is terribly important to understand in racial relationships. A key moment occurs if the object of hatred—in this case, whites—can at least see themselves that as blacks see them. Few whites (or blacks) have experienced such anger!

Malcolm describes the young black man in provocative terms and dialogue. "God spelled backward," the young man reminded Malcolm, "spells dog." He was twenty-one, wearing a T-shirt and jeans. He dropped out of high school. I said to Malcolm that black people seem invisible in Los Angeles. Asian and Latino worldviews seem to dominate and represent a new momentum. Malcolm responds, "Well, we had Tom Bradley," whom Malcolm knew and thought was a great mayor. But do we have any blacks in prominent positions today—the kind who do not represent the schizophrenia of Rodney King and O. J. Simpson? Neither Malcolm nor I could offer a positive answer.

The black kid in Watts and the inability to remember role models made Malcolm and I think about how does one remember well? On several occasions Malcolm challenged me to write more clearly on the matter of remembering the past, especially the tragic past of black people. Like a disciplined coach, Malcolm required that I put my thoughts together coherently about these difficult matters, not only for my sake but for others as well. Perhaps he thought my response to the constant tragedies of black people on this planet could reveal what is often unsaid—and that which should only be said by someone who actually represents the struggle—someone marked by slavery as an affliction that still remains. Malcolm writes me:

> In this present chapter, I realize how important it is for you to "deal with" essential issues and questions. In other words, something specific and relevant and demanding, no bullshit as usual. In this chapter you've dipped into this subject in several different ways on several different occasions. But this lacks centrality or clarity; it needs a more coherent wholeness. Like, maybe: state the proposition; follow with three points; offer a few illustrations; move in a radical confrontation. Offer concrete examples (keep it a bit simple), then bring it home. Let's talk more about this. It is really, clearly, a major part of spiritual direction. Is there (in your own consciousness) a key moment when, perhaps, all this came up in an absolutely major and irresistible way? (Could not be denied)?[17]

Even in Malcolm's own role of fighting against racial discrimination, he doesn't know what black people think about his involvement in black people's lives. Malcolm sadly thinks a number of black persons didn't think Malcolm, or anyone like him, should have bothered being a civil rights activist. I think it's a generational problem of ignorance, indifference, or enmity. "It's interesting," he says. "No black college has ever invited me to speak!" Is there an embarrassment in inviting Malcolm? Is there a lack of information?

As Malcolm grows older, he invites me into these remaining enigmas in his life. Whites don't ask him to speak about race. Blacks don't. A few gays want to talk about gay rights with Malcolm. Some people do want to talk about aging, especially the aging.

"In light of my strange life," Malcolm says matter of factly, "it will be interesting when the book comes out to get the reactions to who I am and have become."

---

17. Malcolm Boyd, "Have Finished Chapter," e-mail message to author, January 13, 2010.

The irony of this conversation about civil rights is that in takes place in the context of Barack Obama running for president of the United States. In May 2008, Malcolm and I were rooting for Obama, but I don't think either of us thought he would win. My big thing was that I thought the "Bradley Effect" would kill his chances to win in America. The "Bradley Effect" is that circumstance in which white people may say in public they may vote for a black candidate; meanwhile, in the voting booth, voting for someone else. I remember telling Malcolm I overheard one of the HBO episodes of Bill Maher's humorous insight about the "Bubbas" (his version of "rednecks" in backwoods America having the opposite of the Bradley effect). He said the "Bubba Effect" could occur if they went into the voting booth and voted for Obama due to his health care policy and his being more of a champion for the poor. Of course, I remember Maher laughing as he recalled that such Bubbas would never want to admit this in public. So, I asked Malcolm about what happened to Tom Bradley being the first black mayor of Los Angeles.

Malcolm told me that Bradley's personality was such that he never hugged you. He looked out and saw his court. As Malcolm reflects deeply about the impact of Bradley, he tells me that someone could write a hell of a book about blacks in LA. The problem, however, is that LA may not have much of a moral compass, a fact that would tie into Malcolm's insight that you can't easily find a significant church leader in LA who is also a strong social and cultural leader. You can have major TV evangelists, but they are major in PR with no gravitas. So maybe LA is a wasteland of the spiritual. So much in LA is theater.

Before I gave the Baccalaureate Address at the University of Southern California (USC), Varun Soni, the first non-Christian Dean of Religious Life, sent me the following article. Varun, a practicing Hindu, asked me to keynote the Baccaulareate probably because of our common ties to South Africa—with Varun finishing a PhD degree at the University of Cape Town. When I read his reflections, I found it interesting how Obama's entry into politics is similar to Malcolm's life confronting the political world. In other words, for both Obama and Malcolm, you can't easily separate religion and politics. Varun writes the following:

> What does it mean for Barack Obama to be an interfaith president? The religious historian Martin Marty described presidents as the priests of public religion, but every president navigates this high-wire act differently. They all have something to say about their faith and the role of faith in the public sphere, and their public religiosity reflects the spiritual

mood of their times. Throughout presidential history, we see how the religious pulse of the nation influences the highest office as much as the holder of that office shapes the public's perception of public religion.[18]

Malcolm notes that Varun's insight is fascinating, relevant, and of primary importance.

I think we're all dumbfounded now because of Barack Obama. We're into a strange new land. Barack and Michelle met the Queen of England and her husband on April 1, 2009. Malcolm's insight was that the men were stiff, but Michelle and the Queen were relaxed. I was sitting at JFK airport watching this scene on CNN. The black anchor on CNN, a male, was doing an interview. Strangely, instead of trying to appear objective and facilitate a conversation with his guests, the black anchor took over the conversation and the white woman correspondent didn't say much, although she was supposed to be recounting the story about the appropriate etiquette for being with the queen. I asked Malcolm about the strangeness of this encounter between the Obamas and the monarchy, "Wasn't the strangeness and confusion a sign of the end of the monarchy?" The slaves of the colony were now in power. Malcolm would say no, because the queen validated the monarchy. If the queen wore the tiara and the pink, instead of simply being natural and herself, she would have messed up.

The end of the civil rights era apparently means the complication of those once powerless now being complicated with power. By no means does such a complication mean that racism or homophobia has ceased; on the contrary, more visible minorities in power may mean higher anxieties among the majority. What the end of the civil rights era may really mean is that there is no more excuse that "a black man" can never be President. This has now been achieved and we can cross this off of our "bucket list."

Wisdom Approaching Death

In a reflective mood, Malcolm sent me the following e-mail about growing older.

> Growing older is a scream. Memory of many names and details seems long gone. The simplest chore requires reserves of energy increasingly in shorter supply.

---

18. Matthew Weiner and Varun Soni, "Dialogue: Obama's High Wire," *Harvard Divinity Bulletin* 37, no. 2 and 3 (Spring/Summer 2009).

So something as basic as the ritual of my morning shave has undergone change. For example, I used to shave with an electric razor. But I've switched to Gillette Fusion Hydragel, "Ultra Sensitive." "You don't have to sacrifice comfort or closeness. This aloe-rich formula with hydrating emollients softens hair and protects skin, so your razor can comfortably glide for an incredibly close shave. Gillette's best razor glide—even for the most sensitive skin."

Lately I've complemented Fusion Hydragel by using my old electric razor beneath my chin. All this seemingly gives me a more romantic Byronic lackadaisical look. Shouldn't a writer at least try, well, to look interesting?

However, let's get serious. Migawd [My God], this entire matter of aging is rapidly changing into something more complex. Which brings up the subject of my driver's license. It would have expired on my eight-sixth birthday last June unless I passed a written driver's exam. I pondered this. I remembered when my mother, Beatrice, stopped driving when she was ninety. (She died nine years later.) She loved driving her car but stopped when she thought the time had come.

So, at eight-six, had my own time come? I weighed the matter carefully. Then I sent for copies of driver's tests that one may study. Also I purchased a tape that the Dept. of Motor Vehicles prepared to assist persons like myself getting ready to take the exam. I played the tape daily. I worked hard. When the day arrived for my written test, I showed up and took it. My score was near perfect. I don't drive at nights or on freeways, but feel secure and confident behind the wheel.

Aging is a constant test of one's capabilities. I believe it's vitally important to appreciate life and live as fully as possible in the moment at hand. Yet life changes. We change within life itself and our own life. Always this is a recurring challenge.

I remember both my father and mother, and how each handled his or her aging challenges magnificently. But earlier Melville, my dad, had failed as an alcoholic and a womanizer. This meant that, as a child, I had neither a father nor a family. I was in middle school in Denver when a large "Christmas box" arrived in a late December mail from my dad in New York City. Energized, anxious to discover what holiday treasure it might contain, I tore the box open. Inside, to my dismay, was a suit I wouldn't be caught dead in. Also a book I would not want to read. I hurled the box against a wall. I sobbed. My heart broke. It seemed my father was a stranger who didn't know me.

Years later Melville's life underwent an astonishing change. He hadn't taken a drink for thirty years. He had a highly successful remarriage that proved lasting. I was able to know him as a mature, charming, wise man. He had been the son of one Episcopal priest and was now the father of another. I served as the priest at his burial.

My mother Beatrice didn't remarry. She lived quietly with her beloved dogs, painted, wrote an unpublished book, enjoyed close friends, including actresses Mary Pickford and Lillian Gish, and volunteered for many years as a teacher at the Children's Hospital of Los Angeles. It honored her with two awards: the Kate Page Crutcher Award in 1977 and the Mary Helm Memorial Award in 1982. One day a small boy asked Beatrice "You're old, aren't you?" "Yes, I am" replied my mother. "Good! Then I can talk to you," he said.

Beatrice's final years were spent in a convalescent hospital after mother broke her hip. I find her high in a roster of contemporary saints. As someone aging myself—and with role models like Melville and Beatrice—who could ask for anything more?[19]

In light of the habits and virtues that Malcolm learned from exemplars like Beatrice and others, I asked him about how he was approaching his own death. What do you believe about death? What happens when you die. Do you believe that there is life after death, a heaven or a hell? Does what you believe about death matter? I asked him to tell me about all of this. I asked specific questions. Malcolm responds as a typical sage by avoiding easy answers. He simply describes how his life is now. He drives from Silver Lake, checks messages and parks, checks messages and mail. He does spiritual direction sessions for two hours, 11 AM to 1 PM.

Malcolm doesn't accept many speaking engagements anymore. Malcolm comments that this refers again to the problem of celebrity. "What's the point?" Malcolm asked. But Malcolm accepts some engagements.

"What are your criteria for accepting a speaking engagement?"

"The meaning of the event, the capacity of what you have to offer. Preaching is something I basically no longer accept. Because I'm an outsider to a parish. The celebrity preaching thing, I don't like it. It makes me an outsider when preaching."

"Do you feel bad about the speaker who parachutes in?"

Malcolm shared with me his wisdom of what works better than the paid expert who swoops into a scene to make people spiritual. Any

---

19. Malcolm Boyd, "Dad and Mom: Growing Older," e-mail message to author, March 8, 2010.

speaker or preacher shouldn't just show up and pontificate. He or she should do a summation speech at first. Malcolm would do this. He might take a second day and meet with small groups on the next day and listen. Have people sit with you for questions and answers. "I don't think it feeds groups to have the celebrity motivational speaker," Malcolm tells me. "You have to know what to do with it. It's potentially a very useful moment, however, if an outside speaker can be a catalyst for an ongoing community."

I asked Malcolm how he learned such wisdom to have these habits. The majority of Malcolm's working days prior to entering a seminary he wasn't going into an office. Malcolm worked in Hollywood, where he would have those constant power lunches with all the gossip and the intrigue. This lasted for about seven years.

"Working at the Samuel Goldwyn studio, on Saturdays no one could reach you. Two men were shouting outside the window. It was Howard Hughes and Samuel Goldwyn. The context of their conversation changed me." Both the shallowness of the debate between Hughes and Goldwyn and the Hollywood environment left Malcolm restless for a deeper life. Such restlessness made Malcolm realize how the habits of executives often led to detrimental lifestyles. It was now or never for Malcolm to make vocational decisions that would provide him deeper life rather than set him on a road to quick decline and despair. This was an epiphany that led Malcolm to seminary, Taizé, and what followed. Even when he lived in the rectory of St. George's Cathedral in Indianapolis, he was looking for opportunities that would further life's choices rather than choices to despair.

As Malcolm looked back over his life with me, he laughed when he recalled an incident that usually would end in despair. At Colorado State University as a chaplain, Malcolm was placed in a Canterbury house-like place called St. Paul's house. He had a secretary, Grace Williams, who addressed him as Father Boyd. Malcolm called her Mrs. Williams. Nothing sentimental occurred in this relationship, no friendship. On the last day when Malcolm was leaving under the cloud of some controversy, Malcolm said, "I guess this is it, Mrs. Williams."

She said, "Father Boyd, let's have a drink. Here's to you, all the best." She pours a glass of bourbon. "Well, now can I have your keys, I think I'll lock up and go home now, Father Boyd." Malcolm's endings always somehow resulted in his beginnings. Such leave-taking was less frightening to Malcolm and yet deeply frightening to others who find it extremely difficult in the face of change and ultimately death.

The Pale Green Rider of Death

The last rider is the Green Knight. His color is paradoxical due the customary association of color green with life. Perhaps this is fitting though as Malcolm's life remains robust even in old age. So much of the last apocalyptic green rider represents angst in the face of change—the ultimate change of death; and yet, I have never met anyone with less anxiety about death than Malcolm. Perhaps this was due to the fire in Malcolm and his ability to reason for his longevity in the midst of harsh circumstances, even desert-like conditions—much like I mentioned in the very beginning of this book. Somewhere in the midst of an extraordinary life, Malcolm learned not to long for a simple peace, the absence of war, but for a deeper sense of peace. Malcolm states it again, "The bottom line is that such a prophet does not desire to be wished—perfunctorily—a superficial, essentially lying, quite dismissive 'peace.'" Like the great theologian Augustine, Malcolm wanted a restless peace.

Indeed, with this deeper kind of peace, this book refers to Malcolm's four apocalyptic personas: the White Horse of Pestilence, the Red Horse of War, the Black Horse of Famine, and the Pale Green Horse of Death. These personas represent many stories of whom Malcolm has become. Malcolm states, "I refer not solely to the mixed plots of my life; I am also a number of different people under the skin. Each one has his or her own story or stories, and all are a part of mine." None of these stories is finished yet. What is brilliant about Malcolm's life is that they are all open to possibility, change, new decisions, unexpected events and moves. This is why I like to see Malcolm's life as apocalyptic—constantly revealing new realities. In the end is the beginning.

Malcolm helps me end this book with a story from his childhood. It is a fitting apocalyptic story that sheds light on how death is not the end but the beginning. Particularly, a life well-lived cannot help but affect others to live well. One cannot know if one lived well apart from dying well. Malcolm explains such interrelatedness through his encounters with Orson Welles's recounting of *The War of the Worlds*. Although our apocalyptic imaginations anxiously move toward pestilence, war, famine, and death, Malcolm's imagination continues to shock and provoke us toward God's deeper relationships.

> One of the great lessons of my life unfolded on an evening in 1938 when I learned that little things I do can affect other people.
>
> Three of my high school friends and I attended a Sunday school supper at a Midwestern cathedral. Bored and seeking excitement, we

concocted a plan to climb into the stone tower after everybody else had departed. We would ring the bells of the cathedral after dark! It seemed like an innocent lark that couldn't possibly hurt anybody. We hid in the sanctuary until doors were bolted, lights turned off, and voices drifted away into the night.

What we did not know was the Orson Welles had just begun the fateful broadcast of his classic radio program about a Martian invasion of earth, one that would shortly result in national terror. But now the three of us moved swiftly through the cathedral's dark interior. Splendid stained-glass windows looked like mere leaded spaces in the night. The sanctuary with its stone altar took on the appearance of a treacherous inky expanse. Did evil spirits lurk there? Would they reach out with powerful tentacles to pull us into a bottomless pit?

We found the door leading to the bell tower. The stairs were narrow and winding. Around the next turn we had no idea what gargoyles or church officials we might encounter. Soon it became apparent to us we were being followed. When we stopped, holding our breath, the footsteps halted. Shouting at the top of our lungs to ward off spirits and confuse the demon in pursuit, we tore up the stairs. Reaching the bell tower, ready to fight pursuers, we realized the demon was our echo.

Now the moment had come to ring the bells. Unknown to us, the city was already locked in deadly fear. To all intents and purposes, the Martians had landed. Switchboards of police stations, newspapers, and broadcasters were swamped with desperate calls. Some people were in the streets, others had started in cars toward safety in the hills beyond the city, when the bells of the cathedral boomed out their note of warning.

Doom! Those who had held back in rational behavior or cynicism now leapt headlong into a cauldron of discombobulation. The gothic cathedral, the fortress of Almighty God, betrayed no evidence of God's intervention in human affairs except that its bell tower heaved with clashing night bells ringing out over the world in disarray.

Shortly, of course, word reached the people that there no Martians. The best thing was to go home and get some sleep. The three of us, breathless with excitement about our achievement of ringing the bells, and without any knowledge of what had transpired about the radio program and Martians, were making our way hilariously down the winding stairway when we heard the ominous sound of police sirens.

Somehow we realized they were coming for us. We raced into the cathedral sanctuary mere footsteps ahead of what appeared to be a small army of police. Crouching behind the bishop's throne in the dark shadows, it seemed to us that the separation between church and state was not entirely adequate. As the police made their way up the stairway to the bell tower, we fled through a convenient cathedral herb garden to our homes.

What did I learn from the experience that continues to stay with me today? When you throw a pebble into a lake, it makes ripples. I learned not to shout "Fire!" in a crowded theater and to share responsibility for living in a world with other people.

www.ingramcontent.com/pod-product-compliance
Lightning Source LLC
Chambersburg PA
CBHW051806230426
43672CB00012B/2659